Communications
in Computer and Information Sc

T0237860

Dominik Ślęzak   Tai-hoon Kim
Stephen S. Yau   Osvaldo Gervasi
Byeong-Ho Kang (Eds.)

Grid and Distributed Computing

International Conference, GDC 2009
Held as Part of the Future Generation
Information Technology Conference, FGIT 2009
Jeju Island, Korea, December 10-12, 2009
Proceedings

 Springer

Volume Editors

Dominik Ślęzak
University of Warsaw and Infobright Inc.
E-mail: slezak@infobright.com

Tai-hoon Kim
Hannam University, South Korea
E-mail: taihoonn@hnu.kr

Stephen S. Yau
Arizona State University, USA
E-mail: yau@asu.edu

Osvaldo Gervasi
University of Perugia, Italy
E-mail: osvaldo@unipg.it

Byeong-Ho Kang
University of Tasmania, Australia
E-mail: bhkang@utas.edu.au

Library of Congress Control Number: 2009939711

CR Subject Classification (1998): C.1.4, C.2.4, C.2.1, D.1.3, D.4.2, D.4.3, E.1, H.2.4, H.3.4

ISSN   1865-0929
ISBN-10   3-642-10548-3 Springer Berlin Heidelberg New York
ISBN-13   978-3-642-10548-7 Springer Berlin Heidelberg New York

springer.com

© Springer-Verlag Berlin Heidelberg 2009
Printed in Germany

Typesetting: Camera-ready by author, data conversion by Scientific Publishing Services, Chennai, India
Printed on acid-free paper   SPIN: 12805679   06/3180   5 4 3 2 1 0

Foreword

As future generation information technology (FGIT) becomes specialized and fragmented, it is easy to lose sight that many topics in FGIT have common threads and, because of this, advances in one discipline may be transmitted to others. Presentation of recent results obtained in different disciplines encourages this interchange for the advancement of FGIT as a whole. Of particular interest are hybrid solutions that combine ideas taken from multiple disciplines in order to achieve something more significant than the sum of the individual parts. Through such hybrid philosophy, a new principle can be discovered, which has the propensity to propagate throughout multifaceted disciplines.

FGIT 2009 was the first mega-conference that attempted to follow the above idea of hybridization in FGIT in a form of multiple events related to particular disciplines of IT, conducted by separate scientific committees, but coordinated in order to expose the most important contributions. It included the following international conferences: Advanced Software Engineering and Its Applications (ASEA), Bio-Science and Bio-Technology (BSBT), Control and Automation (CA), Database Theory and Application (DTA), Disaster Recovery and Business Continuity (DRBC; published independently), Future Generation Communication and Networking (FGCN) that was combined with Advanced Communication and Networking (ACN), Grid and Distributed Computing (GDC), Multimedia, Computer Graphics and Broadcasting (MulGraB), Security Technology (SecTech), Signal Processing, Image Processing and Pattern Recognition (SIP), and u- and e-Service, Science and Technology (UNESST).

We acknowledge the great effort of all the Chairs and the members of advisory boards and Program Committees of the above-listed events, who selected 28% of over 1,050 submissions, following a rigorous peer-review process. Special thanks go to the following organizations supporting FGIT 2009: ECSIS, Korean Institute of Information Technology, Australian Computer Society, SERSC, Springer LNCS/CCIS, COEIA, ICC Jeju, ISEP/IPP, GECAD, PoDIT, Business Community Partnership, Brno University of Technology, KISA, K-NBTC and National Taipei University of Education.

We are very grateful to the following speakers who accepted our invitation and helped to meet the objectives of FGIT 2009: Ruay-Shiung Chang (National Dong Hwa University, Taiwan), Jack Dongarra (University of Tennessee, USA), Xiaohua (Tony) Hu (Drexel University, USA), Irwin King (Chinese University of Hong Kong, Hong Kong), Carlos Ramos (Polytechnic of Porto, Portugal), Timothy K. Shih (Asia University, Taiwan), Peter M.A. Sloot (University of Amsterdam, The Netherlands), Kyu-Young Whang (KAIST, South Korea), and Stephen S. Yau (Arizona State University, USA).

We would also like to thank Rosslin John Robles, Maricel O. Balitanas, Farkhod Alisherov Alisherovish, and Feruza Sattarova Yusfovna – graduate students of Hannam University who helped in editing the FGIT 2009 material with a great passion.

October 2009

Young-hoon Lee
Tai-hoon Kim
Wai-chi Fang
Dominik Ślęzak

Preface

We would like to welcome you to the proceedings of the 2009 International Conference on Grid Distributed Computing (GDC 2009), which was organized as part of the 2009 International Mega-Conference on Future Generation Information Technology (FGIT 2009), held during December 10–12, 2009, at the International Convention Center Jeju, Jeju Island, South Korea.

GDC 2009 focused on various aspects of advances in grid and distributed computing with computational sciences, mathematics and information technology. It provided a chance for academic and industry professionals to discuss recent progress in the related areas. We expect that the conference and its publications will be a trigger for further related research and technology improvements in this important subject.

We would like to acknowledge the great effort of all the Chairs and members of the Program Committee. Out of 100 submissions to GDC 2009, we accepted 29 papers to be included in the proceedings and presented during the conference. This gives roughly a 30% acceptance ratio. Three of the papers accepted for GDC 2009 were published in the special FGIT 2009 volume, LNCS 5899, by Springer. The remaining 26 accepted papers can be found in this CCIS volume.

We would like to express our gratitude to all of the authors of submitted papers and to all of the attendees, for their contributions and participation. We believe in the need for continuing this undertaking in the future.

Once more, we would like to thank all the organizations and individuals who supported FGIT 2009 as a whole and, in particular, helped in the success of GDC 2009.

October 2009

Dominik Ślęzak
Tai-hoon Kim
Stephen S. Yau
Osvaldo Gervasi
Byeong-Ho Kang

Organization

Organizing Committee

General Chairs   Stephen S. Yau (Arizona State University, USA)
                        Osvaldo Gervasi (University of Perugia, Italy)

Program Chairs   Byeong-Ho Kang (University of Tasmania, Australia)
                        Tai-hoon Kim (Hannam University, Korea)

Program Committee

Albert Zomaya
Alex Sim
Bilha Mendelson
BongHee Hong
Chao-Tung Yang
Cho-Li Wang
Chun-His
Damon Shing-Min Liu
Dan Grigoras
Dan Meng
Daniel S. Katz
Danilo Gonzalez
Deok-Gyu Lee
Dimitrios Serpanos
Domenico Laforenza
Domenico Talia
Eung Nam Ko

Gail-Joon Ahn
Geoffrey Fox
George Bosilca
Hai Jin
Hung-Chang Hsiao
Hyeong-Ok Lee
Jan-Jan Wu
Jean-Louis Pazat
Jiannong Cao
John Cavazos
Keecheon Kim
Kenichi Takahashi
Liria Matsumoto Sato
Marcin Paprzycki
Marian Bubak
Mark Baker
Matt Mutka

Minglu Li
Mohamed Jemni
Mohand-Said Hacid
Nabil Abdennadher
Omer F. Rana
Ramin Yahyapour
Ronald Perrott
Ruay-Shiung Chang
Stephane Genaud
Susumu Date
Tomàs Margalef
Yangwoo Kim
Yeh-Ching Chung
Yong Man Ro
Yongik Yoon
Yong-Kee Jun

Table of Contents

Autonomic Management of Object Replication for FT-CORBA Based Intelligent Transportation Systems

Woonsuk Suh[1] and Eunseok Lee[2]

[1] National Information Society Agency
NIA Bldg, 77, Mugyo-dong Jung-ku Seoul, 100-775, Korea
sws@nia.or.kr
[2] School of Information and Communication Engineering, Sungkyunkwan University
300 Chunchun Jangahn Suwon, 440-746, Korea
eslee@ece.skku.ac.kr

Abstract. Intelligent Transportation Systems (ITS) comprises the electronics, communications or information processing used singly or integrated to improve the efficiency or safety of surface transportation. Accordingly, the ITS has to perform collection, management, and provision of real time transport information reliably. It can be deployed based on the Common Object Request Broker Architecture (CORBA) of the Object Management Group (OMG) because it consists of many interconnected heterogeneous systems deployed by independent organizations. Fault Tolerant CORBA (FT-CORBA) supports real time requirement of transport information stably through redundancy by replication of server objects. However, object replication, management, and related protocols of FT-CORBA require extra system resources of CPU and memory, and can degrade the system performance both locally and as a whole. This paper proposes an architecture to enhance performance of FT-CORBA based ITS in terms of CPU and memory by managing object replication adaptively during system operation with an agent. The application of the agent is expected to support fault tolerance of real ITS efficiently.

Keywords: Agent, Fault Tolerance, ITS, Real Time.

1 Introduction

The ITS is deployed by various independent organizations and therefore is operated on heterogeneous platforms to satisfy its characteristics, functions, and performance requirements. FT-CORBA with stateful failover is needed to satisfy real time requirements of transport information considering its update cycle of 5 minutes. In stateful failover, checkpointed state information is periodically sent to the standby object so that when the object crashes, the checkpointed information can help the standby object to restart the process from there [9]. FT-CORBA protocols need additional CORBA objects such as the Replication Manager and Fault Detectors, server object replicas, and communications for fault tolerance, and therefore require accompanying CPU and memory uses, which can cause processing delays, thereby deteriorating the performance. Processing delay can be a failure for real time

D. Ślęzak et al. (Eds.): GDC 2009, CCIS 63, pp. 1–8, 2009.

services of transportation information. This paper proposes an agent based architecture to enhance the performance of FT-CORBA based ITS. Due to the real time and composite characteristics of ITS, the proposed architecture is expected to be applicable to most applications. In section 2, FT-CORBA related work is presented. In section 3, an architecture is proposed to perform object replication of FT-CORBA based ITS autonomously with an agent. In section 4, the performance of the proposed architecture is evaluated by simulation focused on usage of CPU and memory. In section 5, this research is concluded and future research directions are presented.

2 Related Work

The OMG established the FT-CORBA which enhances fault tolerance by creating replicas of objects in information systems based on the CORBA. Active and passive replications are two approaches for building fault-tolerant distributed systems [4]. End-to-end temporal predictability of the application's behavior can be provided by existing real-time fault tolerant CORBA work such as MEAD and FLARe [1][2]. However, they also adopt replication styles of FT-CORBA as they are. A prior research has shown that passive replication and its variants are more effective for distributed real time systems because of its low execution overhead [1]. In the WARM PASSIVE replication style, the replica group contains a single primary replica that responds to client messages. In addition, one or more backup replicas are pre-spawned to handle crash failures. If a primary fails, a backup replica is selected to function as the new primary and a new backup is created to maintain the replica group size above a threshold. The state of the primary is periodically loaded into the backup replicas, so that only a (hopefully minor) update to that state will be needed for failover [6].

FT-CORBA protocols need additional CORBA objects such as the Replication Manager and Fault Detectors, server object replicas, and communications for fault tolerance, and therefore require accompanying CPU and memory uses, which can cause processing delays, thereby deteriorating the performance. Processing delay can be a failure for real time services of transportation information. A research [8] has developed a solution to dynamically configure the appropriate replication style, monitoring style of object replicas, polling intervals and membership style. However, a method to maintain minimum number of replicas autonomously, which means adjusting "a threshold" specified in the warm passive replication style for resource efficiency and overhead reduction of overall system, needs to be developed and improved.

3 Proposed Architecture

The FT-CORBA can be represented as Fig. 1 when an application uses the WARM PASSIVE style.

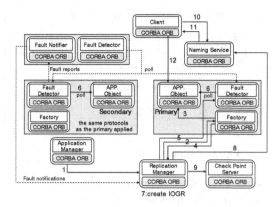

Fig. 1. FT-CORBA Protocol

The processes of Fig. 1 are summarized as follows [7]. 1. An application manager can request the Replication Manager to create a replica group using the create object operation of the FT-CORBA's Generic Factory interface and passing it a set of fault tolerance properties for the replica group. 2. The Replication Manager, as mandated by the FT-CORBA standard, delegates the task of creating individual replicas to local factory objects based on the Object Location property. 3. The local factories create objects. 4. The local factories return individual object references (IORs) of created objects to the Replication Manager. 5. The Replication Manager informs Fault Detectors to start monitoring the replicas. 6. Fault Detectors polls objects periodically. 7. The Replication Manager collects all the IORs of the individual replicas, creates an Interoperable Object Group References (IOGRs) for the group, and designates one of the replicas as a primary. 8. The Replication Manager registers the IOGR with the Naming Service, which publishes it to other CORBA applications and services. 9. The Replication Manager checkpoints the IOGR and other state. 10. A client interested in the service contacts the Naming Service. 11. The Naming Service responds with the IOGR. 12. Finally, the client makes a request and the client ORB ensures that the request is sent to the primary replica. The Fault Detector, Application Object, and Generic Factory in Fig. 1 are located on the same server.

The use of system CPU and memory resources in FT-CORBA is large, which can affect the real time characteristics of ITS due to processing delays because FT-CORBA is an architecture to enhance fault tolerance based on the redundancy of objects. Accordingly, it is possible to enhance resources availability and therefore prevent potential service delays if an autonomous agent (FTAgent) is introduced to the FT-CORBA based ITS, which adjusts the minimum numbers of object replicas autonomously. An autonomous agent is a system situated within and a part of an environment that senses that environment and acts on it, over time, in pursuit of its own agenda, and so as to effect what it senses in the future [5]. The FTAgent has algorithm and database which can help to maintain the number of replicas efficiently which require system CPU and memory resources both directly and indirectly, which can lower performance in terms of the overall ITS. The FTAgent is introduced in Fig. 2 on the same system as the Replication Manager in Fig. 1 which maintains 3 replicas for each object in this paper, i.e., the primary, first secondary, and second secondary replicas.

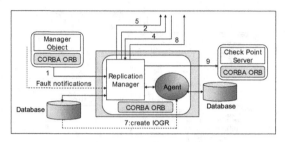

Fig. 2. Architecture to improve FT-CORBA

The FTAgent maintains its DB to support the Replication Manager for management of object replicas whose schema is as shown in Table 1.

Table 1. DB maintained by the FTAgent

IOGR IDs	date(dd/mm/yy)	time	failure 1	failure 2	flag	risky$_k$	NoROR
1	01/01/08	00:00:00~00:04:59	0	0	0	0	0
.	.	.	.	.	.	.	.
100	31/01/08	23:55:00~23:59:59	0	1	0	0	1

The IOGR IDs identify replica groups of each object whose numbers are 100 in this paper. The numbers of records in Table 1 are maintained to be under 1 million because values of the time attribute of Table 1 are measured by 5 minutes per day. The date identifies days of one month. The time is measured every 5 minutes. The failure 1 means failures of primary object replicas which are original or recovered from previous failures. The failure 2 means failures of first secondary replicas after becoming the primary ones. The values of failure 1 and 2 are 0 for working and 1 for failed, respectively. The flag has two values which are 0 when primary or first secondary is working and 1 when both primary and first secondary have failed for respective 5 minutes as a service period. The risky$_k$ is a fault possibility index for object groups, which is assigned to each period of 5 minutes for one hour backward from current time, and is set to zero at first. The k and risky$_k$ are equivalent and they ranges from 0 to 11 because the flag is set to 1 up to a maximum of 11 times for one hour. The values are assigned in the way that 11 and 0 are assigned to the nearest and furthest periods of 5 minutes to current time, respectively. The NoROR stands for the number of reduced object replicas. The FTAgent algorithm is described as follows.

```
FTAgent(int rush hours){
   while(there is no termination condition){
(1)  search whether primary replicas of each object are
     working on the DB maintained by Replication Manager
     (RM) in real time resuming every 5 minutes which
     ranges from previous to next middles of the informa-
     tion service period of 5 minutes, restricted to last
     30 days from current time;
```

```
(2)  if(primary replica is working){failure 1=0 for all
         object groups identified by IOGRs; flag=0;}
(3)  else{failure 1=1 for all object groups;
(4)       confirm whether first secondary of each object pro-
          moted to primary by RM is working on the RM DB;
(5)       if(first secondary is working){failure 2=0;flag=0;}
(6)       else{failure 2=1;
(7)           confirm whether the replica created by RM,
              substituting for crashed primary is working;
(8)           if(it is working){failure 1=0; flag=0;}
(9)           else flag = 1;}}
(10)Decision_Number_of_Replicas(rush hours);}}
```

```
Decision_Number_of_Replicas(int rush hours){
(11)an array for numbers of two successive 1's of flag
    values for all object groups=0;
(12)search successions of two 1's in flag values for all
    object groups;
(13)if(there are two successive 1's of flag values) add
    to the number of two successive 1's of flag values
    for relevant objects;
(14)if{(number of two successive 1's ≥ 1 for last one
       hour)and(rush hours)}{
```

(15)   NoROR=[3-3×{max(risky$_k$)/11}]/3;NoROR$_1$=NoROR;

(16)   if(0≤k≤5){NoROR =$\{\sum_{d=1}^{30}(d \times NoROR_d)\}$/30/30; NoROR$_2$ = NoROR;}

```
(17)  select the smaller one between NoROR₁ and NoROR₂,
      round it off, and assign the result to NoROR;
(18)  let RM keep the number of relevant object replicas
      minus NoROR, whose selection is the order of their
      ID numbers;}
(19)else if{(number of separate 1's≥2 for last one
      hour)and(rush hours)}{
(20)  if(min|tᵢ-tⱼ|<5minutes)let RM keep the number of re-
           levant object replicas 3;
(21)   else let RM reduce the number to 2;}
(22)else let RM reduce the number to 2 which mean the two
    of the 3 replicas which are working at the moment
    and whose priority for selection is the order of
    their ID numbers;}
```

In line (16), NoROR$_d$ means daily minimum number of reduced object replicas for last 30 days. In line (20), t_i and t_j mean the time when flag values are 1, respectively. The proposed architecture in this paper can be applied to the work such as MEAD and FLARe to increase resource availability and decrease overheads by enhancing utilization efficiency of CPU and memory, thereby improving end-to-end temporal predictability of the overall system.

4 Evaluations

The items for performance evaluation are total time of CPU use and maximum usage of memory of servers related to the 11 processes except for the 12th process in Fig. 1 from the beginning to termination of the simulation of two types to maintain 3 and 2 object replicas for fault tolerance [3]. The simulation has been performed on the PC with Intel Pentium M Processor 1.60 GHz, 1.0 GB memory, and Windows XP as the OS. The programs are implemented in Visual C++ 6.0. Firstly, the use rate of CPU during simulation is 100% on the implementation environment, and therefore it is appropriate to measure and compare total times of CPU use from beginning to termination of the simulation programs of two types. They must be measured for all servers related to creation and maintenance of object replicas in Fig. 1. The processes without numbers on arrows in Fig. 1 are not considered. Accordingly, the number of CPUs to be considered is 11.

Secondly, the peak usage is more appropriate for memory rather than continuous measurement of memory use. Therefore, the maximum usage of two types of 3 and 2 replicas is measured respectively. Total time of CPU use and maximum usage of memory are compared in that the Replication Manager maintains 3 and 2 replicas of objects respectively. Namely, the 11 processes prior to the client requesting services in Fig. 1 are simulated with 2 separate programs which describe the two types in terms of CPU and memory use. The components of the FT-CORBA are the same and therefore they are not designed in the programs in terms of memory use. The processing latencies with loops in the programs are set for the type of 3 replicas as follows: 1) latency between internal components: 2 sec. 2) latency between external components: 3 sec. 3) latency for the FTAgent to search the DB maintained by the Replication Manager and itself and to deliver related information to it : 5 sec. Of course, latencies directly related to creating and maintaining 2 replicas are set to two thirds of those for 3 replicas. The values of the established processing latencies are variable due to basic processes of the OS in the implementation environment, which is ignored because the variableness originates uniformly in simulations of both types to be compared. The conditions presented earlier are based on the experimental fact that the processing latency to select records which have the condition of the line (14) in the algorithm is about 3 seconds in case of the Oracle 9i DBMS which maintains 1 million records with 13 columns on IBM P650 with 4 CPUs of 1.24GHz and 12GB memory, and is 34 Km distant from a client.

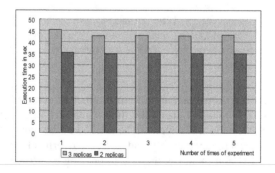

Fig. 3. Total time of CPU use in sec

A commercial internet browser is used as an object to simulate usage of CPU and memory in creation and termination of 3 and 2 object replicas obviously. The browser is called 3 and 2 times by types and kept as processes until the simulation is finished. The types of 3 and 2 replicas are simulated respectively by executing the relevant programs 5 times where www.sersc.org/GDC2009 is filled in the URL of the browser assumed as an object. The results for the total CPU time used are shown in Fig. 3.

The total time of CPU use ranges from 42.75 to 45.45 seconds for the type of 3 replicas. The arithmetic mean is 43.40 seconds and the standard deviation is 1.15 seconds, which is 2.7% based on the minimum of 42.75 seconds. On the other hand, the total time of CPU use ranges from 34.77 to 35.27 seconds for the type of 2 replicas. The arithmetic mean is 34.96 seconds and the standard deviation is 0.19 seconds, which is 0.5% based on the minimum of 34.77 seconds. The deviations result from basic processes of Windows XP, the properties of processed data, and a variable network situation, which causes deviations because the browser is used as an object. The performance improvement in terms of CPU is 19.45% through comparison of the values of the two arithmetic means. Accordingly, the improvement ranges from 0 to 19.45% whose lower and upper bounds correspond to simultaneous failures of 100% and 0% of primary and first secondary replicas, respectively. Therefore, the expected improvement is the arithmetic mean of 9.73% assuming the ratio of simultaneous failures of primary and first secondary replicas is 50% over all objects.

The results for maximum usage of memory are shown in Fig. 4.

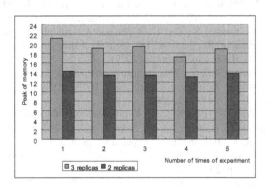

Fig. 4. Maximum usage of memory in MB

The expected improvement is 14.54% assuming the ratio of simultaneous failures of primary and first secondary replicas is 50% over all objects in the same way as CPU.

The simulation has been performed with another URL of www.springer.com to investigate how much the properties of processed data and a variable network situation influence the results. The expected improvement for CPU is 9.26% which is 0.47% lower than that with the previous URL. The expected improvement for memory is 11.53% which is 3.01% lower than that with the previous URL. To sum up, the influence of the properties of processed data and a variable network situation on the ratio of performance improvement in terms of CPU and memory is small although there is a difference in memory.

5 Conclusion

The ITS can be deployed based on FT-CORBA efficiently considering heterogeneous and its real time properties. However, improvement is needed to enhance performance of the ITS based on FT-CORBA because it requires additional uses of CPU and memory for object redundancy. This paper has proposed an architecture to adjust the number of object replicas autonomously with an agent. In the future, additional research is needed to optimize the number of object replicas in real environment of ITS. Firstly, the FTAgent can improve its own performance over time by learning from statistical data related to recovery of replicas by objects such as the interval to check failures and their frequency, which means improvement of the line (14) through (22) of the algorithm. Secondly, the size of the DB maintained by the FTAgent has to be studied experimentally as well which is the record of failures for one month in this paper. It will be decided according to the characteristics of transportation information. The proposed architecture can be applied to other FT-CORBA based systems considering complex feature and strict service requirement of ITS.

References

1. Balasubramanian, J., Gokhale, A., Schmidt, D.C., Wang, N.: Towards Middleware for Fault-tolerance in Distributed Real-time and Embedded Systems. In: Meier, R., Terzis, S. (eds.) DAIS 2008. LNCS, vol. 5053, pp. 72–85. Springer, Heidelberg (2008)
2. Balasubramanian, J., Tambe, S., Lu, C., Gokhale, A.: Adaptive Failover for Real-time Middleware with Passive Replication. In: 15th Real-time and Embedded Application Symposium, pp. 1–10. IEEE, Los Alamitos (2009)
3. FatihAkay, M., Katsinis, C.: Performance improvement of parallel programs on a broadcast-based distributed shared memory multiprocessor by simulation. Simulation Modelling Practice and Theory 16(3), 347–349 (2008)
4. Felber, P., Narasimhan, P.: Experiences, Approaches and Challenges in building Fault-tolerant CORBA Systems. Transactions of Computers 54(5), 497–511 (2004)
5. Franklin, S., Graesser, A.: Is it an Agent, or just a Program?: A Taxonomy for Autonomous Agents. In: Jennings, N.R., Wooldridge, M.J., Müller, J.P. (eds.) ECAI-WS 1996 and ATAL 1996. LNCS, vol. 1193, p. 25. Springer, Heidelberg (1997)
6. Gokhale, A., Natarajan, B., Schmidt, D.C., Cross, J.: Towards Real-time Fault-Tolerant CORBA Middleware. Cluster Computing: the Journal on Networks, Software, and Applications Special Issue on Dependable Distributed Systems 7(4), 15 (2004)
7. Natarajan, B., Gokhale, A., Yajnik, S.: DOORS: Towards High-performance Fault Tolerant CORBA. In: 2nd Distributed Applications and Objects (DOA) conference, pp. 1–2. IEEE, Los Alamitos (2000)
8. Natarajan, B., Gokhale, A., Yajnik, S., Schmidt, D.C.: Applying patterns to improve the performance of fault tolerant CORBA. In: Prasanna, V.K., Vajapeyam, S., Valero, M. (eds.) HiPC 2000. LNCS, vol. 1970, pp. 11–12. Springer, Heidelberg (2000)
9. Saha, I., Mukhopadhyay, D., Banerjee, S.: Designing Reliable Architecture For Stateful Fault Tolerance. In: 7th International Conference on Parallel and Distributed Computing, Applications and Technologies (PDCAT 2006), p. 545. IEEE Computer Society, Washington (2006)

Meshlization of Irregular Grid Resource Topologies by Heuristic Square-Packing Methods

Uei-Ren Chen[1], Chin-Chi Wu[2], Sheng-Wun Li[3], and Woei Lin[3]

[1] Department of Electronic Engineering, Hsiuping Institute of Technology
[2] Department of Information Management, Nan-Kai University of Technology
[3] Department of Computer Science, National Chung Hsing University

Abstract. Traditionally, the assignment problem between tasks and processors is worked out by scheduling methods. In this paper, we have an innovative idea to construct a problem-solving environment for computational grids. To bridge the gap between the parallel processing technology and the heterogeneous computing environment, the grid computing resources are reorganized architecturally to form a virtual regular topology. In this research, we put emphasis on finding a heuristic algorithm of transferring an irregular grid resource topology into a mesh virtually.

1 Introduction

Grid computing [3] is a new generation of computing paradigm that coordinates the use of resources, such as high performance computers, networks, databases, and scientific instruments owned and managed by multiple organizations. In comparison with the previous task-resource mappings by the scheduling algorithms, we have other ideas of constructing a problem-solving environment on computational grids. Figure 1 depicts the major difference between the task scheduling and our methodology. We first perform the transformation called *meshlization* of the resource topology selected from the computational grid, and then we assign tasks to the virtual mesh by using traditional parallel processing techniques, so as to solve the *matrix computing problems* [6]. From the aspect of virtual mesh, the concept is similar to the *mesh-partition* or the *graph-partition* problems [9] which consider how to divide a mesh or a graph into parts. Recent works on partitioning for heterogeneous environments include PART [1], JOSTLE [10], SCOTCH [8], and PaGrid [4]. Huang *et al.* have compared their PaGrid with above and shown the partitions with better quality [4]. In the proposed algorithm, transforming computational nodes into square blocks and permuting them in a virtual mesh, we translate the mesh-partition problem into a variant of the off-line two-dimensional *bin-packing problem* [2] using m square items and a fixed-size bin. Leung *et al.* have proved that the problem of packing a set of squares into a square is NP-complete [5]. The difference between the bin-packing problem and ours are that: i) the square items in this research can be changed in size to pack in a bin; ii) our objective is neither maximizing the items packed in bins nor minimizing the number of bins for packing items; iii) we find the permutation with better computational and communicational abilities.

D. Ślęzak et al. (Eds.): GDC 2009, CCIS 63, pp. 9–16, 2009.
© Springer-Verlag Berlin Heidelberg 2009

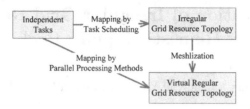

Fig. 1. Comparision of Mappings

2   Proposed Algorithms

The computational grid includes a set of resources, network devices, and links
used to connect them. Theoretically, the grid resource model can be represented
as an undirected connected graph $G = (R, L)$, where R is the *resource set*, and
L is the *link set*. The resource set consists of *computational nodes* and *routing
nodes*. After selecting resources from the computational grid, an example of the
grid resource topology is given in Fig. 2 (a). The *computational node* may be a
supercomputer, a cluster of workstations or computing devices practically and
it is denoted as c with a parameter P_C called *computational ability*. The link can
be defined with a parameter P_B which represents the *communication ability*.

In our meshlization algorithm, the square basic block in Fig. 2 (b) which
represents a computational node is used to permute in a mesh. In Fig. 2 (c),
the edges can be turned into two kinds, that is, *internal links* and *external
links* after placing the basic blocks in a virtual mesh. Internal links are those
edges inside the same basic block or those edges that connect virtual nodes

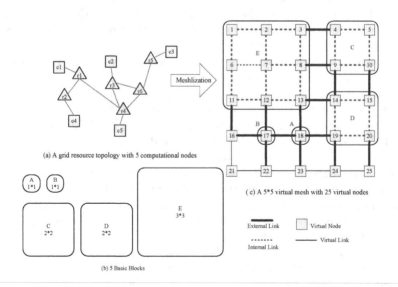

Fig. 2. An Example of Meshlization

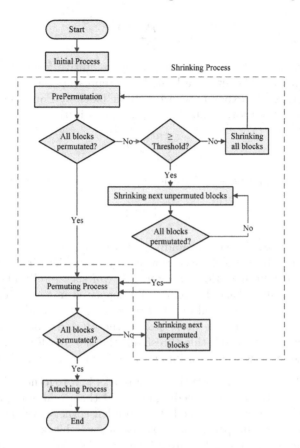

Fig. 3. Flowchart of ISPA algorithm

belong to the same computational node. External links are those edges that connect virtual nodes of basic blocks represent distinct computational nodes. Internal links have better communicational ability than external links because the messages are communicated in the same computational node. The reason of choosing the square block is that it owns the most number of internal links than other rectangulars under the same size.

The input of this algorithm is a virtual mesh and a grid resource topology selected from the computational grid. The output is the mapping result from each computational node to the virtual nodes in the mesh. Figure 3 shows the flowchart of ISPA algorithms.

Initial Process. The ability of computational nodes selected from the grid resource topology is normalized in quantity. The minimal computational ability denoted PC_{min} will be normalized to one; other denoted $PC(c_i)$ for the computational node c_i will be set to the relative ratio nr_i of the minimal one.

$$nr_i = \frac{PC(c_i)}{PC_{min}} \tag{1}$$

The computational node is turned into a representative form of a basic block with size denoted a_i. The size of a basic block represents the number of virtual nodes in this block. We expand the size of basic block by Equation 2. The mesh size denoted N is the total number of virtual nodes in this mesh.

$$a_i = \frac{nr_i}{\sum_i nr_i} \times N \tag{2}$$

The side for each square basic block denoted s_i can be defined as follows.

$$s_i = \lfloor \sqrt{a_i} \rfloor \tag{3}$$

Shrinking Process. To check rapidly that all blocks can fit in the mesh, the pre-permuation of basic blocks is performed by using the First-Fit-Decreasing algorithm [11]. Pre-permutation will stop if it can successfully place all blocks in a mesh. If not all of basic blocks can be deposited in the virtual mesh, the shrinking process will be started up. A *shrinking threshold* is a ratio of the total size of permuted blocks to the mesh size. If the total size of permuted blocks is not larger enough to reach this threshold, the side of all square blocks will decrease by one, otherwise just shrinking the side of remaining blocks by one.

Permuting Process. To make the basic blocks join together, the permuting process will always place the succeeding blocks at the neighbor of previous ones. The first basic block is always placed at the top left corner of the mesh. A search tree can be produced by permuting a series of basic blocks in a mesh. If the search tree is fully expanded, the growth will be highly exponential. To reduce the complexity and find the best placement of basic blocks, a heuristic searching method called A^* *search* is used [7]. Three permuting policies are considered.

1. *Large Block First (LBF)*: The large basic block takes precedence over small ones and it will be selected to permute in the virtual mesh.
2. *Small Block First (SBF)*: The small basic block has higher priority than big one to be selected and permuted in the virtual mesh.
3. *Random*: The order of selecting basic blocks is made at random.

The cost function $f(.)$ used by A^* search consists of two parts, $g(.)$ and $h(.)$.

$$f(.) = g(.) + h(.) \tag{4}$$

The function $g(.)$ can be defined as follow, where $x > 0$ is the total number of internal links, and $y > 0$ is the total number of external links while permuting from the first block to the current one.

$$g(.) = \frac{y}{x} \tag{5}$$

The *estimative function* $h(.)$ is defined as follows, where $x' > 0$ is the total number of internal links after setting the next block, and $y' > 0$ is the total number of external links.

$$h(.) = \frac{y' + y}{x' - x} \tag{6}$$

By definition of the cost function $f(.)$, it has small value while the permutation of blocks in a mesh with small number of external links and large number of internal links. The object of A^* search is to find the solution with small cost.

Attaching Process. For the remaining nodes in the virtual mesh, we have the option of taking one from five policies mentioned below.

1. *Strong Node First (SNF)*: The remaining virtual nodes are attached to the block (represents a computational node) with the maximal computational ability shared by its virtual nodes. We assume that the ability of a computational node is shared by its virtual nodes evenly.
2. *Near Node First (NNF)*: The remaining virtual nodes are attached to the nearest basic block which has the minimal Euclidean distance between them.
3. *First Strong Then Near (FSTN)*: The block with powerful ability has higher attaching priority than the nearest one. The remaining virtual nodes are attached to the block with the maximal shared ability, but if the abilities of two nodes are equal, the near computational node will be attached.
4. *First Near Then Strong (FNTS)*: The nearest computational node will be attached, but if the Euclidean distances of two nodes are equal, the powerful node will be attached.
5. *Random*: Attach virtual nodes to the target randomly.

3   Experiment Results

In the simulation, the mesh size is 70×70. The grid resource topologies with different ratios of computational abilities is listed in Table 1. The communicational abilities in grid resource topologies are set to 100 for external links and 1000 for internal links. The shrinking threshold is set to 0.6.

Table 1. Computational Abilities of Grid Resource Topologies

Topologies	Computational Nodes				
	c_1	c_2	c_3	c_4	c_5
Topology1	500	1000	2000	2500	4000
Topology2	2000	2000	2000	2000	2000
Topology3	500	500	500	4250	4250
Topology4	525	525	2100	2100	4750

Table 2. Abbreviations for Combinations of Permuting and Attaching Policies

Attaching Policies	Permuting Policies		
	LBF	SBF	Random
SNF	lb-s	sb-s	r-s
NNF	lb-n	sb-n	r-n
FSTN	lb-sn	sb-sn	r-sn
FNTS	lb-ns	sb-ns	r-ns
Random	lb-r	sb-r	r-r

The *average computational abilities* $\overline{PC}$ is the optimal shared value for each virtual node and can be defined as follows.

$$\overline{PC} = \frac{1}{N} \times \sum_{i=1}^{N} PC(c_i) \tag{7}$$

In Equ. 8, *variance of computational abilities* evaluates the difference between the abilities of virtual nodes and $\overline{PC}$. N is the total number of computational nodes and $PC(c_i)$ is the computational ability of the computational node c_i.

$$\sigma^2 = \frac{1}{N-1} \times \sum_{i=1}^{N} \left[PC(c_i) - \overline{PC} \right] \tag{8}$$

The *average communicational ability* $\overline{PB}$ is the ratio of total communicational ability to total number of links. In Equation 9, $PB(l_{in})$ is the communicational ability of the internal link l_{in} and $PB(l_{ext})$ is that of the external link l_{ext}. Let N_{in} is the total number of internal links and N_{ext} is that for external links.

$$\overline{PB} = \frac{\sum PB(l_{in}) + \sum PB(l_{ext})}{N_{in} + N_{ext}} \tag{9}$$

Table 2 shows the abbreviations for combinations of permuting and attaching policies mentioned in Section 2.

Table 3(a) shows the Strong Node First and Strong First Then Near policies can effectively reduce the variance of computational abilities in comparison with other attaching policies. Table 3(a) shows that the difference between the ratio of computational ability in the resource topology and its ratio of block size can influence the variance of computational abilities in a virtual mesh. Topology 2 and Topology 4 have the equivalent ratio of computational ability to their block sizes, but Topology 1 and Topology 3 are not. The results in Table 3(a) show that we can get the smaller variance of computational abilities while the ratio of computational ability is close to the ratio of block size such as Topology 2 and Topology 4 in Table 3(a). Moreover, the ISPA has the smaller variance than PaGrid, while the ratio of computational ability approaches the ratio of block size. For the attaching policies of the ISPA algorithm, the First Near then Strong or Near Node First policy can get less number of external links than

Table 3. Performance of the 70 × 70 Mesh for Test Topologies

(a) Variance of Computatonal Abilities

Topology #	lb-sn	lb-ns	lb-s	lb-n	lb-r	sb-sn	sb-ns	sb-s	sb-n	sb-r	r-sn	r-ns	r-s	r-n	r-r	PaGrid
1	0.07	0.56	0.07	1.04	0.40	0.07	0.81	0.07	0.81	0.38	0.07	0.59	0.07	0.22	0.40	0.0003
2	≈ 0	0.34	≈ 0	4.39	1.61	≈ 0	0.34	≈ 0	4.39	1.68	≈ 0	1.97	≈ 0	4.39	1.94	0.0002
3	0.30	1.14	0.30	1.25	1.64	0.30	0.62	0.30	0.56	1.62	0.30	1.08	0.30	0.65	1.60	0.003
4	≈ 0	0.15	≈ 0	0.88	0.10	≈ 0	0.43	≈ 0	0.61	0.09	≈ 0	0.37	≈ 0	0.61	0.10	0.0014

(b) Number of External Links

Topology #	lb-sn	lb-ns	lb-s	lb-n	lb-r	sb-sn	sb-ns	sb-s	sb-n	sb-r	r-sn	r-ns	r-s	r-n	r-r	PaGrid
1	425	220	683	192	1277	214	157	673	204	1285	235	177	458	204	1278	323
2	344	202	406	241	1695	344	202	406	241	1681	344	202	406	241	1711	416
3	223	203	261	246	1761	217	162	261	256	1779	242	196	258	245	1796	336
4	393	228	1885	225	2263	522	135	2035	163	2277	459	171	1893	163	2249	340

(c) Average Communicational Ability

Topology #	lb-sn	lb-ns	lb-s	lb-n	lb-r	sb-sn	sb-ns	sb-s	sb-n	sb-r	r-sn	r-ns	r-s	r-n	r-r	PaGrid
1	957	978	931	981	871	979	984	932	980	872	978	982	953	980	869	967
2	965	980	959	976	827	965	980	959	976	830	964	980	959	979	830	957
3	978	980	974	975	823	978	984	974	974	821	976	980	974	975	819	965
4	961	977	810	977	772	948	986	795	984	771	954	983	810	984	774	965

(d) Branch Amount Visited by A^*

Topology #	lb-sn	lb-ns	lb-s	lb-n	lb-r	sb-sn	sb-ns	sb-s	sb-n	sb-r	r-sn	r-ns	r-s	r-n	r-r
1	16375	16375	16375	16375	16375	13799	13799	13799	13799	13799	8492	18554	18554	17870	8492
2	19358	19358	19358	19358	19358	19358	19358	19358	19358	19358	27058	23710	27058	19358	19358
3	27515	27515	27515	27515	27515	17092	17092	17092	17092	17092	25709	25709	28270	31978	21817
4	25544	25544	25544	25544	25544	14641	14641	14641	14641	14641	28468	28509	23598	14641	21241

others as shown in Table 3(b). The reason is that the First Near then Strong and Near Node First policies assign the neighbor nodes in the mesh to the same computational node so as to reduce the number of external links. In Table 3(b), the ISPA has less number of external links than PaGrid while using the Near Node First and First Near Then Strong attaching policies. As shown in Table 3(c), the average communicational ability of the First Near then Strong or Near Node First is greater than other attaching policies, because they have a larger number of internal links and less number of external links. Table 3(c) shows that the ISPA algorithm with the Near Node First and First Near Then Strong attaching policies can have greater communicational ability than PaGrid. The branch amount in Table 3(d) shows that the A^* search can massively reduce the complexity of block permutation. For example, the branch amount of complete search tree is about 10^8 for permuting five blocks in a 70 × 70 mesh according to our estimation. For test topologies in Table 3(d), their branches actually travelled by A^* search are less than 32000. This result shows that there are above ninty percent of branches reduced by A^* search. Table 3(d) shows that the precedence of permuting basic block has a massive impact on the branch amount of search trees while the difference of the block size is enormous. For instance of Topology

3 in Table 3(d), Small Block First has less branch amount than other permuting policies while the ratio difference of the computational ability and the block size is massive.

4   Conclusions

In this paper, we propose a heuristic square-packing algorithm to transfer a grid resource topology into a virtual mesh. Our experiment results show that the ISPA algorithm can evenly distribute the computational ability of the grid resource to the virtual mesh. Because having more internal links, the virtual mesh gets larger average communicational ability than PaGrid.

Acknowledgment

The equipment assistance of the National Center for High-Performance Computing (NCHC) in Taiwan, ROC is gratefully appreciated.

References

1. Chen, J., Taylor, V.E.: Mesh partitioning for efficient use of distributed systems. IEEE Transactions on Parallel and Distributed Systems 13(1), 67–79 (2002)
2. Coffman, E.G., Garey, M.R., Johnson, D.S.: Approximation algorithms for bin packing: a survey. Approximation Algorithms for NP-hard Problems, 46–93 (1997)
3. Foster, I., Kesselman, C. (eds.): The Grid: Blueprint for a New Computing Infrastructure, 1st edn. Morgan-Kaufman, San Francisco (1998)
4. Huang, S., Aubanel, E., Bhavsar, V.C.: Pagrid: A mesh partitioner for computational grids. Journal of Grid Computing 4(1), 71–88 (2006)
5. Leung, J.Y.T., Tam, T.W., Wong, C.S.: Packing squares into a square. Journal of Parallel and Distributed Computing 10, 271–275 (1990)
6. Modi, J.J.: Parallel Algorithms and Matrix Computation. Clarendon Press (1988)
7. Pearl, J.: Heuristics: intelligent search strategies for computer problem solving. Addison-Wesley Longman Publishing Co., Inc., Boston (1984)
8. Pellegrini, F., Roman, J.: Scotch: A software package for static mapping by dual recursive bipartitioning of process and architecture graphs. In: Liddell, H., Colbrook, A., Hertzberger, B., Sloot, P.M.A. (eds.) HPCN-Europe 1996. LNCS, vol. 1067, pp. 493–498. Springer, Heidelberg (1996)
9. Schloegel, K., Karypis, G., Kumar, V.: Graph Partitioning for High-Performance Scientific Simulations. In: Sourcebook of Parallel Computing, pp. 491–541. Morgan Kaufmann, San Francisco (2003)
10. Walshaw, C., Cross, M.: Multilevel mesh partitioning for heterogeneous communication networks. Future Generation Computer Systems 17(5), 601–623 (2001)
11. Yao, A.C.C.: New algorithms for bin packing. Journal of the ACM 27(2), 207–227 (1980)

An Architecture and Supporting Environment of Service-Oriented Computing Based-On Context Awareness

Tianxiao Ma, Gang Wu, and Jun Huang

School of Software, Shanghai Jiao Tong University,
Dongchuan Road No.800, 200240 Shanghai, China
mysun@sjtu.edu.cn, wugang@cs.sjtu.edu.cn, sbdwhj@gmail.com

Abstract. Service-oriented computing (SOC) is emerging to be an important computing paradigm of the next future. Based on context awareness, this paper proposes an architecture of SOC. A definition of the context in open environments such as Internet is given, which is based on ontology. The paper also proposes a supporting environment for the context-aware SOC, which focus on services on-demand composition and context-awareness evolving. A reference implementation of the supporting environment based on OSGi[11] is given at last.

Keywords: Service-oriented computing, Context awareness, Architecture.

1 Introduction

Open, dynamic and hard to control are inherent attributes of Internet platform. These attributes bring challenges to develop, deploy, run and maintain software in such a platform. In order to tackle these challenges, service-oriented computing (SOC) has emerged as a promising computing paradigm for the next future. In SOC, services are autonomous and platform-independent computational elements which can be described, published, discovered, orchestrated, and deployed with standard protocols[1]. Under this paradigm, the most attractive thing is to let autonomous stand alone services cooperate with each other by certain kind of mechanism which will finally generate a distributed computing network.

To accomplish on-demand service composition and context-aware evolving, many aspects should be studied including context representation, context-aware mechanism, self-adaptation of services, and co-evolution among services.

Context description and collection are the basis for auto-evolvement of SOC style application. Therefore, this paper gives a definition of the context[13] based on ontology, including the static description and dynamical runtime information of services. Then a context-aware architecture is proposed in this paper. The mechanism of service on-demand aggregation and dynamically evolvement under this architecture are described. Moreover, a design of the supporting system which will work as a middleware to help build the application under this architecture is given. Finally we give a reference implementation of the supporting system.

D. Ślęzak et al. (Eds.): GDC 2009, CCIS 63, pp. 17–24, 2009.

The remainder of this paper is organized as follows. Section 2 proposes the context-aware architecture, and explains how the autonomous services composed together cooperate and evolve dynamically with the awareness of the context changing. Section 3 gives the detailed definition of the context ontology. A model of the supporting environment base on the architecture is presented in section 4. The reference implementation of the environment is given in section 5. Section 6 discusses the related work and section 7 concludes the paper with future work.

2   Context Aware Architecture

Service model was introduced to represent the interactive relationship between the stand alone autonomous services. The typical service model includes three actors which are service provider, service requester and service register. With the help of service register, a service requester could locate its required service providers automatically and establish a virtual running environment for certain application requirement.

Definition(Service Entity): Service entity in our context aware architecture is a computing entity which has certain service requirement or some serving abilities or both. It needs other service entities to satisfy its requirements as well as serves other service entities. That is to say, it could be a service requester or a service provider or both.

Definition (Service Context Address): This address is a URL which can be used to fetch the whole context of a service entity. The directory service will hold such addresses. Fig.1 presents the context aware architecture of SOC.

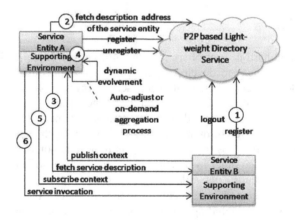

Fig. 1. Context-aware Architecture for SOC

A typical running scene under this architecture is shown as follows. (1) Service Entity B registers itself to the light-weight directory service. (2) After registration, Service Entity A looks for candidate services which can satisfy its requirement through the directory service. The result returned from the directory service is the addresses of context description of candidate service entities. (3) Entity A fetches the context of each candidate service, which includes static information such as ability description and dynamical information such as runtime status. (4) Entity A compares the acquired context with its own requirements to choose a suitable service entity and then builds an aggregation relationship with the selected service entity. Repeating the previous steps several times will form a virtual running environment (VRE). (5) After that, Entity A will subscribe to context transformations which it cares about from every service entity in the VRE. (6) Start the execution of the application by Entity A. If the subscribed context transforms during the execution, it will be published to Entity A. Entity A will adjust the execution according to the transformation based on some rules, such as looking for a new entity which will satisfy the requirements. The VRE evolves dynamically then.

2.1 Light-Weight Directory Service

In this paper, the directory service is light-weight because the information stored by the directory service is not the whole context of a service entity but an address of the context.

The context which can influence the composition of service entities includes both static and dynamical information such as function description, interface, running status and environment description. Even the static information would change during the service entity's lifecycle. If all these information are maintained in the directory server, it will cause bandwidth consumption and heavy loading pressure. As a result, we just store the address instead of the complete context in the directory server since it is relatively stable.

Centralized directory service is also not suitable. For services running on the Internet platform it will become the performance bottle-neck of the whole system. In this paper, P2P technology is used to construct a distributed directory server. The service name is recognized as hash information. Each directory server acts as a P2P node. The address of the context is stored on corresponding server by using the chord algorithm[7].

2.2 Service Discovery and On-Demand Aggregation Based on Context

As mentioned in the previous section, the directory service will store the context address of various service entities. So, through these addresses we can get complete context information of other services entities, which include the services provided by those service entities and related non-functionality abilities. By comparing such context information with the context that belongs to the service requester, we can finally determine which service is most suitable for the service requester. When the context of the service provider transformed, the service requester will reevaluate the suitability of the service provided by the service provider based on the transformed context and determine whether or not to choose another more suitable one.

In the SOC context, an application requirement will be accomplished by several composited service entities. The service entity which issues the requirement is called the main service entity which is responsible for discovering and compositing relative service entities according to their context and the application requirements. The VRE will then be formed after the on-demand integration process. This could be a nesting process, that means service entity A which was chosen by the main service entity might initiate a new process to discover and composite other service entities to help itself accomplish the service used by the main service entity.

This paper focus on how to realize on-demand integration based on context, so we make following assumptions. One is that we only concern which elements in the context will be used to match the application requirements, the exact value of the element is not concerned. We assume that among service entities there is a same semantic interpretation between the value of the context elements and the value of the requirements. For example, the main service entity's functional requirement is "order", and the candidate service entity's context has a functional description called "purchase". The problem whether the two terms have the same meaning is out of the scope of this paper, it could be answered by ontology reconciliation or other similar technologies[2]. Another assumption is that the service provider and requester can reach a consensus on the service interface on semantic level. When the requester gets the interface description from the context, it knows exactly the meaning of each parameter and the return value. Context based service discovery is accomplished by using the light-weight directory service.

2.3 Dynamic Evolvement Based on Context Awareness

The VRE is dynamically changing with the transformation of the context of each involved service entity. This paper introduces a subscribe/publish mechanism to support context awareness. As soon as the composition relationship is formed, the service requester will subscribe to its interested contexts from the selected service entity. When the transformed context of the service provider is published, the service requester can be aware of such transformations and it will check the updated context of the service provider to see if the service provided by the service provider is still satisfy its requirement and if it found the service can never satisfy its requirement it will begin to self-adjust or start a new composition process to implement dynamic evolvement.

Self-adjust behaviors include waiting for some time to see whether the context of the service provider will transform or not. If the context transformed, the service requester will reevaluate the context to decide whether the service provided by the service provider can still be used or not. If the result is positive, there is nothing needs to be changed, or a service discovery process will be launched by the service requester to found new services. The user can also specify their own self-adjust behaviors and associate such behaviors to designated contexts, when these contexts transformed, related user defined self-adjust behaviors will be activated. The context awareness and dynamic evolvement process is transparent to the application user.

3 Service Context Ontology

In an open environment, an explicit and semantic context description for services is needed as the foundation for the evolvement of services and services composition. We have define an internet ontology use RDF/OWL[10] to model service context. For detail about internet ontology, please see [13]. The SOC supporting environment proposed by this paper will use this ontology to represent and maintain the context related to service entities. Note that the service context ontology could be extended and improved continuously.

4 Supporting Environment of Context-Aware Service Composition

The supporting environment for context-awareness services composition is composed of context aware supporting system and runtime supporting system shown in Figure 2.

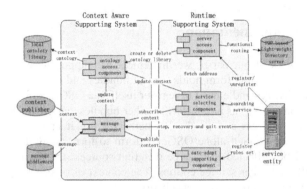

Fig. 2. Supporting environment for context-aware service composition

The context aware supporting system is responsible for collecting, managing, subscribing and publishing context, to give fundamental support for context awareness of the on-demand service composition. Runtime support systems include life cycle management, service invocation and auto-adaptation framework, which provided runtime support for the service entity. The supporting system runs as a middleware for every service entity. The functions of the main components are introduced as follows.

- **Server access component.** This component is used to communicate with the P2P-based directory server, to complete the registration and logout of the service entity, and to fetch the context description address of service entities.
- **Service selecting component.** This is the core component to implement on-demand composition, used by the service entity to select suitable services. With the help of the server access component it gets a list of contexts of candidate service entities and selects a suitable one from them based on the context. After the service provider is chosen, this component will use the context aware supporting system to accomplish two things. One is to update the run-time context ontology library to show which requirement is satisfied by which service entity. The other is to subscribe to the interested context elements from the service provider.
- **Auto-adapt supporting component.** This component is the receiver and processor of the context transformation. In this paper, we use a rule based reasoning mechanism[4] to construct the auto-adapt supporting component to make the service entity evolve dynamically. The service entity can register a set of customized rules to the component for responding to transformation of specific context elements.
- **Context ontology access component.** This component is responsible for creating and maintaining the run-time context ontology library.

- **Message component.** This component is used to maintain the context subscribing relationship. When the subscribed context element changes, it will be published to relevant service entities through message oriented middleware. In this paper we use the Probe-Gauge model in the Rainbow system[8] to acquire the context transformation, and use the Context Provisioning method in paper [9] to transfer the message.

5 Reference Implementation

To validate the work of our paper, we implement the supporting environment based on OSGi[11]. Each OSGi platform holds several bundles and each bundle represents a single service entity. A bundle need to register itself to a OSGi platform along with its service description address as parameter, so other bundles can get the service description based on the address and to check whether to use it or not. We also use R-OSGi[12] to integrating stand alone OSGi platform to form a OSGi platform cluster. The context will be collected from three different sources: the environment, the service entity itself, and other service entities. The context of other services will be collected through the publish-subscribe mechanism.

In our implementation, we treat scalability as the most important part of our supporting environment. We believe our supporting environment can suitable for as many application scenarios as possible. So, many important components in our reference implementation can be extended easily. These include local and remote probes, persistent strategy, context acquisition strategy, service selection strategy and self-adaptation strategy and so on. We also separate the context awareness support system and the runtime support system, so both can be used with other context awareness strategies or on-demand aggregation and self-adaptation strategies. For more detail, please see [13].

6 Related Work

Two key issues need to be tackled when implementing a context-aware service-oriented system. The first one is how to describe the context and second one is how to establish and maintain composition relationships based on the acquired context.

For the former issue, ontology seemed to be the most popular answer for its widely acceptation and semantic functionality. There are two different ways to using ontology to represent context. The first way is to allow independently designed ontology exist and then use ontology reconciliation[2] to hide the difference among ontologies. The second way is to define a unified ontology, and use this ontology as a standard to represent the context. This strategy eliminates the need of reconciliation. The problem of the former way is its complexity and imprecision, as the structure of different ontology may vary very much. And the result of the reconciliation is dependent on the algorithm used. The problem of the second is it is impossible to define an ontology which can represent every concept in every area. In this paper, our strategy to represent the context is much more like the second way aforementioned. The difference is that we are not trying to propose an ontology which includes everything, but we provide an extensible one. If somebody finds the original one is not sufficient, it can be extended easily.

Toward service composition, many research efforts have been put into service on-demand composition and auto-adaptive evolvement. The traditional way to composite services need people to specify composition rules first, for example, specifying the functional and non-functional requirements of each service which form the composition service. It makes the composition service difficult to adapt to the changing environment. This approach is clearly not suitable for a SOC paradigm, since applications are rarely constructed from scratch, but are always composed from existing service components. So, an application transparent method needs to be proposed for this type of service composition. Moreover, such a method also needs to monitor the execution status of the composition service and dynamically adapt the behavior of the composition service response to the rapid changing environment.

Some research focus on how to composite different services based on a context awareness way. Paper [3] and [4] use historical information to aggregate services to form a composition service. Paper [3] proposes an application-specific middleware to composite services adaptively based on a role structure. An organizer is responsible to compose different service based on some QoS information. This method is more suitable for coarse granularity services. For a service which provides the adding operation, it is hard to relate such fine granularity service to a role. Paper [4] uses data mining technology for service selection. The invocation history of a service will be recorded in a warehouse, and during the selection process, the historical information will be used to generate a service selection model. A service will finally be selected based on the user defined quality goals together with its history records.

Agent based solution are also used to tackle the problem of service composition and autonomous evolvement[5][6]. But until now, it is still very hard to construct agents, and this will bring significant complexity to systems for adopting such methods.

The supporting environment provided by this paper aims to balances application transparency and implementation complexity for context-aware service composition. The supporting environment proposed in this paper will support the whole life cycle of context-aware composition service, from service selection to composition service evolvement. With low invasiveness and high extensibility, our supporting environment will satisfies the requirement of context-awareness service composition.

7 Conclusion

This paper focuses on context aware SOC. We concluded which elements should be included in the context of the Internet computing environment and gave a definition of the service context based on ontology. A context-aware architecture for SOC is proposed. This paper explains how the service entities are aggregated together to cooperate under this architecture and evolve dynamically with the awareness of the context changing. Furthermore, the structure of the supporting environment is given and the function of each component is described. The supporting environment acts as the middleware to support the implementation and execution of the context-aware service composition. Finally, a reference implementation is proposed.

The future work includes improving the service context ontology and our reference implementation. We will make our reference implementation support P2P based addressing and provide a better service selection.

Acknowledgments. This work is supported by the National High-Tech Research and Development Plan of China (Grant No.2009AA01Z123). For more information please see [13].

References

1. Singh, M.P., Huhns, M.N.: Service-Oriented Computing: Semantics, Processes, Agent. John Wiley & Sons, Chichester (2005)
2. Huang, J., Dang, J., Huhns, M.N.: Ontology Reconciliation for Service Oriented Computing. In: IEEE International Conference on Services Computing (SCC 2006), pp. 3–10 (2006)
3. Colman, A., Pham, L.D., Han, J., Schneider, J.-G.: Adaptive Application-Specific Middleware. MW4SOC 184 (2006)
4. Casati, F., Castellanos, M., Dayal, u., Shan, M.-C.: Probabilistic, Context-Sensitive, and Goal-Oriented Service Selection. In: International Conference on Service Oriented Computing, pp. 316–321 (2004)
5. Rossi, P., Tari, Z.: Software Adaptation for Service-Oriented System. MW4SOC (2006)
6. Maamar, Z., Mostefaoui, S.K., yahyaoui, H.: Toward an Agent-Based and Context-Oriented Approach for Web Services Composition. IEEE Transactions on Knowledge and Data Engineering 17(5)
7. Stoica, I., Morris, R., Liben-Nowell, et al.: Chord: a scalable peer-to-peer lookup protocol for Internet applications. IEEE/ACM Transactions on Networking 11(1), 17–32 (2003)
8. Garlan, D., Cheng, S.W., Huang, A.C.: Rainbow: Architecture-based self-adaptation with reusable infrastructure. Comput 37(10), 46–54 (2004)
9. Pavel, D., Trossen, D.: Context Provisioning for Future Service Environments. In: International Conference on Computing in the Global Information Technology, p. 45 (2006)
10. http://www.w3.org/2004/OWL/
11. http://www.osgi.org
12. http://r-osgi.sourceforge.net/
13. http://casei.googlecode.com/

Relaxed Time Slot Negotiation
for Grid Resource Allocation

Seokho Son and Kwang Mong Sim*

Multiagent Systems Lab., Department of Information and Communication,
Gwangju Institute of Science and Technology (GIST), Gwangju, Korea
{shson,kmsim}@gist.ac.kr
http://mas.co.to/

Abstract. Since participants in a computational grid may be independent bodies, some mechanisms are necessary for resolving the differences in their preferences for price and desirable time slots for utilizing/leasing computing resources. Whereas there are mechanisms for supporting price negotiation for grid resource allocation, there is little or no negotiation support for allocating mutually acceptable time slots for grid participants. The contribution of this work is designing a negotiation mechanism for facilitating time slot negotiations between grid participants. In particular, this work adopts a relaxed time slot negotiation protocol designed to enhance the success rate and resource utilization level by allowing some flexibility for making slight adjustments following a tentative agreement for a mutually acceptable time slot. The ideas of the relaxed time slot negotiation are implemented in an agent-based grid testbed, and empirical results of the relaxed time slot negotiation mechanism carried out, (i) a consumer and a provider agent have a mutually satisfying agreement on time slot and price, (ii) consumer agents achieved higher success rates in negotiation, and (iii) provider agents achieved higher utility and resource utilization of overall grid.

Keywords: Grid economy and business models, Grid resource allocation, Grid resource management, Negotiation agents, Grid resource negotiation, Advanced reservation.

1 Introduction

Negotiation activities are necessary in a computational grid because it cannot be assumed that a resource provider will unconditionally provide a particular (computing) capability to a consumer [1], and since grid participants are independent bodies, some mechanism is needed to resolve their differences. There are many negotiation issues such as price for resource, time slot (TS), application QoS to increase satisfactions for both parties in grid environment. Most of existing research for negotiation that resolve differences have been focused on price negotiation [2,3,4,5]. Through price negotiation (bargaining), players in a

---

* Corresponding author.

D. Ślęzak et al. (Eds.): GDC 2009, CCIS 63, pp. 25–32, 2009.
© Springer-Verlag Berlin Heidelberg 2009

grid marketplace (providers and consumers) are given the opportunity to maximize their return-on-investment and minimize their cost (the price they pay) respectively. However, there are little works to resolve differences about the preferences of TS between a consumer and a provider. Consumers and providers in a grid environment need allocation procedures to provide or utilize resources in grid environment. Before they allocate grid resource, they have to determine a TS. S. Venugopal and et. al proposed a negotiation mechanism for advance resource reservation at a time slot [6], and O. Waeldrich and et. al proposed a meta-scheduling service to find common TS [7]. However, their negotiation mechanism are focused on searching a co-allocatable TS not resolving differences of time slot preference between a consumer and a provider.

The impetus of this work is designing a relaxed TS negotiation for mutually acceptable grid resource allocation. This is part of a research initiative to develop an TS negotiation mechanism for grid resource management, which consists of (i) designing TS negotiation agents and its protocol by augmenting the alternating offers protocol, and (ii) devising a relaxation algorithm for slightly relaxing agreement criterion to increase the chance of an agreement more successfully.

The agendas of this work are to: (i) devise a decision making model including a formulation of TS strategy as well as a relaxation algorithm for TS agreement (Section 2.1); (ii) design a relaxed time slot negotiation protocol for grid resource allocation (Section 2.2); (iii) evaluate the relaxed TS negotiation by conducting experimentations using a agent-based testbed (Section 3).

2   Relaxed Time Slot Negotiation

In this work, TS negotiation agents negotiate on behalf of consumers and providers in a grid is designed. This section presents (i) a decision making model including a formulation of time slot strategy as well as a relaxation algorithm and (ii) the design of a relaxed TS negotiation protocol.

2.1   Decision Making Model

Negotiation is a bargaining process by which a joint decision is made by two parties. The parties first propose contradictory demands and then move towards agreements. So, a decision making model is important to decide how they move.

Utility Function. The utility $U(x)$ represents the level of satisfaction of x, or in other words, how good x is. To define a TS utility function, we need an analysis of TS preferences of grid participants. Consumers using a grid would like to choose a specific TS (let us assume only one specific TS would be selected for simplicity) to use grid resources, and a TS, far from the TS chose initially, is not preferred. On the other hand, providers would like to select the earliest TS because there is a high chance that resources allocated on later TSs cause additional negotiation failures, and as time goes by, early TSs which have not been used are wasted. So, Allocating resources on an early TS allows providers to utilize resources more efficiently.

Let IT and RT be the most preferred (initial) TS and the least preferred (reserve) TS respectively, and T_{Cons} be the TS that a consensus is reached by both parties. A consumer has a higher preference for a TS that is close to IT_C, and a TS, which is close to RT_C or $2 \times IT_C - RT_C$ (i.e., opposite side of RT_C), is the least preferred TS according to the preference analysis. So, for a consumer, its TS utility $U_{TS}^C(T_{Cons})$ for reaching a consensus at T_{Cons} is given as follows :

$$U_{TS}^C(T_{Cons}) = u_{\min}^T + (1 - u_{\min}^T) \left(\left| \frac{RT_C - T_{Cons}}{RT_C - IT_C} \right| \right) \tag{1}$$

For a provider, its TS utility $U_T^P(T_{Cons})$ is given as follows:

$$U_{TS}^P(T_{Cons}) = u_{\min}^T + (1 - u_{\min}^T) \left(\frac{RT_P - T_{Cons}}{RT_P - IT_P} \right) \tag{2}$$

In Eq. 1 and 4, $u_{\min}^T$ is the minimum utility that an agent receives for reaching a deal at its reserve TS. For the experiment, $u_{\min}^T$ is defined as 0.1.

Negotiation Strategy. A negotiation strategy determines the amount of concession for each proposal. This work considers the bilateral negotiation between a consumer and a provider, where both agents are sensitive to the time and the negotiation deadline. So, both agents adopt the time-dependent strategies in the TS negotiation. Let λ_C and λ_P be the time-dependent strategies of agents.

The provider agent increases the amount of concession according to the negotiation time so that it proposes IT_P initially and the RT_P at the deadline. Proposals between IT_P and RT_P are determined by λ_P. So, the proposal T_t^P of provider at time t, $0 \le t \le \tau_P$, is determined as follows:

$$T_t^P = IT_P + \left(\frac{t}{\tau_P} \right)^{\lambda_P} (RT_P - IT_P) \tag{3}$$

On the other hand, the proposal T_t^C of a consumer at time t, $0 \le t \le \tau_C$, is determined as follows in order to express the consumer's preference:

$$T_t^C = \begin{cases} IT_C - \left(\frac{t}{\tau_C} \right)^{\lambda_C} (RT_C - IT_C), IT_C \ge IT_P \\ IT_C + \left(\frac{t}{\tau_C} \right)^{\lambda_C} (RT_C - IT_C), IT_C < IT_P \end{cases} \tag{4}$$

An agent accepts a counter proposal from its opponent when the counter proposal gives higher utility than utility of the last proposal of itself, and the agreed TS becomes a preliminary agreement result that gives mutually acceptable utility of TS. However, in a grid, the provider is difficult to guarantee that the agreed TS is available because the agreed TS could be already reserved by other consumers. In this case, negotiation will fail eventually.

The Relaxation Algorithm. To enhance negotiation success rate, a relaxation algorithm is proposed for the decision making model. This algorithm relaxes decision level according to provider's situation whether the agreed TS is already reserved. For this algorithm, the provider agent has a priority queue that contains indexes of available TSs, and TS indexes are enqueued in the order of nearness to the preliminary TS. After that, the provider agent and the consumer agent fine a TS in range of $IT_C \leq T_{Cons} \leq RT_C$ and $IT_P \leq T_{Cons} \leq RT_P$ and the closest TS to the preliminary TS by communicating TS indexes in the priority queue. We note that the adjusted negotiation result changes the TS utility initially negotiated. So, it is compensated with other utilities such as price utility.

2.2 Negotiation Protocol

Negotiation activities between a consumer agent and a provider agent are specified by using the relaxed TS negotiation protocol shown in Fig. 1. The TS negotiation protocol consists of two phases. The first phase is the TS negotiation phase based on the alternating offer's protocol [8]. In this phase both agents generate counter proposals according to the negotiation strategy in Section 2.1.2, and evaluate opponent's offers until one of agents accepts an opponent's proposal or reaches it's deadline. If a counter proposal is accepted, agents keep the preliminary agreement result. However, the preliminary agreement is difficult to guarantee the negotiation success because the preliminary TS is possibly occupied by other requests already. Therefore, to enhance the success rate, the relaxation algorithm presented in Section 2.1.3 is combined in the second phase.

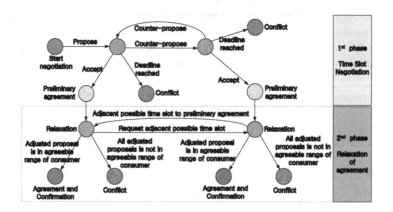

Fig. 1. Protocol of relaxed TS negotiation

3   Simulations and Empirical Results

To evaluate performance of the proposed TS negotiation, an agent-based grid testbed for TS negotiation simulation was implemented. Using the testbed, a series of simulations was carried out to evaluate the relaxed time slot negotiation

Table 1. Performance measures and Experimental settings

Performance measures

TS utility of consumer	$U_{TS}^c = $ TS utilities of consumer (Eq. 1)	
TS utility of provider	$U_{TS}^p = $ TS utilities of provider (Eq. 4)	
Price of resource	$P = U_{TS}^p \times (P_{\max} - P_{\min})$	
Price utility×TS utility	$U_{P \times TS}^c$ and $U_{P \times TS}^p$	
Negotiation success rate	$R_{success} = N_{success}/N_{total}$	
Resource utilization	$R_{utilization} = N_{allocated\_ts}/N_{total\_ts}$	
$P_{\max}$	$P_{\min}$	max. prices of the resource	min. prices of the resource
$U_{P \times TS}^c$	$U_{P \times TS}^p$	$U_{P \times TS}^c = U_P^c \times U_{TS}^c$	$U_{P \times TS}^p = U_P^p \times U_{TS}^p$
U_P^c	U_P^p	$U_P^c = 1 - (P/(P_{\max} - P_{\min}))$	$U_P^p = P/(P_{\max} - P_{\min})$
$N_{success}$	N_{total}	no. of successful negotiations	no. of requests
$N_{allocated\_ts}$	N_{total_ts}	no. of allocated TSs of provider	no. of TSs in provider

Experimental settings

Parameters		Values	
Initial times slot		C:start time + (250 ~ 350), P:start time + (0 ~ 100)	
Reserve times slot		C:start time + (450 ~ 550), P:start time + (280 ~ 380)	
Deadline	Strategy	10 ~ 15 rounds	1/3 ~ 3
Job size	price range	20 ~ 30 0.1MIs	1 ~ 20 $

(RTSN) under different grid loading situations. In this work, one shot agreement (OSA) and adjustable agreement (AA) are used as comparative studies to evaluate the performance of RTSN. AA is a consumer favorable agreement mechanism, and a provider assigns requested resource at the closest TS most preferred by a consumer. If all TSs in serviceable range of the consumer are already allocated by others, AA fails. In addition, OSA is the simplest mechanism for advance reservation. A consumer agent using OSA proposes the most preferred TS, and a provider agent check whether the TS is available. If it is available, the agents succeed in getting the agreement that gives the highest utility to consumer and the lowest utility to provider. If it is not available, the agreement fails.

Performance measures: the performance measures are averages of (i) TS utility of consumers and providers (ii) price of resource (iii) product of TS utility and price utility (iv) success rate of negotiation, (v) Resource utilization, and are summarized in Table 1.

Experimental settings: the testbed simulates the negotiation for grid resources by varying the input parameters shown in Table 1. There are 20 provider agents and 20 consumer agents in the grid. Each provider can execute 10MIPS, a TS represents 0.1MPIS, and the number of requests per second is selected from 1 to 100 to vary market situations. In all the experiments, both agents adopt different time-dependent strategy sets $\{\lambda_C, \lambda_P\} = \{(3, 1/3), (1/3, 3), (2, 2), (1/3 \sim 3, 1/3 \sim 3)\}$ to evaluate RTSN when agents adopt (i)$\lambda_C \gg \lambda_P$, (ii)$\lambda_C \ll \lambda_P$, (iii)$\lambda_C = \lambda_P$, and (iv)λ_C, λ_P are selected randomly. (note that $\{\lambda_C, \lambda_P\} = \{(1/3, 1/3), (1/2, 1/2), (1, 1), (3,3)\}$ show a similar result with $\{\lambda_C = \lambda_P = 2\}$)

Observations: the obs. 1~4 are performance comparisons among OSA, AA, and general RTSN (RTSN adopting λ_C, λ_P randomly within 1/3~3), and the obs. 5 analyzes RTSNs adopting different strategies.

1) RTSN provides a higher value of product of TS utility and price utility to consumers and providers. Fig. 2 (a) and (b) show U_{TS}^c and U_{TS}^p. In Fig. 2 (a), with few requests (<20), AA shows the highest utility for consumers, but AA shows low utility for providers. So, AA has not fairness property for both parties. In this work, providers have a simple charging policy decided according to the U_{TS}^c. So, U_P^c is affected by U_{TS}^p. Fig. 2 (e) shows that general RTSN provides the best price to consumer. Although U_{TS}^c of RTSN is lower than or equal to AA, as aggregated utility of RTSN shows higher $U_{P \times TS}^c$ than other schemes in Fig. 2 (c) because satisfaction of TS can be compensated by low price. Simultaneously, a provider also has higher U_{TS}^p with RTSN and higher $U_{P \times TS}^p$ than other schemes in Fig. 2 (d). Because $U_{P \times TS}^p$ has a low value when either of U_{TS} and U_P is low, higher $U_{P \times TS}$ means a grid user is satisfied with both TS and price. Therefore, with RTSN both a consumer and a provider have higher utilities, and we can conclude that RTSN provides a mutually satisfying agreement on TS and price.

2) Under a number of resource requests (over 20 requests) RTSN and AA show similar U_{TS}^c, and RTSN shows the highest U_{TS}^p. Utilities for a consumer of all schemes decrease under a number of resource requests (over 20 requests) because $R_{success}$ shown in Fig. 2 (f) decreases with many requests. Also, U_{TS}^c of AA and OSA decreases rapidly than RTSN because RTSN has a higher success rate with the relaxation algorithm. RTSN shows the highest U_{TS}^p because it resolves differences in TS preferences of consumers and providers.

3) RTSN shows higher success rate than the other schemes. Fig. 2 (f) shows $R_{success}$. OSA fails when requested TS was already allocated by other consumers, and AA fails when adjusted TS by the provider is not in acceptable range of the consumer. However, RTSN has more chance to succeed negotiation because the relaxation algorithm let them find a next closer TS to preliminary TS. As the level of grid utilization increases, available resources in the grid decrease, and hence, it would be more difficult to successfully find available and agreeable TS (Fig. 2 (g) shows level of grid load is over grid capacity).

4) RTSN shows higher aggregated resource utilization of the grid than the other schemes. In Fig. 2 (h), as the number of requests increase, utilization of all schemes increase. Above all, RTSN shows the highest utilization because high success rate of RTSN directly affects high resource utilization. Grid resource utilization is a same metric with aggregated grid throughput as well.

5) When the provider (respectively, consumer) adopts a conservative strategy (>1), i.e., conceding slowly and the consumer (respectively, provider) adopts a conciliatory strategy (<1) then one would expect that the provider (respectively, consumer) will end up with better utilities. With $\lambda_C \gg \lambda_P$, all performance measures in Fig. 2 shows similar results with AA which is a consumer friendly scheme because $\lambda_C \gg \lambda_P$ gives a more preferred agreement to the consumer by letting the provider impatient. Also, when $\lambda_C \ll \lambda_P$, RTSN shows a provider friendly result because $\lambda_C \ll \lambda_P$ gives an agreement that is more preferred by the provider. So, $\{\lambda_C=1/3, \lambda_P=3\}$ shows the highest U_{TS}^p in Fig. 2 (b) and the highest utilization in Fig. 2 (h).

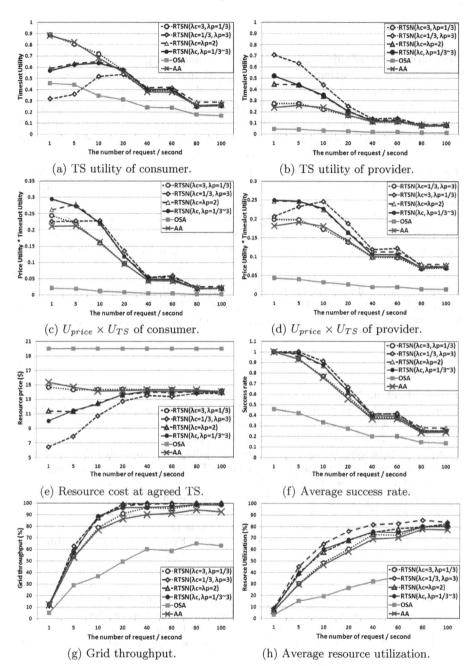

(a) TS utility of consumer.

(b) TS utility of provider.

(c) $U_{price} \times U_{TS}$ of consumer.

(d) $U_{price} \times U_{TS}$ of provider.

(e) Resource cost at agreed TS.

(f) Average success rate.

(g) Grid throughput.

(h) Average resource utilization.

Fig. 2. Experimental results

4   Conclusion

The contributions of this work include: (i) designing a negotiation mechanism for facilitating TS negotiations between grid participants, (ii) developing an agent-based testbed for evaluating relaxed TS negotiation protocol, and (iii) conducting a series of simulations to evaluate the proposed protocol. Empirical results obtained from the simulations show that by following the relaxed TS negotiation protocol: (i) a consumer and a provider have a mutually satisfying agreement on TS and price, (ii) consumer agents achieved higher success rates, and (iii) provider agents achieved higher utility and resource utilization of overall grid. As such, the novelty and significance of this work are that it is one of the earliest works that proposes and devises a TS negotiation for grid resource allocation. However, in real grid environments, providers generally have a local schedular, and utility of provider could be complex. Consequently, as a future work, the utility function has to be carefully revised according to the local scheduler.

Acknowledgments. This work was supported by the Korea Science and Engineering Foundation (KOSEF) grant funded by the Korea government (MEST 2009-0065329) and DASAN International Faculty Fund (project code: 140316).

References

1. Foster, I., et al.: Brain meets brawn: Why Grid and agents need each other. In: 3rd Int. Conf. on Autonomous Agents and Multi-Agent Systems, USA, pp. 8–15 (2004)
2. Sim, K.M.: A Survey of Bargaining Models for Grid Resource Allocation. In: ACM SIGECOM: E-commerce Exchange, vol. 5(5), pp. 22–32 (2006)
3. Lang, F.: Developing Dynamic Strategies for Multi-Issue Automated Contracting in the Agent Based Commercial Grid. In: The IEEE Int. Sym. on Cluster Computing and the Grid (CCGrid 2005), Cardiff (2005)
4. Lawley, R., et al.: Automated Negotiation between publishers and consumers of grid notifications. Parallel Processing Letters 13(4), 537–548 (2003)
5. Sim, K.M., Ng, K.F.: A Relaxed-Criteria Bargaining Protocol for Grid Resource Management. In: Proceedings of the 6th IEEE Int. Sym. on Cluster Computing and the Grid (Agent-based Grid Computing Workshop) (2006)
6. Venugopal, S., Chu, X., Buyya, R.: A Negotiation Mechanism for Advance Resource Reservation using the Alternate Offers Protocol. In: 16th Int. Workshop on Quality of Service (IWQoS 2008). University of Twente, Netherlands (2008)
7. Waeldrich, O., Wieder, P., Ziegler, W.: A meta-scheduling service for co-allocating arbitrary types of resources. CoreGRID Technical Report (December 2005)
8. Rubinstein, A.: Perfect equilibrium in a bargaining model. Econometrica 50(1), 97–109

A Brokering Protocol for Agent-Based Grid Resource Discovery

Jaeyong Kang and Kwang Mong Sim*

Multiagent Systems Lab., Department of Information and Communication,
Gwangju Institute of Science and Technology (GIST), Gwangju, Korea
{kjysmu,kmsim}@gist.ac.kr
http://www.mas.co.to/

Abstract. Resource discovery is one of the basic and key aspects in grid resource management, which aims at searching for the suitable resources for satisfying the requirement of users' applications. This paper introduces an agent-based brokering protocol which connects users and providers in grid environments. In particular, it focuses on addressing the problem of connecting users and providers. A connection algorithm that matches advertisements of users and requests from providers based on pre-specified multiple criteria is devised and implemented. The connection algorithm mainly consists of four stages: selection, evaluation, filtering, and recommendation. A series of experiments that were carried out in executing the protocol, and favorable results were obtained.

Keywords: Grid Computing, Resource Discovery, Agent, Brokering Protocol.

1 Introduction

In a grid environment, proving effective resource discovery [3] is challenging as resources are geographically distributed, heterogeneous in nature and may span numerous administrative domains. Resources are identified based on a set of desired attributes, which have various degrees of dynamism, from mostly static attributes, like operating system version to highly dynamic ones, like CPU load or network bandwidth. Satisfying the scalable need to handle huge amounts of data from multiple sources has become one of the key issues as well as discovering effectively the resources required by users' applications in grid environment. In our proposed system, we use an agent-based approach [2][4][5][6] and enhance the brokering protocol in [1] which contains a broker agent and trading agents by using multiple broker agents to address the scalability issue.

This paper is organized as follows. Section 2 provides the description of the connection algorithm that matches user and provider agents through four stages (selection, evaluation, filtering, and recommendation). The simulations and empirical results in terms of average connection time and average utility and success rate are shown in section 3, and finally conclusion and future work are illustrated in section 4.

---

* Corresponding author.

D. Ślęzak et al. (Eds.): GDC 2009, CCIS 63, pp. 33–40, 2009.
© Springer-Verlag Berlin Heidelberg 2009

2   Connecting User and Provider

While issues of the connection problem in the domain of electronic trading have been addressed by Sim and Chan [1], this research explores the issues of matching profiles of users and providers in grid environments. In this work, the connection consists of: four stages: selection, evaluation, filtering, and recommendation.

Selection : In this stage, the requests of each user is compared with the advertisements of each provider to find the providers that fulfill the minimum requirement of resource. In selecting providers for a request, three section criteria are used. The algorithm prefers to select advertisements

1) That have available resources;
2) With resources (CPU Speed, Memory, OS, Disk Capacity) that fulfill the requirement of a user;
3) That have a common range of timeslot and price between user and provider.

Criterion 1) ensures that only valid advertisements are selected. Criterion 2) ensures that users select providers that have suitable resources such that CPU Speed and Memory and Disk Capacity are equal to or higher than the requirement of user to execute an application smoothly. OS Type is equal to the requirement of user because of compatibility. For example, the resource of provider has CPUSpeed with 2.0 GHz and Linux OSType and the request of user contains the CPUSpeed with 1.0 and Window OSType. In that case, CPUSpeed is satisfied but OSType is different from the user, so this provider is not selected. Criterion 3) ensures that a provider can allocate the timeslot of a user and also the price of the provider is less than acceptable maximum price of the user so that the user can negotiate with the provider.

Evaluation : In this stage, the utility of each of the connection between users and providers is determined.

The utility U is determined as follows.

$$U(C_i) = w_1 \times U(P) + w_2 \times U(Ts) \tag{1}$$

Utility U is the sum of price utility U(P) with weigh w_1 and time timeslot utility U(Ts) with weigh w_2. w_1 and w_2 are user-specified values and determine the weight of price utility U(P) and timeslot utility U(Ts), and $w_1 + w_2 = 1$. Hence, the range of values of utility U is between 0 and 1.

Price utility U(P) is defined as follows.

$$U(P) = \frac{P_{max} - P_{min}}{P_{max}} \tag{2}$$

U(P) is determined by the acceptable maximum price P_{max} of user and the acceptable minimum price P_{min} of provider. If P_{min} is close to P_{max}, U(P) will be low because a user is more likely to get small difference between acceptable maximum price P_{max} (Initial price) and agreement price. If P_{min} is far from P_{max}, U(P) will be high because user is more likely to obtain a large difference between acceptable maximum price P_{max} (Initial price) and agreement price.

Timeslot utility U(P) is determined as follows.

$$U(Ts) = \frac{Ts_{user} \cap Ts_{provider}}{Ts_{user}} \qquad (3)$$

U(Ts) is determined by the range of timeslot of a user and the range of timeslot of a provider. If the timeslot between a user and a provider is close to the timeslot of the user, timeslot utility U(Ts) would be high. Otherwise, U(Ts) would be low.

Filtering : This stage filters out the connections between users and providers which are lower than user-specified thresholds. For instance, if the total utility U is 0.7 and the user-specified threshold is 0.8, then this connection is filtered out because the total utility is less than the user-specified threshold. If the threshold is high, a user would find providers that provide resource with more matching conditions in terms of time-slot and price. However, the number of providers that a user finds would be small. If the threshold is low, a user would find providers that provide resources with less matching conditions in terms of timeslot and price. However the number of providers that a user finds would be large.

Recommendation : In this stage, a broker agent sends a recommendation message to user agents which failed to be matched to provider agent(s). The message contains the information of broker agents which are neighbors of the broker agent. The recommendation procedure consists of 4 steps as follows.

In Figure 1, there are six user and provider agents, and two broker agents. User agents U_1, U_2, U_3 are involved in broker agent B_1 and user agents U_4, U_5, U_6 are involved in broker agent B_2, and the neighbor of B_1 is B_2 and also the neighbor of B_2 is B_1. For the first step, the broker agent finds user agents that fail to connect with provider agents. Figure 1 shows that U_1 successfully connected to P_1, and P_2 and U_2 is also successfully connected to P_2 but U_3 failed to connect to provider agents under broker agent B_1. Also U_5 and U_6 successfully connect to provider agent P_6 and P_5, but U_4 failed to connect to provider agent under broker agent B_2. In step 2, a broker agent sends a recommendation message to user agents which failed to connect to provider agents. The message contains the information of broker agent which is neighbor of the local broker agent. This figure shows that broker agent B_1 sends a message to U_3 which fail to connect to provider agents. The content of message is "Recommendation B_2". "Recommendation" is the type of message and "B_2" is the neighbor of the broker agent. In step 3, after receiving a recommendation message, the user agent sends a request to another broker agent and the broker agent carry out connection procedure such as selection, evaluation, filtering and so on. After step 3, this figure shows that user agents U_3 which failed to connect under broker agent B_1 finally connect to a provider agent P_4 under broker agent B_2 and user agents U_4 which failed to connect under broker agent B_2 finally connect to a provider agent P_3 under broker agent B_1. After the recommendation procedure, the success rate would be enhanced.

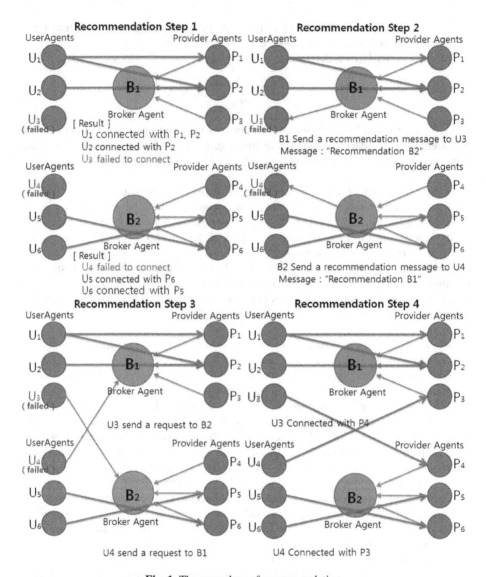

Fig. 1. The procedure of recommendation

3   Simulations and Empirical Results

A series of simulations was carried out to evaluate the brokering protocol for agent-based resource discovery.

Experimental settings: Requests and advertisements contain the information of price range, timeslot range, CPU speed, memory, disk capacity and OS type. The values of these parameters are randomly generated within the ranges shown in Table 1.

Table 1. Input parameters used for simulations

	Request	Advertisement
Price range	4500~10000	0~5500
Timeslot range	0~1000	0~1000
CPU Speed (GHz)	0.1~2.0	1.5~3.5
Memory (Mb)	{128, 256, 512, 1024, 2048}	{512, 1024, 2048}
Disk Capacity (Mb)	0~100	50~1000
OS Type	{Windows, Linux, Mac}	{Windows, Linux, Mac}

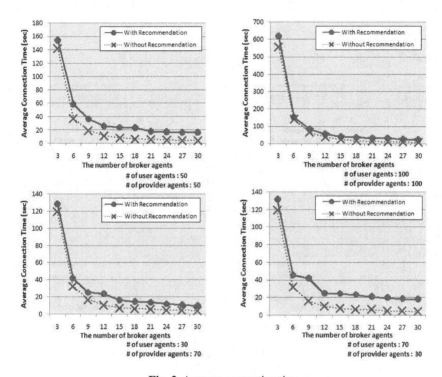

Fig. 2. Average connection time

Average connection time: In Figure 2, deploying a larger number of broker agents results in shorter average connection time than deploying fewer broker agents. This is because with fewer broker agents, each broker agent has to manage more user and provider agents. Without recommendation, the average connection time is shorter. When there is recommendation, more computations are needed. Hence, the average connection time is longer. Without recommendation, although the connection procedure is completed and there exist user agents which failed to be matched to provider agent(s), there is no further connection procedure. Hence, fewer computations are needed. Also the results show that the case with larger numbers of users and providers requires more computations than the case with smaller numbers of users and providers. This is because if the number of users and providers is large, the broker agent needs more computations to compare the requests of users and the advertisements of providers. The case with fewer users and more providers shows slightly better performance than the case with more users and fewer providers. This is because in the case with fewer users and more providers, the user agent is more likely to connect to providers using fewer steps than the case with more users and fewer providers so that average connection time will be shorter.

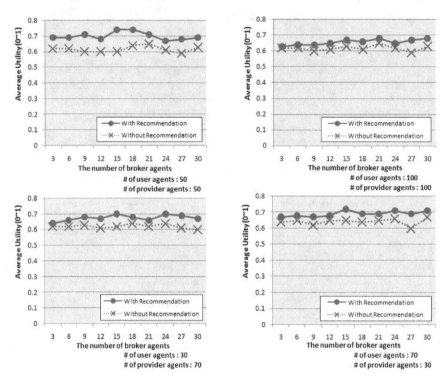

Fig. 3. Average utility

Average utility: In Figure 3, the results with recommendation show better performance than the results without recommendation in terms of average utility. This is because with recommendation, user agent can do the discovery procedure again by receiving recommendation messages although they failed to connect with provider agents so that user agents are more likely to discover provider agents with closer matching resources. Furthermore, the results also show that with varying numbers of user and provider agents (e.g., more users and fewer providers) user agents achieve higher average utilities if the recommendation stage is executed.

Success Rate: In Figure 4, the results with recommendation show significantly better performance than the results without recommendation in terms of success rate. This is

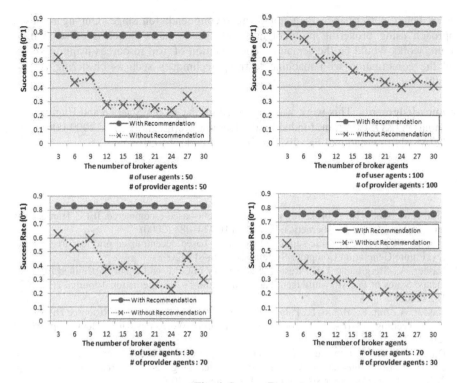

Fig. 4. Success Rate

because with recommendation, user agent can do the discovery procedure again by receiving recommendation messages although they failed to connect with provider agents so that user agent has higher chance to discover closely matching resources. However if the recommendation stage is not executed, if the user agents failed to connect to provider agents, they cannot do the discovery procedure again so that success rate will be low. Also the results show that regardless of the number of user agents, the success rates increased with the number of provider agents. This is because if the number of provider agents is larger, the user agents have higher chance to find closely matching resources.

4 Conclusion and Future Work

The agent-based brokering system exposed in this paper solves the connection problem in grid environment. The design and engineering of the brokering system that consists of user agents, provider agents, and broker agents was briefly introduced. The approach of making connection based on multiple factors was described. In this paper, the stages of the broker protocol that define the brokering process were outlined. Finally, favorable results from the three experiments show that the system has relatively good performance and deploying many broker agents has a good scalability rather than one or small number of broker agents and using recommendation stage shows better performance than not using recommendation stage. Our agent-based approach using brokering protocol has good performance in terms of scalability. Future works would be the semantic representation of grid resources using ontology and the combination with machine learning techniques such as clustering is also possible.

Acknowledgments. This work was supported by the Korea Science and Engineering Foundation (KOSEF) grant funded by the Korea government (MEST 2009-0065329), and DASAN International Faculty Fund (project code: 140316).

References

1. Sim, K.M., Chan, R.: A brokering protocol for agent-based e-commerce. IEEE Transactions on Systems, Man, and Cybernetics, Part C 30(4), 474–484 (2000)
2. Han, L., Berry, D.: Semantic-supported and agent-based decentralized grid resource discovery. Future Generation Computer Systems 24, 806–812 (2008)
3. Naseer, A., Stergioulas, L.K.: Resource Discovery in Grids and Other Distributed Environments: States of the Art. Multiagent and Grid Systems - An International Journal 2(2), 163–182 (2006)
4. Naseer, A., Jun, K., Bolon, L., Palacz, K., Marinescu, D.: Agent-based Resource Discovery. In: Proceedings of IEEE Heterogeneous Computing Workshop (HCW 2000), pp. 43–52 (2000)
5. Ding, S., Yuan, J., JiubinJu, H.L.: A heuristic algorithm for agent-based grid resource discovery. In: IEEE International Conference on e-Technology, e-Commerce and e-Service, pp. 222–225. IEEE Computer Society Press, Los Alamitos (2005)
6. Aversa, R., Marino, B.D., Mazzocca, N., Venticinque, S.: Terminal-Aware Grid Resource and Service Discovery and Access Based on Mobile Agents Technology. In: Proceedings of the 12th Euromicro Conference on Parallel, Distributed and Network-Based Processing (EUROMICRO-PDP 2004), pp. 40–45 (2004)

Towards a Better Understanding of Locality-Awareness in Peer-to-Peer Systems[*]

Hongliang Yu[1], Guangyu Shi[2], Jian Chen[2], Xiongfei Weng[1], and Weimin Zheng[1]

[1] Department of Computer Science, Tsinghua University, Beijing, 100084, China
[2] Huawei Technologies Co., Ltd, Shenzhen, 518129, China

Abstract. Peer-to-Peer(P2P) applications such as BitTorrent and Coolstreaming ignore inter-AS traffic costs at ISPs and generate a large amount of cross ISP traffic. As a result, ISPs always restrict the BT application to control the inter-AS traffic cost. In this paper, we designe a new locality-awareness selection approach: multi-metric neighbor selection algorithm, to enhance local traffic. Based on pwhois query, the algorithm selects the neighbors within the same AS and district as source peers, and uses roulette method based on link bandwidth and latency to choose the final partner peers. Redundancy traffic calculation were implemented to prove the effectiveness of our approach. We evaluate two widely deployed P2P system: BitTorrent and CoolStreaming, under the real dataset from PlannetLab in our evaluations. The results demonstrate our algorithm effects both improving the download time and reducing the inter-AS traffic. Further more, the network congestion can be eased under our algorithm.

1 Introduction

Locality-awareness is one of the essential characteristics for peer-to-peer (P2P) systems, which build and operate their topology independently of the underlying physical network topology. Few of popular P2P applications take physical network topology into consideration. The selected neighbor host in a randomly constructed overlay network may actually be on the opposite side of the globe when the same file can be serviced by a peer a few hops away. For example, a BitTorrent node in Los Angeles may download a 2 hour long MPEG-4 Olympic video clip from a node in Athens because of the topology mismatch problem between the overlay and physical networks, while the same file is available at a node in Atlanta.

Many previous researches have focused on presenting locality-aware algorithms, in which locality can be defined as different network metrics. In this paper, we designed a Multi-Metric Neighbor Selection Algorithm based on the location of the adjacent nodes to choose the profit node for data transmit. We employ a series of novel approaches for conducting deep analysis. First, we study the performance optimization goals between P2P users and Internet service providers (ISP) and define the performance optimization goal of the ISPs for reducing cross-ISP traffic. Then we design a mathematical

---

[*] This work is supported by NSFC under Grant No. 60603071, the Major State Basic Research Development Program of China(973 Program) under Grant No.2007CB311100 and Huawei Research Fund under contract No.YBCB2009032.

D. Ślęzak et al. (Eds.): GDC 2009, CCIS 63, pp. 41–48, 2009.

model to compute the intro-AS traffic, and find that the amount of redundant traffic is in correspondence with the global network's diameter. After that, we designed another mathematical model to compute the potential benefit loss unless they didn't use our algorithm and proved that our Multi-Metric Neighbor Selection Algorithm can bring in distinct benefits to the ISP providers. Finally, we carry out extensive simulations using real dataset from PlanetLab. We choose two widely-deployed P2P systems: BitTorrent, a content-distribution system, and CoolStreaming, a P2P media streaming system, for the tests. We compare our algorithm to the other familiar neighbor selection strategies such as: Random algorithm (RAND), maximum bandwidth clustering algorithm (MBC), intra-AS clustering algorithm in download time and traffic locality improvement ratio. The results show that our algorithm Multi-Metric Neighbor Selection Algorithm can improve traffic locality ratio significantly and release congestion gracefully. On the other hand, Random algorithm (RAND), maximum bandwidth clustering algorithm (MBC) and intra-AS clustering algorithm should not be encouraged for choosing the most usable candidate as this may lead to network congestion and does not improve traffic locality inefficiently.

The remainder of the paper is laid out as follows. In section 2, we introduce the Multi-Metric neighbor selection algorithm. section 3 formally defines the mathematical model to calculate the redundant traffic. And section 4 shows the evaluation results followed by the conclusions in Section 5.

2   Multi-Metric Neighbor Selection Algorithm

In this section, We introduce a algorithm used when the source destination choose its neighbors to transmit data. The design of the algorithm is based on the analysis of redundant traffic described in section 2. With the Algorithm, the source peer can only select neighbors from the same AS in homology district. We drop other inter AS candidates that additions more cross-AS traffic. In accordance with sub-level thinking, we designed two Bloom filters, AS/ISP filter : detect whether the source's neighbor nodes in the same domain of autonomy and clusters the intra AS candidate; and Geo filter , detect whether the source's neighbor nodes are in the same district area and clusters the intra district candidates. The Roulette method is used to choose the exact destination peer in accordance with the weighted bandwidth. However, our perspective differs from much previous modeling studies [1]. We focus on performance evaluation from the P2P user's side and the ISP's side.

2.1   Physical vs. Logical Network

Our models are motivated in part by the work of Liu et.al. [1]. We model a physical network as a directed graph $G = (V, E)$ as Figure 1, where V is the set of nodes, and E is the set of directed links between nodes. We use a or (i, j) to denote a link and C_a to refer the capacity of link a. For the overlay network, we use $G' = (V', E')$. In G' , we use i' to represent the overlay node built upon physical node i in underlay graph G. Overlay node i' is connected to j' by a logical link (i', j') , which corresponds to a physical path from i to j in G . Figure 2 summarizes the notations used in the formulations.

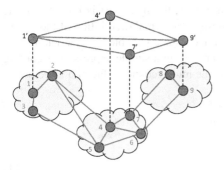

(i', j')	Logical link
$d^{(s,t)}$	Data transferring from pair (s, t)
$d^{(s',t')}$	Data transferring from pair (s', t')
$a = <i, j>$	Physical link a connecting node i to j
C_a	Capacity of a physical link a
$v_a^{(s,t)}$	Flow of $d^{(s,t)}$ on link a
$A_{(s,t)}$	the distance between s and t

Fig. 1. Correlation between overlay and physical networks

Fig. 2. Notaions

2.2 AS/ISP Filter and Geo Filter

Autonomous System (AS) presents a unified management, unified network routing strategy. It characterizes the source peer in the network's position. Namely, for P2P traffic to have ISP locality, the neighbors need to be chosen well. Depending on the pwhois[2] query, Source peer make a judgment on whether the target peer is in the same AS. If the IP address of the neighbor peer is in the same AS as the source peer, we add it to the new neighbor set. The strategy seems brief but is efficient. The filter access all the neighbor nodes, local peers are pushed into the neighbornodes array.

As AS/ISP filters didn't concern the peers in the same AS but the distant away, that still brings in latency to the data transmission. The number of ISPs in the internet and the AS number correlate. Some large ISPs take advantage of their resource and price, and their dimensions become so large that two peers within one AS still take many routers to transmit packages. So the latency is still very large. Considering this factor, Geo filter was build to achieve this goal. Geo filter filtrate the neighbor nodes sets depending on the position of the candidate peers. The peers that within a same district were pushed into the neighbor peers array. If no neighbor is selected, the source chooses randomly from the last filtered neighbor set. This makes the candidate peers cluster becoming small but more efficient.

After filtered by AS-Geo, all the members in the adjacent neighbor set can be represented by the area of pie chart. The size of pie chart is in proportionate to the bandwidth of the link between source and destination. Weakest link has smallest share of the roulette wheel. Then the wheel with a ball inside rotated, the ball's position decides the final data transfer partner. This can guarantee that a near neighbor has a high hit probability, and avoids multi-transfer convergence in large bandwidth link that could trigger congestion.

3 Network Benefit Model

The recent P2P network research focuses on two optimization goals: one is the network transmission speed whose evaluation indicators are deeply analyzed by previous studies. Another goal is to reduce redundant traffic, the most part is inter-AS traffic which enables ISP provider's burden. We construct a formal description of the redundant cross-AS traffic in this section. Our research defines a variable δ to characterization redundancy traffic. A mathematical deduction brings in a simple expression according to the network diameter i. We formally define the multi redundant factor δ as below:

$$\begin{cases} min\delta \\ s.t. \forall a \in E, v_a^{s,t} \leq C_a \end{cases}$$

$$\delta = \frac{J}{J_{opt}} \tag{1}$$

$$J = \sum_{a \in E} (\sum_{(s,t)} A(s_a, t).v_a^{(s,t)})$$

$$J_{opt} = \sum_{a \in E} (\sum_{(s,t)} A_{min}(s_a, t).v_a^{(s,t)})$$

In our formula, the meaning of each parameter can be found in Figure 2. and J represents the amount of traffic on each link of the P2P data transmission times and the distance between source and destiny of the link. J_{opt} is the traffic and without redundant traffic times the distance. δ is made up of J divided by J_{opt}. In that case, because when computing redundant traffic, redundancy factor should be multiplicand. So that bigger δ indicates heavier redundant traffic.

We further compute how much of redundant traffic can be reduced. we define d as the global amount of traffic. the P2P node A chooses an adjacent neighbor for transmission. The adjacent neighbor set has n nodes. Then we define the fastest distance from the source destination as i. The nodes A conform uniform distribution across the whole internet.

In the optimal situation, the source peer choose destination peer from its neighbors. Fortunately the neighbors are all within the same AS/ISP, we calculate:

$$J_{opt} = \sum_{a \in E} (\sum_{(s,t)} A_{min}(s_a, t).v_a^{(s,t)}) = 1 \times d = d \tag{2}$$

We will discuss the value of δ under two strategies:

Strategy 1: (Rand Strategy) In Strategy 1, ISPs do not attempt to change the P2P traffic, which is common in most cases. As a result, P2P nodes choose neighbors in the random way. Due to the mismatching problem, a huge volume of inter-ISP traffic is generated.

Strategy 2: (Best-case Traffic-locality Strategy) The Strategy 2 represents a best-case strategy to minimize inter-ISP traffic without losing service quality. If at least one replica of the object requested by a P2P node resides within the ISP, the inter-ISP traffic can be avoided. Otherwise the object is searched for in the whole P2P community. The optimization target of Strategy 2 is reducing transit cost to minimum under the prerequisite of guaranteeing service quality of P2P systems.

After we filtered redundant cross-AS traffic, the source peer choose a replica peer within the same AS(strategy 2):

$$J = \sum_{a \in E} (\sum_{(s,t)} A(s_a, t) \cdot v^{(s,t)_a}) = 1 \times d = d \tag{3}$$

so putting the equation together:

$$\delta = \frac{J}{J_{opt}} = 1 \tag{4}$$

Without taking the Multi-Metric neighbor selection algorithm, we choose replica peers randomly across internet (strategy 1). In this case:

$$J = \sum_{a \in E} (\sum_{(s,t)} A(s_a, t) \cdot v_a^{(s,t)})$$

$$= \frac{d}{i} \times \frac{i^3 + 3i^2 - 4i + 6}{6}$$

Where the amount of flow $v_a^{(s,t)}$ conform random distribution from 1 to i. From the equation we conclude that Rand strategy brings $o(i^3)$ times than best-case strategy.

$$\delta = \frac{J}{J_{opt}} = \frac{i^3 + 3i^2 - 4i + 6}{6i} \tag{5}$$

If we compute the redundant flow δ under different situations of global distances between ASes, we will find that the redundant flow in random node chosen strategy are much heavier than that in adjacent chosen strategy. So in theory our strategy can reduce the amount of redundant flow.

The network congestion can be reduced in our strategy. Due to the large bandwidth of a set of network nodes,a large amount of flow come to the single set. This can lead to congestion and even deadlock. Random chosen strategy would make nodes which have small bandwidth face congestion. But our chosen strategy, which based on probability of the bandwidth of their adjacent nodes,can neither bring congestion to the large bandwidth nodes nor the small ones.

4 Evaluation

Based on the HP S3 project and pWhois project, we compared our algorithm to three other algorithms, and the result dist demonstrate AS-Geo with Roulette algorithm works well. We use S3(Scalable Sensing Service)[4] on PlanetLab for the test. The end-to-end delay and end-to-end bandwidth data from 405 available PlanetLab nodes are used in our simulation.

For locality information, WhoIs [2] is used. We obtain the AS-number of each PlanetLab node and use the latitude, longitude, city and country information to represent the geographical location of each PlanetLab node. We use algorithms below for the test.

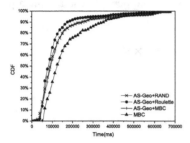
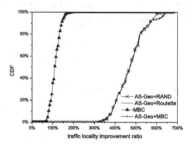

Fig. 3. Download Times of All Blocks in BT   **Fig. 4.** Traffic Locality Improvement in BT

- Maximum bandwidth clustering algorithm(MBC). Many P2P applications are sensitive to bandwidth more than transmission latency. In order to emphasize that the low bandwidth may lead to degraded performance and poor user experience, we study the MBC algorithm. In MBC, each peer selects the neighbors with the maximum available bandwidth on the network path between the two.
- AS-Geo with Random algorithm(AS-Geo+RAND). First the peers select their neighbors using AS/ISP filter and Geo filter, after that they choose their final partner randomly from all the neighbors left.
- AS-Geo with maximum bandwidth clustering algorithm(AS-Geo+MBC). First the peers select their neighbors using AS/ISP filter and Geo filter, after that they choose their final partner using MBC algorithm from the neighbors left.

The algorithms take a graph G=(V,E) as we mentioned in Figure1 as an input. We design and implement a discrete-event simulation platform to simulate BitTorrent and CoolStreaming. We only simulate the heterogeneous network by mapping each overlay node ID to a PlanetLab node IP to read network parameters. The simulator simulates the peer behaviors such as peer join/leave, data transferring and propagation delay/ latency of control messages in the network.

BitTorrent. We simulate 405 BT peers including 1 tracker, 1 seed and 403 leechers. Each leecher requires 20 neighbors from the tracker, and shares a file with the size of 100 MB (divided into 400 blocks with each 256 KB). The simulator initializes the torrent with only one seed who permanently stays in the system until terminating the simulation. 403 new peers join the system in 20 seconds, following the uniform distribution, and start file sharing. We run multiple simulations for arbitrary lengths of time and find that the summary statistics do not show significant changes after 10000 seconds. Therefore we run the simulations for 10000 seconds.

Figure 3 depicts the BitTorrent download time. From Figure 3, AS-Geo with Roulette has the fastest file transmission speed, While AS-Geo filtering with RAND and AS-Geo with MBC has the same download time. And MBC has nearly the most download time. Figure 3 (b) shows that 95% peers finish downloading in 300s when AS-Geo+ Roulette is deployed in the system, while it takes nearly 400s to share the file to the same number of peers when using AS-Geo with MBC and RAND.

There are several reasons why AS-Geo has significant improvement than MBC algorithm. First, the source peers prefer to fetch data from intra-AS nodes that can significantly reduce the transmission time and latency. Secondly the bandwidth is increased because within a same AS, there are less bottleneck links. And AS-Geo with Roulette has the least download time compared to AS-Geo with MBC and AS-Geo with RAND. As AS-Geo with Roulette is a flexible algorithm which deals with congestion and download time appropriate. Each node chooses their neighbor according to bandwidth but not completely, Roulette is used so that AS-Geo with Roulette does not lead to that peer always retrieves data from the most bandwidth neighbor. Instead, Roulette method brings larger probability to larger bandwidth links. In this way, AS Geo with Roulette avoids congestion and still gives priority to the nearby neighbors.

To measure the traffic locality, we define a normalized metric: traffic improvement ratio=number of blocks transferring within the same AS/the average number of blocks transferring within the same AS at RAND. We first run 100 simulations at RAND to calculate the basic value, and then run 100 simulations for each algorithm. Figure 4 shows the results. Under AS-Geo with RAND, AS-Geo with Roulette and AS-Geo with MBC, the traffic locality is significantly improved. They can improve the traffic locality by 464%, 461%, 460% at the mean level, and even at the worst case they can bring in 300% improvement in traffic locality. And MBC algorithm can only improve traffic locality by 108% at the mean level. In the worst case it is slower than RAND.

CoolStreaming. CoolStreaming [6] is one of the most famous P2P media streaming systems. A CoolStreaming node establishes and maintains partnership with other nodes. CoolStreaming requires new coming nodes to contact the origin server to obtain partner candidates and uses Scalable Membership protocol (SCAMP) to distribute membership messages. In our simulation the system contains a pool of 405 peers. The play-back bit rate is 512Kbps and basic time unit is 1 second. To minimize the influence of experiment parameters, we normalize our results. We test different length of the stream and the variance in the results from multiple runs is very low. We here adopt the steam length of 100 seconds. We first run 100 simulations at RAND to calculate the basic value, and run 100 simulations for each locality-aware algorithm to compare the performance improvement with RAND.

The primary objective of P2P media streaming applications is maintaining the continuous play-back. The play-back stalls if current data chunk is not fetched in time, and significantly influenced users' interests. We define a fail-state as a user suffers from the stream lag. And we define the playback continuity improvement ratio= the average number of fail-state under RAND/ the number of fail-state under current locality-aware algorithm. Figure 5 depicts that AS-Geo with Roulette and MBC works better than AS-Geo with RAND and AS-Geo with MBC, even in the worst case, 100% improvement ratio can be made. Because Scalable Membership protocol (SCAMP) is employed in CoolStreaming [7]. When a node receives a forwarded subscription inviting establishing neighborhood relationship, it integrates the new subscriber in its view with a probability p which depends on the size of its neighbor list. If it doesn't keep the new subscriber, it forwards the subscription to a node randomly. Latency based algorithm MBC and Roulette outperform RAND algorithm.

Figure 6 shows the improvement of traffic locality using traffic locality improvement ratio as the main metric. The four algorithms perform nearly the same, the mean improvement ratio of the three locality-aware algorithms (115% of AS-Geo with RAND,

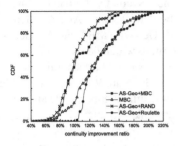
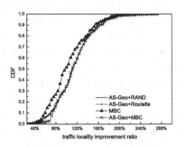

Fig. 5. Playback continuity improvement in CoolStreaming

Fig. 6. Playback continuity improvement in CoolStreaming

113% of AS-Geo with MBC, 116% of AS-Geo with Roulette) works better but not significant.And this is because of the SCAMP protocol.

5   Conclusions

This paper concluded that increasing inter-AS traffic and decreasing of download time in the P2P system can be achieved at the same time. We first proved in mathematics that in uniform distribute of ASes the amount of the redundant traffic is proportional to the diameter of the network. Then we proved that the potential losses if ISP do not use local domain strategy is related to N^2, where N is the number of ISP's P2P users. So based on the analyses we introduce a Multi-Metric Neighbor Selection Algorithm to approach this goal. We simulate an environment using Dataset from PlanetLab and pWhois to obtain the AS and geographic information of the candidate peers. Two popular systems BitTorren and CoolStreaming are run on this platform, the result proving that, Multi-Metric Neighbor Selection Algorithm significantly improves the efficiency of the P2P systems, and reduces the inter-AS traffic. Furthermore network congestion is eased though the method.

References

1. Liu, Y., Zhang, H., Gong, W., Towsley, D.: On the interaction between overlay routing and underlay routing. In: INFOCOM (2003)
2. pWhoIs: http://pwhois.org/
3. PlanetLab: http://www.planet-lab.org/
4. S3 PlanetLab Data: http://networking.hpl.hp.com/s-cube/PL/
5. Cohen, B.: Incentives build robustness in bittorrent. In: P2PEcon (2003)
6. Zhang, X., Liu, J., Li, B., Yum, T.: CoolStreaming/DONet: A Data-Driven Overlay Network for Efficient Live Media Streaming. In: INFOCOM (2005)
7. Ganesh, A., Kermarrec, A.-M., Massouli, L.: SCAMP: Peer-to-Peer Lightweight Membership. Service for Large-Scale Group Communication. In: Networked Group Communication (2001)

Default α-Logic for Modeling Customizable Failure Semantics in Workflow Systems Using Dynamic Reconfiguration Constraints

Hasan Davulcu[1], Supratik Mukhopadhyay[2], Prabhdeep Singh[1], and Stephen S. Yau[1]

[1] Arizona State University, Tempe, AZ 85287-8809, USA
{hdavulcu,prabhdeep.singh,yau}@asu.edu
[2] Utah State University, Logan, UT, USA
supratik@cc.usu.edu

Abstract. In this paper, we propose a logic based framework to handle failures that occur during the execution of workflows by encoding the failures in formalism of *a default normal modal logic*. Default logic provides a set of rules for adding premises to logical arguments. Since the specifications of services are encoded in α-logic, defaults can be added to this logic to accommodate the failure semantics for the predicates. We encode predicate failures as predicates and provide a dynamic proof system that handles failures at the execution time. Workflow adaptations are re-synthesized from proofs in our logic using a Curry-Howard style correspondence.

Keywords: Adaptive Workflows, Failure Semantics, Default Modal Logic.

1 Introduction

Nowadays, heterogeneous networked systems involving sensors, actuators, access points, and control stations connected through wired/wireless networks are being widely used in many mission-critical applications, such as agriculture, healthcare, military, power systems, automobile and space applications. These systems often need to operate in a rapidly changing environment and satisfy various requirements simultaneously, such as real-time, fault-tolerance, and security, and may need to be run in resource-poor environments with bandwidth limitations and shortage of memory space and/or other critical resources. In order to operate in a rapidly changing environment, such systems need to adapt their behavior in response to changes in the environment.

We present Adaptable Situation-aware Secure Service-based (AS³) Systems that provide dynamic service composition and can reconfigure themselves in response to changes in the environment. Reconfiguration can include dynamic substitution of an existing service by another, (incremental) re-synthesis of an agent in response to changes in requirements, etc. Our methodology facilitates rapid development, deployment, and operation of robust and secure service-based systems to achieve declarative specified mission goals with multiple QoS requirements, such as security,

D. Ślęzak et al. (Eds.): GDC 2009, CCIS 63, pp. 49–56, 2009.
© Springer-Verlag Berlin Heidelberg 2009

SAW and real-time, in dynamic and unreliable environments. We introduce a non-monotonic version of the α-logic [15] that supports the specification and automated synthesis of AS^3 systems with various QoS requirements, such as security, SAW and real-time as well as dynamic reconfiguration and redeployment of agents in response to changes in the environment such as services failing or changes in requirements. We will use the AS^3 calculus to model agents; it provides a formal programming model for executing workflows for AS^3 systems.

In a perfect world, synthesized workflows satisfying their initial conditions and goals for the AS^3 system would execute successfully and perform all the needed tasks. However, various things may go wrong during execution such as; a service may fail to terminate successfully, an unperceived exception condition may arise at run-time or more resources may be needed in order to fulfill a user's goal. Since, it is almost impossible to identify all control and correction steps before execution time; it must be possible to adapt the workflow at run-time with *dynamic reconfiguration constraints* such as *resource failure, service failure, or exception condition.*

In this paper, we propose a framework to handle failures that occur during the execution of agents by encoding the failures in formalism of *a default normal modal logic.* Default logic provides a set of rules for adding premises to logical arguments. Since the specifications of services are encoded in AS^3 logic, defaults can be added to this logic to accommodate the failure semantics for the predicates. We encode predicate failures as predicates and provide a dynamic proof system that handles failures at the execution time. Agents are (re-) synthesized from proofs in our logic using a Curry-Howard style correspondence.

The rest of the paper is organized as follows. Section 2 provides background on default logic. We present an overview of failure handling in workflow systems in Section 3 and introduce how we can model and reason with failures using default logic. Section 4 presents the default α-logic. We conclude the paper with a realistic case scenario in Section 5.

2 Background on Default Logic

Default logic provides a set of rules for adding premises to logical arguments. "Defaults function as meta-rules whose role is to further complete an underlying incomplete first order theory" [13]. Default logic was invented by Reiter [13], and has been most fully investigated by Etherington [5]. Poole, Goebel and their colleagues have empirically investigated a simple case of default logic [11,12]. Besnard [2] gives a comprehensive overview of theoretical work in default logic.

A default theory is a pair <D, F> where:

F is a set of closed formulae, called the "facts";
D is a set of "defaults" of the form

$$\frac{\alpha(x):\ \beta_1(x),\ ...\ \beta_m(x)}{w(x)}$$

where $\alpha(x),\ \beta_1(x),\ ...\ \beta_m(x),\ w(x)$ are formulae whose free variables are amongst those of x.

The default rules specify formulae that can be used as premises of a logical argument. The above rule means, intuitively that a ground instance of $w(x)$ can be used if the corresponding instance of $\alpha(x)$ is proved and the corresponding instances of $\beta_i(x)$ are consistent with everything believed.

Consider the following normal default representation of "birds fly, but baby birds are exceptional" [11]:

$$D=\{ \cfrac{bird(x) : flies(x) \wedge \neg baby(x)}{flies(x) \wedge \neg baby(x)} \}, F=\{bird(Tweety), baby(Polly), bird(Polly)\}$$

Here we can explain $flies(Tweety)$ and $\neg baby(Tweety)$ by assuming the default for $x=Tweety$. However, we cannot explain $flies(Polly)$ since $\neg baby(Polly)$ is not consistent with the facts.

3 Overview of Failure Handling in Workflow Systems

The failures that our system handles can be characterized by whether they are caused at the resource-level or at the task-level.

The overview of our system is presented in Figure 1. After the specifications and constraints are sent to the planner, the planner builds a plan using standard backward-chaining procedure. During the execution of the plan, whenever there is a failure, our handling system detects the type of failure and processes it accordingly. If it is a re-source-level failure, then the system attempts to dynamically repair the workflow by addition or deletion of event predicates thereby handling the resource conflicts. If the

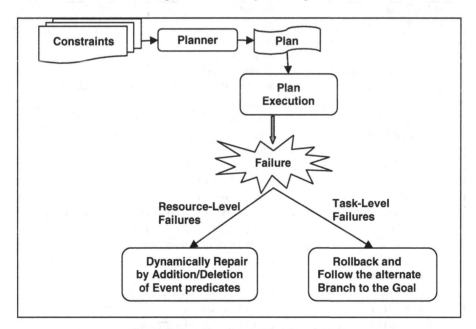

Fig. 1. Failure Handling in Workflow Systems

failure is caused at task-level, then the workflow is rolled back and checked if there is a branching state in the history and if an alternate branch can followed to reach the goal. If the system is not able to recover from the failure, then the constraints that cause the system to fail are identified and the agent is resynthesized to accommodate the new constraints.time), can be used in temporal reasoning.

4 Default α-Logic

α-logic is a hybrid normal modal logic [16], which has been used for specifying SBS [15]. The logic has both temporal modalities for expressing situation information as well as modalities for expressing communication, knowledge and service invocation. It provides atomic formulas for expressing relations among variables and nominals for identifying agents. The α-logic supports developers to declaratively specify situation awareness requirements. Models for the logic are (annotated) processes in the α-calculus. These processes provide constructive interpretations for the logic. We present here a default version of a proof theory for the α-logic. Following a Curry-Howard style isomorphism [17], in which proofs are interpreted as processes, α-logic proofs can support the synthesis of α-calculus terms from declarative α-logic specifications.

Here, we will only summarize the parts of syntax and the proof-theoretic semantics of the default α-logic, which will be used in this chapter, and provide some intuitive explanations to the logic. Table 1 shows the part of the syntax of α-logic.

Table 1. A partial syntax of Default α-logic

$\Phi 1, \varphi 2 ::=$	formula
T	true
0	inactivity
U	nominal
$pred(x_1,...,x_n)$	atomic formula
$x \sim c$	atomic constraint $// \sim ::=> | < | \leq \geq, c$ is a natural number
$\varphi 1 \vee \varphi 2$	disjunction
$\neg \varphi$	negation
$E(\varphi 1 \; u \; \varphi 2)$	until
$E(\varphi 1 \; s \; \varphi 2)$	since
$\varphi 1 \| \varphi 2$	parallel composition
$K(u; \varphi)$	knowledge of u
$sense(u; \varphi; I)$	senses u through a push service
$serv(x;u;\sigma;\varphi)$	invocation of a service σ, with input x by φ and returning u
$\exists \varphi$	existential quantification on time
$<u> \varphi$	behavior after sending message
$\varphi 1 \wedge \varphi 2$	conjunction
$@T(I, \sigma)$	constraint σ becomes true
$@F(I, \sigma)$	constraint σ becomes false
$@C(I, x)$	variable x changes
$PREV(x)$	previous value of variable x
$INIT(x, u)$	initial value of x is u

In the above table, we assume that every variable x has a type. Intuitively, the nominals act as identifiers to processes. The knowledge formula intuitively states that after a process receives the item named u from another process, the process satisfies φ. Sensors such as voltmeters, ampere meters as well as observers can be modeled as services disseminating results in a "push" mode. On the other hand, components such as power system simulators and static VAR compensators can be modeled as services disseminating computation results in the "pull" mode. The logic is hybrid in the sense that it allows terms, called nominals, denoting states to be used as formulas. We assume a finite set of nominals (the participants in a computation). α-logic specifications can express QoS requirements such as context awareness and timeliness. The logic has a sometime/eventually modality for temporal evolution, and a somewhere modality for spatial location. There are atomic formulas with typed signatures for describing relations among variables. We provide a constructive/intuitionistic interpretation of the logic, i.e. classical negation is not allowed and for any formula φ, the formula $(\varphi \vee (\varphi \rightarrow F))$ is not a tautology. Such interpretation of the logic is necessary for generating constructive proofs of formulas from which software agents will be synthesized.

We provide a brief explanation of important formulas of the logic as follows:

- The formula *serv(u; v; φ1; I)* describes the properties of a software/hardware service disseminating results in the pull mode declaratively. The formula states that (1) a service exported by the entity with nominal I can be invoked by a process that matches the pattern $\varphi 1$, and (2) the service, to which an object u is passed as the parameter, returns object v as the result. Note that the nominal I also indicates the location of the entity, and the patterns that can be used in the logic are limited to regular patterns.

- The formula *sense(u; φ; I)* states that the object u is sensed by a sensor, i.e. a service that disseminates its results in the push mode, and received by an agent that matches the pattern φ. The service is exported by an entity with nominal I.

- The formulas *@T(I, σ)*, *@F(I, σ)*, and *@C(I, x)* state that the entity with nominal I knows that the constraint σ has changed from false to true, the constraint σ has changed from true to false, and the value of variable x has changed, respectively.

- The formula *PREV(x)* (a term used as a formula since this is a hybrid logic) denotes the previous value of the variable x. The formula *INIT(x, u)* states that the initial value of x is u.

- The formula *<u>φ* describes the behavior of a process after sending out u.

5 A Case Study of Failure Modeling in Workflow Systems Using Dynamic Reconfiguration Constraints

In this section, we will demonstrate our failure handling system using a case study with dynamic reconfiguration constraints in default α-logic.

5.1 An Example Scenario

Consider a workflow system, as shown in Figure 2, connecting the Intelligent Transportation System (**ITS**), Police Departments (**PD**), Fire Departments (**FD**), and Ambulance Services (**AMS**), for maintaining traffic safety and coordinating various responders (**ITS, PD, FD** and **AMS**) in emergency situations. **ITS, PD, FD** and **AMS** provides various capabilities as services in the system. A Mission Planner (**MP**) service in the system is used to automatically synthesize workflows using these services to fulfill various mission goals. The following *Accident Response* scenario illustrates the need for adaptability, situation-awareness and security provided by AS³ system.

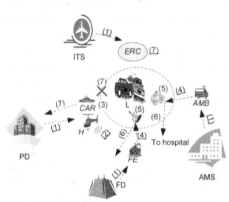

Fig. 2. Traffic Emergency

A <u>911 call center</u> gets a report specifying an accident at location **L** on a road during rush hour. In response to such a situation, the following workflow (as shown in Figure 2) is automatically generated by the **MP** to coordinate field rescue operations and mitigate the effects of the accident. The following is the step-by-step description of the control flow logic in the workflow:

We use the eventuality connective ($\Diamond$) in α-logic to state that an event can eventually occur sometime in the future. The logical order of the occurrence of these events is as follows:

1. K("accident", location;MP)$\rightarrow\Diamond$(<"accident", location>MP) (C0)
2. When 911 request comes to MP, it is announced to the PD.

    <Loc>MP : K(x; PD)

    -------------------------- (C1)

        K(x; PD)

3. Upon receiving the accident location PD is dispatched: K(x;PD) $\rightarrow \Diamond$PD
4. After the police car arrives, it attempts to setup the perimeter.

    PD : $\Diamond$PS

    ----------- (C2)

    $\Diamond$PS

5. After the perimeter is setup, eventually the ambulance and the fire engine arrive at the accident scene: PS$\rightarrow\Diamond$(AMB $\wedge$ FE) (C3)
6. After the ambulance and the fire engine arrive, FESearch operation is performed to search for the fire: (AMB $\wedge$ FE)$\rightarrow\Diamond$FESearch (C4)
7. After the FESearch operation is successfully completed, the injured passengers are rescued from the location: FESearch$\rightarrow\Diamond$RES (C5)

In a perfect world, the above workflow would execute successfully and perform all the needed tasks to complete the rescue operations. However, various things may go wrong during execution such as; a service may fail to terminate successfully, an unperceived exception condition may arise at run-time or more resources may be needed in order to fulfill a user's goal. To accommodate these failures in our model, we identify the predicates that are likely to fail and develop contingency plans with *dynamic reconfiguration constraints* that would automatically adapt the workflow using default α-logic as follows:

❖ **Resource failure:** An ambulance can transport at most two injured passengers at the same time hence; the **MP** should send another ambulance to carry additional injured passengers.

$$: K(injuries; MP), @F(MP, injuries <= 2)$$
$$\text{-- (C6)}$$
$$MP \rightarrow K(injuries; MP), @F(MP, injuries <= 2), \Diamond AMB2$$

❖ **Service failure:** If the police fail to set up a perimeter within five minutes after the 911 call center gets an accident report, FE and AMB can enter the accident site regardless a police perimeter has been set up or not.

$$\Diamond PD : K(delay; MP), @T(MP, delay > 5mins), \neg\Diamond PS$$
$$\text{--- (C7)}$$
$$MP \rightarrow K(delay; MP), @T(MP, delay > 5mins), \neg\Diamond PS, \Diamond(AMB \wedge FE)$$

❖ **Exception Condition:** If the paramedics determine that one of the injured passengers is in *critical condition* in Step (6), and the accident site is too far from nearby hospitals, a closest hospital with sufficient resources is notified to start preparing, and another helicopter (H1) is discovered and used to transport the passenger in critical condition to the hospital.

$$\Diamond FESearch : K(inj\_status; MP), @T(MP, inj\_status = \text{`critical''})$$
$$\text{--- (C8)}$$
$$MP \rightarrow K(inj\_status; MP), @T(MP, inj\_status = \text{`critical''}), \Diamond HEL1$$

Acknowledgment

The work reported here was supported by the NSF under the CAREER Program Award Number: 0644459.

References

1. Beguiling, A., Seligman, E., Stephan, P.: Application level fault tolerance in heterogeneous networks of workstations. Journal of Parallel and Distributed Computing on Workstation Clusters and Networked-based Computing (1997)
2. Besnard, P.: An Introduction to Default Logic. In: Symbolic Computation. Springer, Berlin (1989)
3. Condor manuals, http://www.cs.wisc.edu/condor/manual/
4. Elder, M.C.: Fault Tolerance in Critical Information Systems. PhD thesis, University of Virginia (2001)
5. Etherington, D.W.: Relating default logic and circumstription. In: Proceedings of 11th International Joint Conference on Artificial Intelligence (IJCAI 1989), Milan, Italy, pp. 489–494 (1987)

6. Gartner, F.C.: Fundamentals of fault-tolerant distributed computing in asynchronous environments. ACM Computing Surveys 31(1) (1999)
7. Hwang, S., Kesselman, C.: GridWorkflow: A Flexible Failure Handling Framework for the Grid. In: Proceedings of the 12th IEEE International Symposium on High Performance Distributed Computing, HPDC 2003 (2003)
8. Leon, J., Fisher, A.L., Steenkiste, P.: Fail-safe pvm: A portable package for distributed programming with transparent recovery. Technical Report CMU-CS-93-124, Carnegie Mellon University (1993)
9. Plank, J.S., Beck, M., Kingsley, G., Li, K.: Libckpt: Transparent checkpointing under unix. In: Proceedings of the the USENIX Winter Technical Conference, New Orleans, Louisiana (1995)
10. Poole, D., Goebel, R., Aleliunas, R.: Theorist: A logical reasoning system for defaults and diagnosis. In: Cercone, N., McCalla, G. (eds.) The Knowledge Frontier: Essays in the Representation of Knowledge, pp. 331–352. Springer, New York (1987)
11. Poole, D.: A logical framework for default reasoning. Artificial Intelligence 36(1), 27–47 (1988)
12. Poole, D.: Default Logic, Handbook of Logic for AI & Logic Programming (1998)
13. Reiter, R.: A logic for default reasoning. Artificial Intelligence 12(1,2), 81–132 (1980)
14. Stellner, G.: Cocheck: Checkpointing and process migration for mpi. In: 10th International Parallel Processing Symposium, pp. 526–531. IEEE Computer Society, Los Alamitos (1996)
15. Yau, S.S., Davulcu, H., Mukhopadhyay, S., Huang, D., Gong, H., Singh, P., Gelgi, F.: Automated Situation-Aware Service Composition in Service-Oriented Computing. International Journal of Web Services Research on Services Engineering (JWSR) 4(4), 59–82 (2007)
16. Blackburn, P., de Rijke, M., Venema, Y.: Modal Logic (Paperback)
17. Sørensen, M.H., Urzyczyn, P.: Lectures on the Curry-Howard Isomorphism. Studies in Logic and the Foundations of Mathematics, vol. 149 (Hardcover)
18. Goebel, R.G., Goodwin, R.G.: Applying theory formation to the planning problem. In: Proc. of of the Workshop on the Frame Problem in AI, pp. 207–232 (1987)

A Back Propagation Neural Network for Evaluating Collaborative Performance in Cloud Computing

Biao Song, Mohammad Mehedi Hassan, Yuan Tian, and Eui-Nam Huh

Department of Computer Engineering, Kyung Hee University, Global Campus
Seocheon-dong, Giheung-gu, Yongin-si, Gyeonggi-do 446-701, South Korea
{bsong,hassan,ytian,johnhuh}@khu.ac.kr

Abstract. The partner selection is an important decision problem in the formation of dynamic collaboration among Cloud Provides (CPs). To acquire optimal collaboration, both individual and collaborative performance of candidate partners should be considered. In the existing methods for partner selection, the collaborative performance is evaluated by using linear functions which cannot address the comprehensive relationships among candidate partners. This paper proposes an evaluation approach using Back Propagation Neuron Network (BPNN) instead of any fixed objective function. Through training, the BPNN can achieve function approximation and provide estimates of collaborative performance. The experiment results show that our approach is effective and accurate in the evaluation.

Keywords: Back Propagation Neuron Network, Partner Selection, Dynamic Collaboration.

1 Introduction

In the last years, Cloud computing [1] has become a critical issue in the development of computer science. It was defined as "a style of computing in which dynamically scalable and often virtualized resources are provided as a service over the Internet" in [5]. To make Cloud computing truly scalable, one huge Cloud that is controlled by one huge vendor running just a very narrow set of applications is not feasible. Interoperability is becoming an important issue for Cloud services since many enterprises will not want to tie their most important applications to specific providers' remote infrastructure or platforms [2]. One approach for achieving interoperability is to establish dynamic collaboration [3] among CPs.

To achieve scalable services and pursue mutual profit, dynamic collaboration was introduced to Cloud providers [6]. One of the major challenges for achieving optimal collaboration is the partner selection problem. What deserves special mention is that an improper partner selection may result in many problems such as many conflicts during negotiation, low QoS or high cost of collaborative services. As we mentioned in the abstract, it desires to use an efficient partner selection approach if possible.

Multi-objective genetic algorithm (MOGA) [4] is a fruitful solution to increase the efficiency of partner selection because of its optimization capability on a variety of

D. Ślęzak et al. (Eds.): GDC 2009, CCIS 63, pp. 57–64, 2009.
© Springer-Verlag Berlin Heidelberg 2009

objectives such as cost and reliability. In [7], a MOGA algorithm using both individual information and collaborative information was applied to address the member selection problem of R&D teams. In particular, a linear function was used to evaluate the collaborative performance by summing up all pair-wise collaboration information. Obviously, it is too simple to illustrate the complex relationships among collaborative partners. An efficient evaluation approach needs to be developed to address this problem.

It is widely accepted that BPNN is an efficient alternative tool for modeling of complex systems. In [8], it was tested and proved as a successful approach for achieving function approximation. In this paper, we propose an approach using a three layer BPNN for evaluating collaborative performance. The function approximation ability of BPNN is utilized in our approach. The BPNN can provide reliable estimates of collaborative performance to any group which may or may not exist in the training set. It provides a novel and efficient method to solve the critical problem in partner selection. We simulate our approach and test it by using a variety of data sets which are generated from different functional forms. The experiment results show that our approach has high accuracy and good flexibility in the evaluation.

The rest of this paper is organized as follows: Section 2 presents the proposed evaluation approach using BPNN. In Section 3, we simulate the existing and our proposed approach and present our experiment results. We conclude our work by presenting summary and future directions in Section 4.

2 Proposed Evaluation Approach

In this section, we introduce a mathematical model to illustrate our proposed BPNN for evaluating collaborative performance. First of all, the notations of parameters and variables for the system are illuminated.

2.1 Notations

$P = \{p_i | i=1,...,n\}$: a set of n candidate CPs that may join into a group. Especially, if any CP can provide two or more services at the same time, we can give an identical symbol to each service. For instance, if CP_1 can provide CPU service and memory service, we can define them as p_1 and p_2 to verify these two services.

$G = \{p_j | j=1,...,m\}$: a formed or unformed group G contains m CPs where $G \subseteq P$ and $m \leq n$. Besides, we also define m_{max} denoting the maximum number of CPs in a group. Thus, $m \leq m_{max}$.

$A_G = \{a_{12},...,a_{1n}; a_{23},...,a_{2n};...; a_{(n-1)n}\}$: a $n \times n$ matrix denotes to pairs of CPs appearing in group G. The elements in diagonal and lower-triangle part are not listed since they are not used in our design. If both p_x and p_y ($x < y$ & $x, y \leq n$) participate in G, set $a_{xy} = 1$. Otherwise, $a_{xy} = 0$. In our BPNN, the number of input neurons is same as the number of elements listed in A_G. Consequently, there are $n(n-1)/2$ neurons in input layer.

$Co_G = \dfrac{C_{m_{max}}^2}{C_m^2} = \dfrac{m_{max}(m_{max}-1)}{m(m-1)}$: a coefficient for input-output normalization. As our approach support different size of groups, we need this coefficient to standardize the input signals.

$E(G)$: an estimate for the collaborative performance of group G. It is produced from the output layer of BPNN.

$T(G)$: a value representing the true collaborative performance of group G. The difference between $E(G)$ and $T(G)$ is the error we need to correct by adjusting the connection weight in BPNN.

2.2 Proposed BPNN Model

Our proposed BPNN consists of three layers, input, output and hidden layer. In the input layer, each neuron represents a pair of candidate participants. If both of them appear in a group G, the corresponding neuron receives a signal Co_G and delivers it to the neurons in hidden layer. Otherwise, it delivers 0. As we known, the collaborative performance of a group depends on the collaborative performance between each pair of participants. If a group contains more excellent pair-wise collaborations, the collaborative performance of the whole group will be better. Thus, our design originates from the assumption: the pair-wise collaborations contained in a group are the features of that group. Through training, BPNN needs to judge whether these features are good or bad and how they can affect the performance of a group.

Each neuron in hidden layer or output layer receives weighted inputs from a previous layer and transmits output to neurons in the next layer. The summation of weighted input signals in hidden layer and output layer are calculated by Eq. (1) and Eq. (2) respectively. This summation is transferred by a nonlinear activation function given in Eq. (3). The evaluation result of network $E(G)$ is compared with the true result $T(G)$ and the network error is calculated with Eq. (4). The training process continues until this error is reduced to an acceptable value.

$$Y_j = \sum_{i=1}^{n(n-1)/2} X_i \times w_{ij} + w_0 \tag{1}$$

$$Y_k = \sum_{j=1}^{M} X_j \times w_{jk} + w_0 \tag{2}$$

$$Y = f(Y_{net}) = \frac{1}{1+e^{-Y_{net}}} \tag{3}$$

$$Er = \frac{1}{2} \times (E(G)-T(G))^2 \tag{4}$$

In above equations, X_i and X_j represents the input signals from input layer and hidden layer respectively. Y_j denotes the summation of weighted inputs in hidden layer and Y_k denotes the summation of weighted inputs in output layer. w_{ij} and w_{jk} are weight coefficients of each neuron input, w_0 is bias. $f(Y_{net})$ is sigmoid activation function , Y_{net} can be any Y_j or Y_k . In particular, our BPNN has only one neuron in output layer, which means it always exists $k = 1$. Moreover, M is the number of hidden neurons in hidden layer. We refer to Eq. (5) proposed in [4] and calculate M as follows:

$$M = \sqrt{(p+q)} + a \qquad (5)$$

Where p is the number of nodes in input layer; q is the number of nodes in output layer; a is a constant between 1 to 10.

Er in Eq. (4) is the error between the evaluation result of network $E(G)$ and the true result $T(G)$. To diminish the error, we implement the simplest back propagation algorithm to updates the network weights and biases. The training of the network is based on the delta training rule method [9]. As we use the same training method, it is not necessary to present the details in this paper.

3 Simulation Results

In our simulation, we selected 3 functional forms to generate training data and testing data (See Table 1).

Table 1. Models for Generating Data

Functional Forms	Functions
Linear Functional Form	$T(G) = \sum_{i=1}^{m-1} \sum_{j=i+1}^{m} T_{ij}$
Squared Functional Form	$T(G) = \sum_{i=1}^{m-1} \sum_{j=i+1}^{m} (T_{ij})^2$
Exponential Functional Form	$T(G) = \sum_{i=1}^{m-1} \sum_{j=i+1}^{m} e^{T_{ij}}$

T_{ij} denotes the collaborative performance between participant p_i and p_j. In addition, T_{ij} is randomly generated following uniform distribution $U(0, 1)$. Other parameters can be found in Table 2. As we mentioned above, n is the total number of candidate participants and m is the number of participants in a group. Tr_G is the total number of groups we generated for training the network, Te_G is the total number of groups we generated for testing the network. The participants of any group are randomly selected from n candidate participants.

Table 2. Models for Generating Data

Parameters	Values
n	40
m	3-10
Tr_G	5000-50000
Te_G	100

To test proposed BPNN, we use pair-wise testing method which simulates the pair-wise comparisons used in MOGA for partner selection. Suppose two groups are G_1 and G_2, $T(G_1)$ and $T(G_2)$ are the true collaborative performance of G_1 and G_2. The estimates produced by BPNN are $E(G_1)$ and $E(G_2)$. First, if fault tolerance is not considered, we say the estimates are correct in a pair-wise comparison under any of following conditions:

$$T(G_1) > T(G_2) \& E(G_1) > E(G_2) \text{ or}$$
$$T(G_1) < T(G_2) \& E(G_1) < E(G_2) \text{ or}$$
$$T(G_1) = T(G_2) \& E(G_1) = E(G_2)$$

Besides, it is also reasonable to enable fault tolerance since small faults do not result in too much bad effect during the partner selection process. If small faults can be tolerated, we add another condition:

$$|T(G_1) - E(G_1)| + |T(G_2) - E(G_2)| < \alpha \text{ where } \alpha \text{ is the tolerable fault}$$

In testing set, the estimates for each pair of groups were checked to verify the accuracy of BPNN.

3.1 Fixed Number of Participants

In our first simulation, we fixed number of participants in all groups as 5. The experiment results are show in Fig. 1, Fig. 2 and Fig. 3:

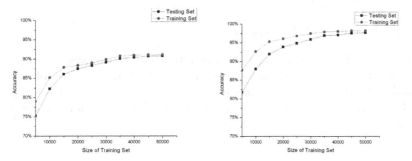

Fig. 1. Experiment results of linear functional form. The right one has fault tolerance.

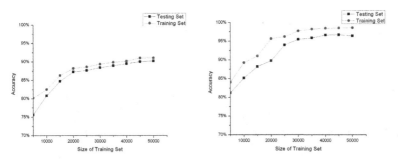

Fig. 2. Experiment result of squared functional form. The right one has fault tolerance.

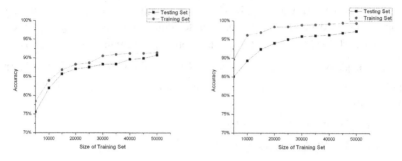

Fig. 3. Experiment result of exponential functional form. The right one has fault tolerance.

In above graphs, "Training Set" denotes the testing set is selected from the training set and "Testing Set" means the testing set is a new set which is randomly generated. As we can see, the network can always produce more accurate estimates when the testing set is selected from the training set. Usually, after the size of the training set is increased to 20000, further enlargement of the training set cannot bring too much increase on accuracy. To verify the performance in real case, we need to focus on the tests using new data set. Without fault tolerance, the accuracy of BPNN can be increased to 90% when the size of training set is 50000. With fault tolerance, it can be improved a lot and reach 95%. Besides, the differences between the results of three functional forms are very small, which means proposed BPNN can adapt to all of these three functions very well.

3.2   Variable Number of Participants

Secondly, we varied the number of participants from 3 to 10. To generate any group for training or testing, the simulation program first generates the value of m, and then randomly selected m participants from all candidates. The flexibility of proposed BPNN can be investigated in this simulation. The results are presented as follows:

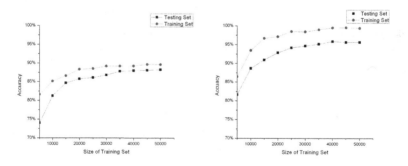

Fig. 4. Experiment result of linear functional form. The right one has fault tolerance.

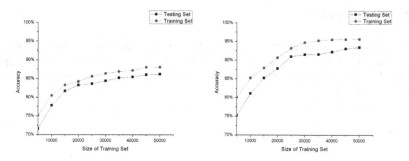

Fig. 5. Experiment result of squared functional form. The right one has fault tolerance.

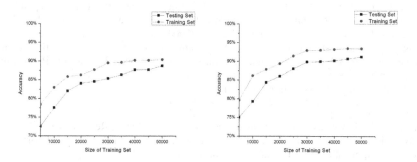

Fig. 6. Experiment result of exponential functional form. The right one has fault tolerance.

Not surprising, comparing with previous simulation results, the accuracies are reduced by 3%-5%. However, no obvious difference can be found between fig. 1 and fig. 4. Meanwhile, we can see the increasing trend from fig. 5 and fig. 6. If a larger training set is provided to the BPNN, the accuracy can be further improved. Even if the size of training set is 50000, with fault tolerance, the accuracy is still acceptable as it can reach 90%. Thus, we can conclude that our proposed BPNN has good flexibility to support variable number of participants.

4 Conclusion

In this paper, we addressed the issue of collaborative performance evaluation in partner selection. An approach using a three layer BPNN was introduced as an effective solution. We utilized the function approximation ability of BPNN. Since the approach is novel, we simulated proposed BPNN and tested it. The experiment results show that our approach has high accuracy and good flexibility in the evaluation. In our future work, a virtual collaborative Cloud environment will be created as a test bed for related researches.

Acknowledgment

This research was supported by the MKE (Ministry of Knowledge Economy), Korea, under the ITRC (Information Technology Research Center) support program supervised by the IITA (Institute of Information Technology Advancement) (IITA-2009-C1090-0903-0011).

References

1. Weiss, A.: Computing in the Clouds. Net Worker 11(4), 16–25 (2007)
2. Interoperability: A key Challenge for Cloud Computing (2009),
   http://www.lightreading.com/document.asp?doc_id=172033
3. Yamazaki, Y.: Dynamic Collaboration: the model of new business that quickly responds to changes in the market through "The integrated IT/Network Solutions" provided by NEC. NEC Journal of Advanced Technology 1(1), 9–16 (2004)
4. Wang, Z.-J., Xu, X.-F., et al.: Genetic Algorithms for collaboration cost optimization-oriented partner selection in virtual enterprises. International Journal of Production Research 47(4) (2009)
5. Gruman, G.: What cloud computing really means,
   http://www.infoworld.com/article/08/04/07/
   15FE-cloud-computing-reality_1.html
6. Nepal, S., Zic, J., Chan, J.: A Distributed Approach for Negotiating Resource Contributions in Dynamic Collaboration. In: Proc. of the 8th IEEE Int. Conf. on Parallel and Distributed Computing Applications and Technologies, vol. 1, pp. 82–86 (2007)
7. Fan, Z.P., Feng, B., Jiang, Z.Z., Fu, N.: A method for member selection of R&D teams using the individual and collaborative information. Expert System with Applications 36, 8313–8323 (2009)
8. Marquez, L., Hill, T.: Function Approximation using Backpropagation and General Regression Neural Networks, 0-8186-1060-3425/93. IEEE, Los Alamitos (1993)
9. Zilouchian, A., Jamshidi, M.: Intelligent Control Systems Using Soft Computing Methodologies. CRC Press, Florida (2001)

SCAIMO – A Case for Enabling Security in Semantic Web Service Composition

Amir Vahid Dastjerdi[1], Sayed Gholam Hassan Tabatabaei[2], Wan M.N. Wan Kadir[2], Suhaimi Ibrahim[2], and Elahe Sarafian[3]

[1] Department of Computer Science and Software Engineering,
The University of Melbourne, VIC, Melbourne, Australia
amirv@student.unimelb.edu.au
[2] Department of Software Engineering, Faculty of Computer Science & Information Systems,
Universiti Teknologi Malaysia (UTM), 81310 Skudai, Johor, Malaysia
gtsayed2@siswa.utm.my, {wnasir,suhaimiibrahim}@utm.my
[3] Shahid Bahonar University of Kerman, Kerman, Iran
elahe.sarafian@gmail.com

Abstract. Web service is a novel distributed computing paradigm, trying to address the problem of enabling interaction between heterogeneous applications distributed over the Web. A problem that has become one of the recent critical issues is automated composition of Web services. A number of approaches like AI-planning have been proposed to resolve the problem. Despite the importance of AI-planning techniques for Web service composition, previous works in that area do not address security issues, which is the focus of this paper. Based on our prior work, i.e. AIMO, we present an approach called SCAIMO to achieve security conscious composition of Semantic Web services. We test our approach on a case study and the result shows SCAIMO can provide an applicable solution.

Keywords: Web Service Security, Semantic Web Service, Web Service Composition, Web Service Modeling Ontology, AI-planning.

1 Introduction

Nowadays, the term "Web services" has been used very often. According to W3C, "A Web service is a software system identified by a URI [1], whose public interfaces and bindings are defined and described using XML. Its definition can be discovered by other software systems. These systems may then interact with the Web service in a manner prescribed by its definition, using XML based messages conveyed by Internet protocols "[2].

Currently, an increasing number of companies and organizations implement their applications over Internet. Thus, the ability to select and integrate inter-organizational and heterogeneous services on the Web efficiently and effectively at runtime is an important step towards the development of the Web service applications.

In this paper, a significant portion of our work has been dedicated to scenarios aimed at secure automating Web service composition functionality. When no atomic Web service can fulfill the user's requirements, there should be a possibility to

D. Ślęzak et al. (Eds.): GDC 2009, CCIS 63, pp. 65–72, 2009.
© Springer-Verlag Berlin Heidelberg 2009

combine existing services together in order to satisfy the request requirement. This trend has inaugurated a considerable number of research efforts on the Web service composition (WSC) both in academia and industry.

Most of current approaches related to WSC applied following techniques: HTN [3], Golog [4], classic AI-planning [5], rule-based planning [6], model checking [7], theorem proving [8], etc. However, considering security issues in WSC have not been carefully addressed by most of previous works. In this paper, we propose an automated approach for Security Conscious composition of Semantic Web services, called SCAIMO, in order to tackle that problem. The aim is to insert security consideration for composition into our prior work, i.e. AIMO [26] which is an effective approach for WSC based on AI-planning, Web Service Modeling (WSMO) [9], and Description Logic (DL) [10].

The remainder of this paper is organized as follows. The section 2 discusses some related work in the area of WSC. The next two sections form the technical core of this paper, section 3 describes security capability and constraint types in SCAIMO, and section 4 details the proposed SCAIMO architecture. We test our approach on a case study and the result is described in section 5. The paper is concluded in section 6.

2 Related Work

Based on our evaluation of the state-of-the-art approaches for WSC [25], the HTN-DL formalism [17] can be considered as an optimized AI-planning technique which has some problems to be solved, that are addressed in [26].

Other current approaches which are being used to address the issue of WSC and similar to the SCAIMO framework are HTN-planning based approaches described in [7] and [16]. Sirin et al. [16] proposed an approach to translate process models and service descriptions written in OWL-S into the problem and domain description language of the HTN planner SHOP2 [22], and then, shows how to solve service-composition problems using SHOP2 based on that translation methodology.

Rao et al. [5] focus on the discovery and composition of Web services and propose a mixed initiative framework for Semantic Web service discovery and composition. The major weakness of all formerly presented approaches to service composition based on planning is lack of security mechanism.

BPEL4WS [24] addresses compositions where the BPEL4WS specification benefits from WS-Security [15] to ensure messages integrity and confidentiality.

As cited in [23], security has been a key factor that was holding companies back from adopting Web services. In 2005, the landscape is different especially after the emergence of several specifications for Web service security such as WS-Security [15], WS-Trust [13], and WS-Federation [11]. Nevertheless, these specifications have not found their way to composite Web services and among them AI-planning techniques. Due to the importance of AI-planning techniques for Web service composition, their security issues needed to be answered carefully, which is the focus of this work.

3 Security Capability and Constraint Types in SCAIMO

This section provides a brief overview on both security capability and constraint concepts. Service capability simply means what the service can do, and they can be used for discovery, advertising, and matchmaking. Security capabilities are defined as a type of service capability to express the security features of a Web service, based on the specified security terms. We introduce WSMO security vocabulary for providing those security terms as depicted in Fig. 1. On the other hand, security constraints are security features which are required. For example, a security constraint can be the X.509 authentication mechanism required by a service requestor.

```
/*****************************
* ONTOLOGY
******************************/
ontology _"http://www.example.org/ontologies/Security"
    nfp
        dc#title hasValue "WSML example ontology"
        dc#subject hasValue "Security Vocabulary"
        dc#description hasValue "fragments of a security ontology"
        dc#date hasValue _date(2009,7,10)
        dc#format hasValue "text/html"
        dc#language hasValue "en-US"
        wsml#version hasValue "$Revision: 1.1 $"
    endnfp
...
concept privacyAccessControl
hasType impliesType privacyAccessControl

instance P3P memberOf privacyAccessControl
    hasName hasValue "P3P"
instance REI memberOf privacyAccessControl
    hasName hasValue "REI"
instance EPAL memberOf privacyAccessControl
    hasName hasValue "EPAL"
instance XACML memberOf privacyAccessControl
    hasName hasValue "XACML"
...
concept authentication
hasType impliesType authentication

instance WS-Security memberOf authentication
    hasName hasValue "WS-Security"
instance SAML memberOf authentication
    hasName hasValue "SAML"
instance X.509 memberOf authentication
    hasName hasValue "X.509"
```

Fig. 1. Security terms in WSMO

Security constraints further categorized into three types as follows:

Security-related goal constraints: Every single requestor requirement must have a corresponding capability on the provider side to satisfy it. These requirements are described as goal constrains and have to be defined in preconditions (which are used to express constrains on the inputs, the requestor should be able to provide to the service) of Web services description as depicted in Fig. 2. For example a constraint can be a specific encryption algorithm that a user would like to be supported by requested Web services.

```
goal _"http://example.org/OnlineConferenceRegistrationSystem"
  capability _"http://example.org/OnlineConferenceRegistrationSystem#cap1"
  sharedVariables {?date, ?origin, ?participant, ?authentication, ?encryption}
  precondition definedBy
                  ?date memberOf _date and
                  ?origin memberOf cont#Location and
                  ?participant memberOf conf#participant and
                  ?authentication memberOf scr#authentication and
                  ?encryption memberOf scr#encryption
  assumption definedBy exists
  ...
  effect definedBy exists
  ...
```

Fig. 2. Security-related Goal constraints

Security-related choreography constraints: this category of constraint describes
security requirements of Web service providers which have to be satisfied by service
requestor capabilities. For describing this type of constraint, we use the syntax of
WSMO Choreography [18] with a slight extension, based on control state ASMs [14].
Therefore, only Web services will be selected by security matchmaker which can
successfully reach the security confirmed state as illustrated in Fig. 3. The figure
shows Transition rules and states for the orchestration case; for the choreography case
exactly the same format and structure is used, therefore it has not been added to the
example of Fig .3.

```
wsmlVariant _"http://www.wsmo.org/wsml/wsml-syntax/wsml-rule"
namespace { fl    _"http://www.example.org/BookFlight",
            htl   _"http://www.example.org/BookHotel",
            OCRS _"http://www.example.org/OnlineConferenceRegistrationSystem",
            scr  _"http://www.example.org/Security"}
/*********************************
* COMPOSITE WEBSERVICE
*********************************/
webService OCRS_"http://example.org/OnlineConferenceRegistrationSystem"
interface _"http://example.org/OnlineConferenceRegistrationSystem#OCRSInterface"
    choreography
        .....
    orchestration
        stateSignature
            importsOntology { fl#bookFlightOntology, htl#bookHotelOntology,
                              scr#SecurityOntology"}

        state{OCRS#start, OCRS#flightRequested, OCRS#hotelRequested, OCRS#noFlight,
              OCRS#noHotel, OCRS#booked, OCRS#securityCheck, OCRS#securityConfirmed, OCRS#noSecurity}

        transitionRules

        //Request a flight
        if (state = OCRS#start) then
            add (_#fReq[OCRS#date hasValue ?date, OCRS#statrt hasValue ?start,
                       OCRS#destination hasValue ?dest, fl#client hasvalue ?client]
                       memberOf fl#FlightRequest)
            state = OCRS#flightRequested
        endIf

        //No flight available: terminate with failure
        ...
        //Flight offer received: request and Security Check for Book Hotel Service
        if (state = OCRS#flightRequested and
            exists {?fo, fn } {?fo [OCRS#date hasValue ?date, OCRS#statrt hasValue ?start,
                               OCRS#destination hasValue ?dest, fl#flightNumber hasValue ?fn,
                               fl#client  hasValue ?client]
                               memberOf fl#FlightOffer)
        then
            ?flight = ?fo
            add (_HoSecReq{ scr#authentication hasValue ?authentication,
                           scr#encryption    hasValue ?encryption] memberOf scr#SecurityCheck)
            state = OCRS#SecurityCheck
        endIf

        //Security requirement checked: Request Hotel
        ...
        state = OCRS#securityConfirmed
        //No security requirement available: terminate with failure
        if (state = OCRS#SecurityCheck and
            exists {?sna} ?sna [ scr#authentication hasValue ?authentication,
                               scr#encryption    hasValue ?encryption] memberOf scr#SecReqNotAvailable)
        then
            state = OCRS#noSecurity
        endIf

        //Hotel offer received: confirm both flight and hotel and terminate successfully
        ...
        //No hotel available : cancle the flight and terminate with failure
        ...
```

Fig. 3. Choreography and Orchestration constraints

Security-related Orchestration constraints: it can be named as cooperation constraints which refer to conditions that a Web service can require from another Web
service in order to cooperate with. For example as depicted in Fig. 3, *bookFligh* Web
service uses transition rules in WSML notation to describe its security-related orchestration constraints. Then, it only cooperates with *bookHotel* Web services which can
reach confirmed security state.

4 SCAIMO Architecture

In order to realize SCAIMO, some specific extension has to be added to the WSMO framework. Fig. 4 shows main components of the proposed framework for the Web service composition. The architecture of the SCAIMO framework consists of four main components:

EHTN-DL Planner: This component is the heart of the framework, where composition of services for making higher level ones is done. The component is responsible to compose two or more operators or methods to satisfy the task request using task decomposition. The planner uses the WSML-DL reasoner to find the matching operators and methods for a given task. The reasoner is again used by the planner to evaluate the preconditions of actions to determine applicability. Note that in our framework, if an atomic Web service can satisfy the user's goal, the planner will not be used.

SCAIMO Translator: This component is used in SCAIMO to translate each *WSMO capability of service* into an element in the *task ontology* (T_{ont}) using *WSMO ontologies*. In addition, the translator provides translating of *WSMO service interfaces* into a set of methods and operators.

WSMX: This component [12] has a component-based architecture and is a reference implementation of WSMO. In addition, it takes the full conceptual model of WSMO into consideration. Some of its components are used in our framework such as *discovery*, *data mediation*, and *process mediation*. Furthermore, the SCAIMO architecture takes care of non-functional properties during matching the Semantic capability descriptions of Web services and goals, using discovery component of WSMX.

Secure Task Matchmaker: Secure task matchmaker function is used by WSML-DL Reasoner to select for each task a Web service satisfying the specified security requirements, which are described in the form of goal choreography and orchestration constraints to achieve security conscious composition.

WSML-DL Reasoner: This component captures the expressive Description Logic SHIQ (D) and consists of a wrapper of WSML-DL expressions to a classical Description Logics syntax [19]. Using this component we can, among others, perform the reasoning tasks of checking ontology consistency, entailment and instance retrieval.

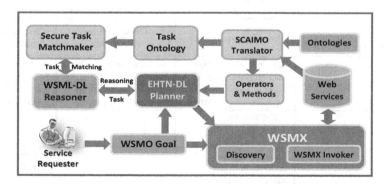

Fig. 4. High-level architecture of SCAIMO framework

In the following, the mechanism for using WSMO and planner is described. Firstly, the users' request will be presented to the WSMO with a WSMO Goal that formally describes what they would like to achieve.

In the next step, WSMX uses the Discovery component to find Web services, which have Semantic descriptions registered with WSMX that can fulfill this Goal. Security constraints of a service requestor can be defined in the form of goal capabilities. They are described in preconditions and explains the requestors constrains which should be satisfied by all candidate services participating in composition. A set of properties strictly belonging to a goal are defined as non-functional properties of a WSMO goal. A goal may be defined by reusing one or several already-existing goals by means of goal mediators.

If no single Web service can satisfy the request then the request will be offered to the planner. The planner then tries to combine existing Semantic Web services and generate the process model. Therefore, first the goal will be decomposed into two or more tasks. Next, WSML-DL Reasoner will be queried one by one for the existence of each task. In order to respond to queries, WSML-DL Reasoner has to communicate with secure task matchmaker for matching possibilities between the task and operators or methods described by Task Ontology. In that case, security-related choreography and orchestration constraints of Web services will be considered by secure task matchmaker.

5 Case Study

The case study illustrated in this section is based loosely on a scenario described in [20]. Suppose *Hassan* wants to participate in an international conference in *Kuala Lumpur* for a given period of time (e.g., staying there from December 1 to December 5). Therefore, it is not sufficient to register, but he should also take care of submitting the camera-ready version of the paper, booking a flight, reserving a hotel, renting a car, and look at weather forecast. In that case, AES encryption is required for all Web services and Hassan is only capable of supporting X.509 authentication mechanism and AES encryption.

Table 1. Security capabilities and constraints of Web services

Demanded Task	Candidates	Security capabilities	Orchestration constraints	Choreography constraints
BookFlight	WS1	Authentication=X.509 Encryption=DES, AES	Authentication=X.509 Encryption= DES	Authentication= X.509
	WS2	Authentication=SAML Encryption=AES, DES	Authentication=SAML Encryption= DES	Authentication= SAML
BookHotel	WS3	Authentication= WS-security Encryption=DES		
	WS4	Authentication=X.509 Encryption=AES, DES		Authentication= X.509
	WS5	Authentication=SAML Encryption=AES, DES		

For the sake of simplicity only composition of two Web services namely as *Book-Fligh* and *BookHotel* is explained. Table 1 shows candidate services for *BookFligh* and *BookHotel* along with their security capabilities and constraints. In order to fulfill the Hassan's request, which is depicted in Fig. 2 and illustrated with WSML notation [21], we need an automated Online Conference Registration System (OCRS). OCRS finds an execution path based on these predefined task decompositions, and then we can perform Hassan's Web Service discovery and composition task automatically. Indeed, the participant sends his request to the OCRS, which shows the weather forecast based on the request, and then the OCRS has to build a package including a travel to/from *Kuala Lumpur*, a hotel for all the nights spent in *Kuala Lumpur*, and a car based on the dates which are specified by the participant.

With regards to the constraints explained before, only Web services which can satisfy precondition constraints, including security-related goal constraints are selected. In this case, WS1, WS2, WS3, WS4 are capable of satisfying the security goal constraint (supporting of AES encryption). Next, choreography constraints is considered, as the user only supports X.509 authentication, therefore WS2 will be removed from list of candidates. Consequently, the WS1 is the only candidate for *BookHotel* in this stage. In addition, orchestration constraints are considered which refer to conditions that a Web service can require from another Web service in order to cooperate with. It means that the *BookFlight* Web service candidate (WS1) requires to the consequent Web services (book hotel Web service candidates) to support X.509 for authentication and DES for encryption. Therefore, in this simple example WS1 and WS5 are selected for execution path.

6 Conclusion and Future Work

In this paper, we have summarized ongoing work on the development of a security conscious composition of semantic Web services, called SCAIMO. In contrast to most works in AI-planning Web service composition, our approach concerns about security issues. The SCAIMO framework takes care of security requirements of both Web service requestors and providers using *Secure Task Matchmaker*.

There are several directions for future work to further enhance SCAIMO features. Future research can look into other non-functional constraints and capabilities in WSC such as reliability, persistence, trust, and QoS for the proposed architecture. We are currently working on developing a prototype to validate the benefits of the proposed approach. In this case, the implementation of the matchmaker is currently under investigation.

Acknowledgments. This research is supported by the Ministry of Science & Technology and Innovation (MOSTI), Malaysia and Universiti Teknologi Malaysia.

References

1. Berners-Lee, T., Fielding, R., Masinter, L.: Uniform Resource Identifiers (URI): Generic Syntax, IETF RFC 2396, http://www.ietf.org/rfc/rfc2396.txt
2. Web Services Architecture Requirements (2004),
   http://www.w3.org/TR/wsa-reqs/

3. Sirin, E., Parsia, B., Hendler, J.: Templatebased composition of semantic Web services. In: AAAI fall symp. on agents and the semantic Web, Virginia, USA (2005)
4. McIlraith, S., Son, T.C.: Adapting Golog for composition of Semantic Web services. In: Knowledge Representation and Reasoning (KR 2002), Toulouse, France (2002)
5. Rao, J., et al.: A Mixed Initiative Approach to Semantic Web Service Discovery and Composition: SAP's Guided Procedures Framework. In: The IEEE Intl. Conf. on Web Services, ICWS 2006 (2006)
6. Medjahed, B., Bouguettaya, A., Elmagarmid, A.K.: Composing Web services on the Semantic Web. VLDB Journal (2003)
7. Kuter, U., et al.: A Hierarchical Task-Network Planner based on Symbolic Model Checking. In: The Intl. Conference on Automated Planning & Scheduling, ICAPS (2005)
8. Rao, J., Kungas, P., Matskin, M.: Logic-based Web services composition: from service description to process model. In: The 2004 Intl. Conf. on Web Services, San Diego, USA (2004)
9. WSMO working group, http://www.wsmo.org
10. Baader, F., et al. (eds.): The Description Logic Handbook: Theory, Implementation, and Applications. Cambridge University Press, Cambridge (2003)
11. IBM, Web Services Federation Language (WSFederation) (July 2003)
12. WSMX working group, http://www.wsmx.org
13. BEA, Web Services Trust Language (WSTrust) (May 2004)
14. Gurevich, Y.: Evolving Algebras 1993: Lipari Guide, pp. 9–36. Oxford University Press, New York (1995)
15. OASIS, Web Services Security: SOAP Message Security. WSS TC Working Draft (2003)
16. Sirin, E., Parsia, B., Wu, D., Hendler, J., Nau, D.: HTN planning for Web service composition using SHOP2. Journal of Web Semantics 1(4), 377–396 (2004)
17. Sirin, E.: Combining Description Logic Reasoning with AI Planning for Composition of Web Services., PhD thesis, Department of Computer Science, University of Maryland (2006)
18. Scicluna, J., Polleres, A., Roman, D., Feier, C., Fensel, D.: Ontology-based choreography and orchestration of WSMO services. WSMO (2005)
19. McIlraith, S., Son, T., Zeng, H.: Semantic Web services. IEEE Intelligent Systems 16(2), 46–53 (2001)
20. Martínez, E.: Web service composition as a planning task: an agent-oriented framework, MSc thesis, Department of Computer Science, York University (2005)
21. The ESSI WSML working group, http://www.wsmo.org/wsml/
22. Nau, D., et al.: SHOP2: An HTN planning system. In: JAIR, December 2003, vol. 20, pp. 379–404 (2003)
23. IBM, Microsoft. Security in a Web Services World: A Proposed Architecture and Roadmap (April 2002)
24. Andrews, T., et al.: BPEL v1.1 (2007), http://www.ibm.com/developerworks/library/specification/ws-bpel/
25. Tabatabaei, S., Wan-Kadir, W., Ibrahim, S.: A Comparative Evaluation of State-of-the-Art Approaches for Web Service Composition. In: The 3rd Int'l Conf. on Software Engineering Advances (ICSEA 2008). IEEE Computer Society, Malta (2008)
26. Tabatabaei, S., Wan-Kadir, W., Ibrahim, S.: Semantic Web Service Discovery and Composition Based on AI-planning and Web Service Modeling Ontology. In: IEEE Asia-Pacific Services Computing Conference (IEEE APSCC 2008). IEEE Computer Society, Taiwan (2008)

Automatic Synthesis and Deployment of Intensional Kahn Process Networks

Manuel Peralta[1], Supratik Mukhopadhyay[2], and Ramesh Bharadwaj[3]

[1] Utah State University, Logan, UT 84322
[2] Louisiana State University, Baton Rouge, 70810
[3] Naval Research Laboratory, Washington DC, 20375
m.peralta@aggiemail.usu.edu, supratik@csc.lsu.edu,
ramesh@itd.nrl.navy.mil

Abstract. In this paper we introduce and study, theoretically, a clean slate "formal" foundational approach for developing and deploying high-assurance distributed embedded systems deployed in mission-critical applications. We propose a simple formal distributed asynchronous framework extending Kahn Process Networks with intensional specification. More precisely, we present a model-driven approach based on a platform-independent language and an intensional specification logic that allows us to synthesize distributed agents that can handle interactions with external resources asynchronously, ensure enforcement of information flow and security policies, and have the ability to deal with failures of resources. Our approach allows rapid development and automated deployment of formally verified embedded networked systems that provide guarantees that clients' requirements will be met and QoS guarantees will be respected. Moreover, it allows modeling (and programming) reliable distributed systems for multi-core hosts. Such a capability makes our framework suitable for next generation grid computing systems where multi-core individual hosts need to be utilized for improving scalability.Given an intensional logical specification of a distributed embedded system, that includes Quality of Service (QoS) requirements, a set of software resources and devices available in a network, and their formal interface specifications, a deductive system can automatically generate distributed extended Kahn processes and their deployment information in such a way that the application requirements—including QoS requirements—are guaranteed to be met. The generated processes use the inputs of the sensors/meters/probes and the management policies of the customer to generate real-time control decisions for managing the system. The processes are deployed automatically on a distributed network involving sensors/meters/probes tracking system parameters, actuators controlling devices, and diverse computing and communication elements such as PDA's, etc.

1 Introduction

We present a new approach for intelligent on-demand development, deployment, and co-ordination of service-delivering and service-receiving entities in heterogeneous embedded networks consisting of disparate computing and sensing elements such as control stations, sensors, personal digital assistants (PDAs), smart phones, notebook

D. Ślęzak et al. (Eds.): GDC 2009, CCIS 63, pp. 73–87, 2009.

computers, and actuating physical devices (e.g., process controllers) connected through wired/wireless networks. *A service is an abstraction for a software or a hardware component running on a host of a distributed network providing certain utilities to clients; e.g., printers, gps, google, etc.* To satisfy the demands of the clients running on heterogeneous platforms (e.g., different operating systems) and computing elements (e.g., PDA's) and devices (e.g., sensors) embedded in physical environments on a network, coordination and collaboration between services running on different nodes of the network is of paramount importance. Such collaboration and coordination is determined by the current context or situation (e.g., data obtained from sensor networks) and must respect the diverse local policies governing computation and communication in individual nodes and local networks and account for unexpected disturbances such as failures/compromises of individual network nodes or even entire subnetworks.

The approach presented here is based on formal semantics-based, demand-driven automatic synthesis of context-aware resource coordination agents from the functional logic of the clients and the quality of service (QoS) goals specified by them. The QoS goals can include real time deadlines, security, availability etc. Our approach is based on a simple formal distributed asynchronous framework extending Kahn Process Networks [41] with intensional specification [1]. More precisely, we present a model-driven approach based on a platform-independent language and an intensional specification logic that allows us to synthesize distributed agents (an agent is a Kahn process) that can handle interactions with external resources asynchronously, ensure enforcement of information flow and security policies, and have the ability to deal with failures of resources. Our approach allows rapid development and automated deployment of *formally verified* embedded networked systems that provide guarantees that clients' requirements will be met and QoS goals will be respected. Moreover, it allows modeling (and programming) reliable distributed systems for multi-core hosts. Such a capability makes our framework suitable for next generation grid computing systems where multi-core individual hosts need to be utilized for improving scalability. Thus our approach can be viewed as a first step towards realizing an embedded grid where diverse computing elements connected through heterogeneous communication media provide services that are coordinated through decentralized agents.

Given an intensional logical specification of a distributed embedded system, that includes Quality of Service (QoS) requirements, a set of software resources and devices available in a network, and their formal interface specifications, a deductive system can automatically generate distributed extended Kahn processes and their deployment information in such a way that the application requirements—including QoS requirements—are guaranteed to be met. The generated processes use the inputs of the sensors/meters/probes and the management policies of the customer to generate real-time control decisions for managing the system. The processes are deployed automatically on a distributed network involving sensors/meters/probes tracking system parameters, actuators controlling devices, and diverse computing and communication elements such as PDA's, etc.

Compared to existing techniques (see Section 3. for a description of the current-state-of-the art), the presented approach provides formal guarantees that the functional requirements of the clients in the network are met and the QoS goals specified by them are respected even under changing environments like services changing their configuration or network nodes failing or getting compromised. The technique can synthesize agents automatically from declarative specification of the functional logic, mission and QoS goals and formal models of available devices and services and can even deal with resources with side-effects in contrast with existing techniques. Because of the model-driven nature of the synthesis process, the presented technique is able to coordinate information and service delivery in networks consisting of disparate physical devices such as wireless sensors and actuators as opposed to existing middleware. Changing environments are handled by dynamic reconfiguration of a coordinating agent by a monitoring agent. The monitoring agents also ensure that the policies (e.g., access control policies) of the network and individual elements are enforced and issues reconfiguration actions for automated recovery when there is a possibility of violation.

2 Related Work

☐ Intensional dataflow networks were introduced as part of Wadge and Ashcroft's Lucid [2] programming language and its later version TransLucid [3] and the GIPSY framework [4]. Operational semantics of pure dataflow programs have been provided in terms of infinite games by Faustini [5]. However, none of these authors considered automated synthesis of Kahn process networks from intensional declarative specifications. In [6], the authors consider compilation of declarative network specifications in datalog into overlay networks. However, their work does not consider intensional specification of resources or third-party services

☐ In the area of context-aware coordination of services, Yau et. al has developed a situation-aware middleware, RCSM [7], which provides the capabilities of context data acquisition and situation-aware communication management, and a middleware-based situation-aware application software development framework. RCSM is not based on a formal framework and provides no guarantees that the service level agreements (SLA) will be respected. Ranganathan and Campbell [9] propose a context aware middleware GAIA for ubiquitous systems. Even though GAIA uses first order logic to implement situation awareness, GAIA does not provide (composed) services with formally verified properties. In particular, GAIA does not tie security with the middleware technology. In [8], the authors present PrismMW, a middleware architecture for small, meagre-resource, mobile computing environments. In contrast with the wide applicability of our technique and architecture, [8] is applicable only in restrictive domains. Besides they do not provide the reliability guarantees provided by the technique and the architecture presented in this paper. In [19], the authors introduced a control-theoretic framework for quality of service configuration in heterogeneous networked environments.

☐ In [10], the authors develop a proactive middleware platform MIDAS for mobile computing.

☐ In [12], the authors introduce EnviroTrack, an object-based distributed middleware system that raises the level of programming abstraction for distributed sensor networks by providing a convenient and powerful interface to the application developer geared towards tracking the physical environment. In contrast with ours, this work is not applicable to domains other than wireless sensor networks. In particular it does not provide any framework for automatically synthesizing processes that stitch together services. Besides it does not provide techniques for building sensor-based systems that provide provable guarantees of meeting their requirements

☐ Roemer et. al. [20] survey middleware challenges in the area of wireless sensor networks. According to [20], adaptability and data-centric communication should be important issues in coordinating services in networks that involve wireless sensors. We augment the desirable properties of coordination frameworks for wireless sensor networks stated in [20] with the capability of intelligent data/service fusion.

☐ Lang [11] shows how the concepts of model driven software engineering can be applied to security in an infrastructure. In particular, he presents a flexible model driven security framework where a technology independent abstract representation of the security policy is stored in a policy repository, which is integrated with the underlying platform and security technology in a flexible manner. However, Lang's architecture provides an informal framework lacking precise semantics and does not consider issues like context-awareness, failure handling etc.

☐ In [13,14], the authors present a framework for adaptable service composition in an agent-based architecture.

☐ Sirin, Hendler and Parsia [16] describe a technique for semi-automatic service composition in the context of web services using semantic description of the services. They use non-functional properties to filter the set of services that match a requirement. However, the architecture of [16] is not dynamically reconfigurable under changing contexts. Duan et. al. [17] describes a logical model-based verification and synthesis procedure for web services. Their logical model does not allow expressing QoS goals like security or deadlines. In [33], the authors describe a framework for web service composition based on deduction in predicate logic. Compared to their approach our approach captures the notion of a state and can thus express both functional as well as non-functional requirements.

☐ Ankolekar et. al. [24] attempt to provide a Erlang/Concurrent Haskell-based concurrent execution semantics of BPEL4WS. Their semantics does not incorporate the ability of reacting and dynamically reconfiguring based on context by the participants of a workflow.

☐ In the healthcare domain, [34] provides integrated web-based delivery of health services. . The services of [34] can be easily delivered using our technique and architecture. In addition, we provide interoperation with drug models and devices for automated therapeutic drug monitoring as well as automatic reconfiguration under changed situations such as failures in networks, different operating environment etc.

☐ Labview [36], marketed by National Instruments, provides a graphical domain-specific object-oriented language for programming controllers, testing, and measurement systems for hardware devices. It is mostly used for calibration and testing of instruments. It facilities analysis of data obtained from the tests as well as share them with relevant authorities. Compared to the wide applicability of our work, Labview is suitable for a particular only for a particular domain. Functionality-wise, the technique described below provides more intelligent and broader capabilities than Labview. The Labview programming language does not provide constructs for specifying non-functional requirements like context-awareness, availability, application-dependent security, etc. Compared with our approach, Labview systems are not dynamically reconfigurable; do not provide: any way of reducing spurious triggers, fault-tolerance, and large-scale distributed operation. Our framework can interoperate with the conventional web services framework in contrast with Labview. Unlike Labview, the service coordination framework described in this paper is agnostic of the communication media or the networking technology used.

☐ Several architectural platforms have been proposed for component-based software development aimed at promoting easy integration, interoperabilty and deployment of distributed applications some of which provide specific functionalities or services while others may use them. For example, service-oriented architectures (SOAs) [22] are nowadays being widely used for building and deploying loosely coupled distributed systems. SOAs promote component reuse as well as provide separation of concerns by separating the functional logic of an application from the implementation details. A service can be viewed as a stand-alone software/hardware module performing a specific function. For example, a sensor can be viewed as a stand-alone hardware module that provides the service of "sensing its environment".

3 Our Approach

In contrast with previous techniques for service coordination in heterogeneous networks, our technique and architecture builds on advanced concepts in automated deduction and programming languages to provide smart composition and orchestration of services/devices that formally guarantees that the client's business requirements as well as its QoS goals are met.

The method and the architecture relies on decentralized context-aware intensional Kahn processes that model agents for processing of information about the current context and discovering and composing services in order to adapt to future contexts. *The programming model encompasses an inbuilt security model (that subsumes standard Bell-La-Padula-like [27] models of multilevel security) for providing security guarantees.* The programming model *has formal operational semantics and incorporates, communicating processes, hierarchical group structure, group communication,and logical and physical migration by processes. It is also capable of talking about time constraints, space constraints and failures and has constructs for control flow.* It has capabilities for dynamic reconfiguration using. The model also ensures that the provenance of any data exchanged between processes is certified. A software engine can formally verify if a model satisfies safety properties like deadlock-freedom, mutual exclusion etc.

Our approach also involves a declarative logical specification language for specifying the business goals of a client at a very high level along with the QoS constraints. A network of intensional Kahn processes can be synthesized automatically from a declarative specification of the business goals and QoS constraints of a client. The language has atomic constructs for describing real time and space constraints (for describing complex dynamical behavior of devices embedded in physical environments like sensors, actuators etc.) and is realizable meaning that given a specification one can automatically construct a network of intensional Kahn processes that satisfies the specification. It can express temporal evolution, spatial relationships, communication, leaving and joining domains protected by firewalls, network topologies, and can describe the models of services and devices (e.g., sensors) involving their temporal as well as input/output behaviors along with their pre-conditions and post-conditions. *The language can be used to specify QoS goals like context-awareness, availability, deadlines etc.* Safety properties like deadlock freedom, data consistency etc. can also be expressed. *The language provides the expressiveness to describe models of complex heterogeneous physical devices.* Devices and services can communicate with databases of specifications through an UPnP interface. A software engine can query databases of specifications and can synthesize networks of intensional Kahn processes from specifications.

Given a set of services and devices available in a network, the UPnP [28] models of services and devices (available as a UPnP database) are compiled to an intensional Kahn logic (IKL) specifications using a UPnP to IKL compiler. The resulting IKL specifications are used to populate a database called the Master Directory. The devices and services can wirelessly interact with the Master Directory through a gateway called the Control Point through which they can register any changes in their configuration autonomously as well as populate the Master Directory. The Master Directory provides an interface for querying and updating records. Temporal as well as input/output behaviors of services and devices along with their pre and post conditions as obtained from the service providers and the device manufacturers can be used to update the IKL specifications in the Master Directory through the interface. The IKL records (a IKL record is a set of IKL sentences) for devices and services also includes the local policies (e.g., security) enforced by the services and devices, if any. In the event of any change in the configuration of the services/devices, they can inform a Control Point of the changes through UPnP. The Control Point in turn can update the corresponding record in the Master Directory through its interface. The Master Directory also stores records which contain information about which services/devices are logically equivalent, i.e., provide equivalent functionalities. This information is used for fault tolerance purposes. The Master Directory also contains a IKL record corresponding to the current network topology which gets updated by the Control Point as the topology changes. The Master Directory has a notification interface through which it can notify other components in the architecture of updates to its records. The Master Directory can be replicated for fault-tolerance purposes with standard techniques being used to maintain consistency. The Master Directory can be viewed as a set of (non) logical axioms of a logical theory of available services and devices (along with an equational theory). Logical inferences based on such a theory forms a template for all the functionalities that can be offered by composing the capabilities of the available devices and services. Such "global" inferencing is computationally expensive. Hence, below we will follow a demand-driven local inferencing scheme to logically compose services in order to meet the requirements of a client.

The inputs to our synthesis procedure are

(i) the functional goals of an application (i.e., application requirements) along with possible triggers for the application (along with the possible devices that can provide the trigger), the possible global policies (security etc.) enforced by the application (application-specific security policies), the exception handling schemes (application-specific failure handling policies) and the QoS constraints respected by the application (application-specific context-awareness policies, application-specific timeliness requirements), all expressed in IKL (Model Generator input)

(ii) Non-functional safety properties like deadlock freedom, mutual exclusion etc. (if any) again expressed in IKL (Analyzer input)

The following describes the various components of the architecture. We will use the following automated emergency response scenario as a running example in the ensuing discussion.

4.1 Example Application

Consider a scenario for an emergency management service in a rural town as shown in Figure 1. In the event of an accident at location L, an observer informs a "911" service station through her cell phone. The "911" service station in turn informs the police department (PD), the ambulance management service (AMS) and the fire department (FD) of the accident and its location by sending an accident report (composition of services). Each of these three services has several vehicles already roaming in different parts of the town. The cars are equipped with PDA's and can communicate through wireless networks. The police service requests one of the patrol cars (PCAR) that is nearest the site of the accident to move there. In case this car breaks down, it should be able to communicate the information to another car that is nearest the accident site to replace it (failure handling). Similar is the case for the other two services. The QoS requirement is that a patrol car (PCAR), a fire engine (FE) and an ambulance (AMB) should converge at the accident site within two minutes. In case it is found that the accident has resulted in a serious injury, the ambulance informs the ambulance management service which in turn informs the county helicopter service for a helicopter evacuation (context-awareness). The security policies include among others: only the ambulance management service should be able to call for a helicopter

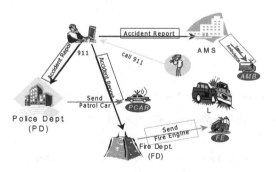

Fig. 1. Example Emergency Management Scenario

evacuation. Other non-functional requirements include for example that a patrol car/fire engine/ambulance already serving one accident site should not be called on to serve another accident site at the same time.

4.2 Intensional Kahn Processes

The syntax of the modeling language is given below as recursive EBNFs. The terminals start with small letters while the nonterminals are capitalized. IKP is built on the top of Kahn Processes [31, 32] and provides a formal programming model for resource coordination. It has operational semantics involving interactions between: external actions: communication and internal computations. It can model timeouts and failures (in monadic style) [38]

N :: = N par N | Proc (Intensional Kahn Network)

Proc :: =   (Intensional Kahn Process)
  channels Channels   process ProcName [:: Loc]   ArgList   Begin   VarDecl   Statlist;
[ExportList] End

Channels :: = TypedChannel Channels | ε

TypedChannel :: = Type Channel

Channel :: = string

ProcName :: = string   (Process Name)

Loc :: = string   (location)

ArgList :: = '(' Type In InArgList; Type Out OutArgLIst ')'

InArgList :: = string, InArgList | ε

OutArgList :: = string, OutArgList | ε

Type:: = b (base type) | Constructor Type

VarDecl :: = Type VarList; VarDecl | ε

VarList :: = Var, VarList | ε

Var ::= string

StatList :: = Stat; StatList | ε

Stat :: =

let Var = Invoke instantiate Stat | Var = [] Guard -> Expr

Guard :: = bexpr | fail(ProcName) | @C(Expr) | @T(Bexpr) | @F(Bexpr) | @Comp(Cont) |
K(Bexpr) | otherwise

Expr :: = Bexpr | Aexpr | wait(Channel) | send Var on Channel

Aexpr :: = Const | Var | Var Arithop AExpr | PREV(Var)

Bexpr :: = Var Relop Aexpr

Invoke :: = ProcName : API^ Cont \ replace(Invoke)

API ::= APIname '(' FormalParList ')'

ExportList :: = API .. pre .. post ; ExportList \ ε

Cont :: = string

pre :: = Bexpr

post :: = Bexpr

A IKP network can consist of several subnetworks. Each subnetwork consists of one or more processes in parallel. A process can perform external actions, internal computation, detect and handle failures, and export methods that can be invoked by itself or other processes. External action involves communication. Internal computation takes place by calling methods of identified services. It can also involve failure handling and dynamic reconfiguration. Service methods are described by their interfaces that include pre and post conditions that hold before and after invoking a method. The pre and post conditions can be simple type judgements (the types of the parameter passed) and arithmetic constraints. Consider an agent for the Police Department (PD) in the example above. The IKP system describing PD is below.

```
process PD(AccidentReport In x; pcarResponse Out z)
Begin
PDResponse y;
let y= pcar:dispatchPCAR(x) instantiate
z=
[] y== 'car sent' -> y
otherwise -> 'error'
End
```

One thing to notice is that when we specify a network using intensional Kahn processes, we assume that communication is synchronous. However, in the original formulation of Kahn, asynchronous communication is assumed. This leads to channels becoming unbounded queues resulting in Turing-completeness of the model. This would render the synthesis problem outlined below undecidable. In our formulation, we will first specify a system using synchronous Kahn processes which can then be refined to asynchronous intensional Kahn networks using a compiler that preserves the semantics under certain guarantees provided by the underlying target infrastructure.

Structural congruence rules of intensional Kahn process networks are as follows.

$N \equiv N$
$N1 \equiv N2, N3 \equiv N4 \rightarrow N1 \ par \ N3 \equiv N2 \ par \ N4$
$Stat \equiv Stat$
$Expr \equiv Expr \ [y/x]$

$Invoke1 \equiv Invoke2, Stat1[y/x] \equiv Stat2 \rightarrow let \ x = Invoke1 \ instantiate \ Stat1 \equiv let \ y = Invoke2 \ instantiate \ Stat2$

4.3 Logic for Intensional Kahn Processes

The specification language (IKL) is a logical language based on an intuitionistic intensional logic [29]. It can describe both temporal and spatial evolution and has atomic constructs for describing relations among variables. The basic syntax is given below as the following EBNFs. We assume a finite set of nominals (participants in a computation). For example, the set of nominals for the example above consist of 911, AMS, PD, FD, AMB, FE, PCAR. Let the variable *I, II* range over a finite set of nominals. Let *NOM* denote the set of nominals.

$P ::=$

	prop	*(property/predicate definition)*
	u	*(type definition)*
	T	*(constant true)*
	F	*(constant false)*
	OR(P1,P2)	*(disjunction)*
	→(P1,P2)	*(Lewis-style strict implication)*
	Eventually P	*(temporal eventuality)*
	I	*(nominal I ∈ NOM)*
	[Knows](u; P)	*(knowledge of an object by agent satisfying P)*
	[Invoke](u\v\P1\P2\P3)	*(invocation of service agent satisfying P)*
	[Send](u,P)	*(Message sent by agent satisfying P))*
	T	*(constant true)*
	Exists(I,P)	*(quantification over nominals)*

@T(P, prop)   *(property prop becomes true for agent satisfying P)*

@F(P, prop)   *(property prop becomes false for agent satisfying P)*

@C(P, x)   *(variable x becomes changes for agent satisfying P)*

prop::=
               ID Varlist
            ~ Var Constant
~::=> | <| ≤| ≥

Essentially, the language includes nominals or identifiers standing for state and constructs for expressing communication, service description, knowledge, etc. Services/resources are defined in terms of their properties. A property can be a predicate or a constraint. *[Knows](u; P)* denotes that a process that satisfies *P* knows the object of type *u*. A process can know an object only if it has received a communication of it. *[Invoke](u;v;P1; P2; P3)* describes the properties of a service declaratively. Basically it describes a service to which an object (of type) *u* is passed as parameter, returns object (of type) *v*, satisfies the specification *P1*, can be invoked by a process satisfying *P2*, is exported by an agent satisfying *P3*. Consider the PD process in the example above. If the PD process receives an accident report *x* (i.e., comes to know of an accident report) it will use that report to send a patrol car to the accident location by invoking some service. This is specified in the IKL as follows:

→ ([Knows](x; PD) ,Eventually([Invoke](AccidentReport; pcar_response; ; W ; PD)))

Here *W* is a placeholder since we do not yet know the name of the service or the entity exporting it. Once these things are discovered, the proper nominal will get instantiated by the model generator. Example specifications: the negation of a security policy stating that an agent *I* should not receive the type *u* is specified as *Eventually ([Knows](→(u,F), I)→F)* which states that eventually there will be a "world" in which it will not be the case that in all worlds possible from it *u* is not known (i.e., not received) where the possibility relation defined in the model-theoretic semantics is a reflexive one. The denotation of *→(u,F)* is *U\\{u}*

5   Synthesis of Intensional Kahn Processes

The model generator (MG) is an engine that synthesizes IKP models from a declarative specification of the functional and QoS goals of a distributed application as IKL sentences. It is a deduction engine that can interpret IKL sentences (as theories) and can syntactically deduce all their logical consequences. IKP models (in short called models) are synthesized from deductions using a Curry-Howard-style correspondence [30]. The MG queries the Master Directory for possible services/devices whose input matches the trigger(s) provided and uses the IKL sentences returned by the Master Directory to deduce the responses returned by the services/devices corresponding to the trigger(s). These responses are used by the MG to consult the Master Directory for further devices/services whose inputs match these responses and their resulting responses are deduced in a similar way. This process is used to develop a forward chaining natural deduction whose end result is the functional goals of the application as provided by the user. The deduction is obtained from a finite branching finite deduction tree generated as a result of the process. For better space utilization, the deduction tree can be built in an on-demand basis reusing space. Throughout the deduction, the policies respected by the application and the individual services/devices as well as the QoS goals provided are used as constraints in the deduction steps. The MG also uses the information about the network topology as obtained from the Master Directory to impose deployment constraints in the deduction. In case the specification is inconsistent (by itself or with respect to the available services and devices), the MG will terminate reporting inconsistency. In the case where the available services/devices are not adequate to implement the required functionality, the MG will terminate reporting that. The deduction can be compiled to an IKP in a straightforward way using a Curry-Howard style correspondence. *The deductive synthesis of the IKP is carried out automatically and it contains a resource composition that meets the requirements of the user. Since the IKP is generated corresponds to a "proof" of the functional goals of the application from the service/device definitions under the constraints imposed by the QoS requirements of the user and the policies enforced by the individual services/devices as well as the application, it formally guarantees that functional goals of the user are met, the QoS constraints required by the users are respected and none of the policies imposed by the individual services/devices or the application are violated.* An IKP carries with it its deployment information. We explain the synthesis procedure with an example.

Consider a few of the coordination requirements of the emergency response example. We use *P && Q* as a shorthand for *→(OR(→(P,F), →(Q,F)), F)*.

Eventually([Knows]("accident", location; 911) &&
C0 && C1 && C2 && ...)
C0: →([Knows]("accident", location; 911), Eventually([Send](<"accident", location>911)))
C1: →(<u>911 , Eventually([Knows](u; PD)) && Eventually([Knows](u; AMS)) && Eventually([Knows](x; FD)))
C2: →([Knows](u;PD) ,Eventually(Invoke(u; pcar_response; ;W ; PD))))
...

Then MG synthesizes the 911 process as a model as follows.
From *[Knows]("accident",location; 911)* it synthesizes
process 911 (Accident In z, AccidentLocation In x;)
(since a process only knows an object only if it receives it).

From *Knows("accident",location; 911)* and C0, it infers *[Send](<"accident", location>911).* From *[Send](<"accident", location>911)* and C1 it infers *[Knows]("accident", location; PD), [Knows]("accident", location; AMS), [Knows]("accident", location; FD).* Based on these deductions, it expands the model for 911 as

process 911 (Accident In z, AccidentLocation In x; Accident Out t, Accident-Location v)
Begin
Accident z1;
Accident x1;
z1 = wait(z);
x1 = wait(x);
send z1 on t;
send x1 on v;
end

It also generates the PD process as
process PD(Accident In x, AccidentLocation In y)

and instantiates channels
Accident z, t;
AccidentLocation x,v;
911(z,x,v,t) par PD(v,t)

Similar is the case for the AMS and FD processes. This way the MG continues the deduction and simultaneously synthesizing the processes until no more new facts are produced. The deductive synthesis above is similar in principle to knowledge-based programming [40]. The next part of the synthesis procedure binds the unknown service invocations to suitable service compositions. For automatically synthesizing service compositions, the MG uses natural deduction [35]. Consider the ambulance dispatch service in the example scenario above. It is specified in IKL as

→(dispatchAMB(u;amb;W),
Eventually([Invoke](u; amb_response; ;W;amb)))
Let us call this specification S1.
Additionally the specification C3 for the application provides
C3: →(Knows(x; AMS), Eventually([Invoke](u; amb_response; ; AMS; S)))

From *Knows("accident", location; AMS)* MG uses C3 to deduce *[Invoke]("accident", location ; amb_response; ; AMS; S))* where S is a variable. Now it assumes in natural deduction style` Using S1, it deduces *[Invoke]("accident", location ; amb_response; ; AMS; amb))*. Using standard implication-introduction rule in natural deduction, it deduces

$\rightarrow$*(dispatchAMB("accident", location ;amb;AMS), [Invoke]("accident", location ; amb_response; ; AMS; amb))))*

Based on this deduction it refines the model for AMS as

...

let y= amb:dispatchAMB(x) instantiate

...

Notice the automated discovery of the ***amb:dispatchAMB*** service using deduction. The basic deduction is conducted as a forward-chaining procedure and whenever a goal involving a Service construct is encountered, a companion natural deduction proof tree is developed to discover the appropriate service. The deduction as well as synthesis of processes is carried out completely automatically; the computational complexity of the synthesis procedure is $O(|F|. |S|^{|S|})$ where $|F|$ is the length of the specification and $|S|$ is the number of available resources/services.

6   Conclusions

We have presented a formal approach for developing high-assurance distributed embedded grid computing systems. Our technique allows automatic synthesis and deployment of IKPs from declarative specification of the functional logic and QoS goals and formal models of available devices and services. Correctness of the synthesized IKPs is guaranteed by construction.

References

1. Montague, R.: Pragmatics and Intensional Logic. Synthese 22, 68–94 (1970)
2. Wadge, W.W.: Lucid, the Dataflow Programming Language. Academic Press, London
3. Ditu, G.: The Programming Language TransLucid, PhD Dissertation, University of New South Wales (2007)
4. Paquet, J., Wu, A., Grogono, A.: Towards a Framework for the General Intensional Programming Compiler in the GIPSY. In: Proceedings of OOPSLA 2004 (2004)
5. Faustini, A.: Towards an Operational Semantics of Pure Dataflow. In: Nielsen, M., Schmidt, E.M. (eds.) ICALP 1982. LNCS, vol. 140, pp. 212–224. Springer, Heidelberg (1982)
6. Loo, T.B., Condie, T., Garofalakis, M.N., Gay, D.E., Hellerstein, J.M., Maniatis, P., Ramakrishnan, R., Roscoe, T., Stoica, I.: Declarative Networking: Language, Execution, and Optimization. In: Proceedings of SIGMOD 2006 (2006)
7. Yau, S., et al.: Reconfigurable Context-Sensitive Middleware for Pervasive Computing. IEEE Pervasive Computing 1(3), 33–40 (2002)
8. Mikic-Rakic, M., Medvidovic, N.: Adaptable Architectural Middleware for Programming-in-the-Small-and-Many. In: Endler, M., Schmidt, D.C. (eds.) Middleware 2003. LNCS, vol. 2672, pp. 162–181. Springer, Heidelberg (2003)

9. Ranganathan, A., Campbell, R.H.: A Middleware for Context-Aware Agents in Ubiquitous Computing Environments. In: Endler, M., Schmidt, D.C. (eds.) Middleware 2003. LNCS, vol. 2672, pp. 143–161. Springer, Heidelberg (2003)
10. Popovici, F.A., Alonso, G.: A Proactive Middleware Platform for Mobile Computing. In: Endler, M., Schmidt, D.C. (eds.) Middleware 2003. LNCS, vol. 2672, pp. 455–473. Springer, Heidelberg (2003)
11. Lang, U.: Access Policies in Middleware, PhD Thesis. University of Cambridge (2003)
12. Abdelzaher, T., Blum, B., Cao, B.Q., Chen, Y., Evans, D., George, J., George, S., Gu, L., He, T., Krishnamurthy, S., Luo, L., Son, S., Stankovic, J., Stoleru, R., Wood, A.: Enviro-Track: Towards an Environmental Computing Paradigm for Distributed Sensor Networks. In: The 24th International Conference on Distributed Computing Systems. Tokyo, Japan, March 23-26 (2004)
13. Yau, S., Davulcu, H., Mukhopadhyay, S., Huang, D., Yao, Y.: Adaptable, Situation-aware, Secure Service-based (AS3) Systems. In: Proceedings of the IEEE International Symposium Object-oriented, Real-time, Distributed Computing, ISORC 2005 (2005)
14. Bharadwaj, R., Mukhopadhyay, S., Padh, N.: Service Composition in a Secure Agent-based Architecture. In: Proceedings of the IEEE International Conference on E-Technologies, E-commerce and E-Service (EEE 2005), pp. 787–788 (2005)
15. Internet2 Medical Middleware (MedMid) Working Group: Draft Workplan Scenarios (2003)
16. Sirin, E., Hendler, J.A., Parsia, B.: Semi-automatic Composition of Web Services using Semantic Descriptions. In: WSMAI 2003, pp. 17–24 (2003)
17. Duan, Z., Bernstein, A.J., Lewis, P.M., Lu, S.: Semantics Based Verification and Synthesis of BPEL4WS Abstract Processes. In: ICWS 2004, pp. 734–737 (2004)
18. Necula, G.C.: Enforcing Security and Safety with Proof-Carrying Code. Electr. Notes Theor. Comput. Sci. 20 (1999)
19. Li, B., Nahrstedt, K.: A Control-based Middleware Framework for Quality of Service Adaptations. IEEE Journal on Selected Areas in Communication 17(9) (September 1999)
20. Roemer, K., Kasten, O., Mattern, F.: Middleware Challenges in Wireless Sensor Networks. Mobile Computing and Communications Review 3(2) (2002)
21. Curbera, F., et al.: Business Process Execution Language for Web Services (2002)
22. Christensen, E., et al.: The Web Services Description Language (WSDL), IBM
23. Berners-Lee, T., et al.: The semantic web, Scientific American (May 2003)
24. Ankolekar, A., Huch, F., Sycara, K.: Concurrent Execution Semantics for DAML-S with Subtypes. In: Proceedings of The First International Semantic Web Conference, ISWC (2002)
25. Newcomer, E.: Understanding Web Services. Addison Wesley, Reading (2002)
26. Endrei, M., Ang, J., Arsanjani, A., Chua, S., Comte, P., Krogdahl, P., Luo, M., Newling, T.: Patterns: Service-oriented Architecture and Web Services. IBM Redbook, ISBN 073845317X (2004)
27. Bell, D., La Padula, L.: Secure Computer Systems: Unified Exposition and Multics Interpretation, Technical Report, Mitre Corporation (1975)
28. http://www.upnp.org
29. Blackburn, P., de Rijke, M., Venema, Y.: A course in modal logic. Cambridge University Press, Cambridge
30. Barendregt, H.: The lambda calculus, its syntax and semantics. North-Holland, Amsterdam (1984)
31. Milner, A.J.R.J.: Communication and Concurrency. Cambridge University Press, Cambridge
32. Charatonik, W., Dal-Zilio, S., Gordon, A.D., Mukhopadhyay, S., Talbot, J.M.: Model Checking Mobile Ambients Theoretical Computer Science (1-3), 277–331 (2003)

33. Ponnekanti, S., Fox, A.: SWORD: A Developer Toolkit for Web Service Composition. In: Proceedings of WWW 2002 (2002)
34. http://www.carematix.com/
35. Troelstra, A.S., Schwichtenberg, H.: Basic Proof Theory (Cambridge Tracts in Theoretical Computer Science). Cambridge University Press, Cambridge, ISBN 0-521-77911-1
36. http://www.ni.com/labview/
37. Brachman, R.J., Levesque, H.J.: Readings in Knowledge Representation. Morgan Kaufmann, Los Altos (1985)
38. Wadler, P.: Comprehending Monads. In: 6'th Conference on Lisp and Functional Programming, vol. 2, pp. 461–493 (1992)
39. Baumann, A., Heiser, G., Appavoo, J., Da Silva, D., Krieger, O., Wisniewski, R.W., Kerr, J.: Providing Dynamic Update in an Operating System. In: USENIX Annual Technical Conference, General Track, pp. 279–291 (2005)
40. Fagin, R., Halpern, J., Moses, Y., Vardi, M.Y.: Reasoning About Knowledge. MIT Press, Cambridge
41. Kahn, G.: The Semantics of a Simple Language for Parallel Programming. In: Proceedings of IFIP Information Processing (1974)

Extended Heartbeat Mechanism for Fault Detection Service Methodology

Ahmad Shukri Mohd. Noor[1] and Mustafa Mat Deris[2]

[1] Department of Computer Science, Faculty of Science and Technology,
Universiti Malaysia Terengganu, 21030 Kuala Terengganu, Malaysia
ashukri@umt.edu.my
[2] Faculty of Multimedia and Information Technology Universiti Tun Hussein Onn Malaysia
86400 Parit Raja, Batu Pahat, Johor Darul Takzim, Malaysia
mmustafa@uthm.edu.my

Abstract. Fault detection methodology is a crucial part in providing a scalable, dependable and high availability of grid computing environment. The most popular technique that used in detecting fault is heartbeat mechanism where it monitors the grid resources in a very short interval. However, this technique has its weakness as it requires a period of times before the node is realized to be faulty and therefore delaying the recovery actions to be taken. This is due to un-indexed status for each transaction and need to wait for a certain time interval before realizing the nodes has failed. In this paper, fault detection mechanism and service using extended heartbeat mechanism is proposed. This technique introduced the use of index server for indexing the transaction and utilizing pinging service for pushing mechanism. The model outperformed the existing techniques by reducing the time taken to detect fault in approximately 30%. Also, the mechanism provides a basis for customizable recovery actions to be deployed.

Keywords: Fault Detection, Heartbeat Methodology, Grid Computing Environment, system failure.

1 Introduction

Nowadays, grid is popular among organizations so as to achieve high performance computing. It has fascinated a great deal of interest and various infrastructure and software projects have been undertaken to comprehend numerous vision of grids [1].

Since grid computing is vulnerable against failures, the ability to tolerate failures while efficiently exploiting the grid computing resources in an accessible and transparent manner must be an integral part of grid computing infrastructure. Hence, fault-detection service is a necessary requirement to fault tolerance and fault recovery in grid computing .In developing the fault detection mechanism, there are few requirements has been identified in order to ensure that this mechanism is built within the grid context.

One of the most popular fault detector service is the Globus Heartbeat Monitor (HBM) [2]. HBM provides a fault detection service for applications developed with

D. Ślęzak et al. (Eds.): GDC 2009, CCIS 63, pp. 88–95, 2009.

the Globus toolkit. However they are developed under the assumption that both the grid generic server and the heartbeat monitor run reliably [3]. Moreover, they scale badly in the number of members that are being monitored [4], require developers to implement fault tolerance at the application level [2]; difficult to implement [7] and have high-overhead [5].

Failure Detection and Recovery Services (FDS) [7] improves the Globus HBM with early detection of failures in applications, grid middleware and grid resources. The FDS also introduce efficient and low-overhead multi-layered distributed failure detection service that release grid users and developers from the burden of grid fault detection and fault recovery .However, this technique has its weakness as it require a period of times before the node is realized to be faulty and delaying the recovery actions to be taken. This is due to unindex status for each transaction and need to wait for a certain time interval.

The Extended Heartbeat Mechanism is proposed in intention to reduce the time required to detect failure system by utilizing pinging service for pushing mechanism. Furthermore all the transactions status needs to be indexed for references and further action to be taken during recovery process.

The rest of the paper is organized as follows: Section 2 presents the proposed fault detection service architecture and details of the proposed fault detection service along how it enables the detection of the failure is illustrated. The performance of existing model and proposed model is discusses in section 3 as well as it comparison. The research findings and conclusion is given in Section 4 and section 5 respectively.

2   Extended Heartbeat Mechanism

The extended heartbeat mechanism (EHM) is proposed by utilizing heartbeat mechanisms with index server and ping service. This mechanism methodology will detect the failure occurrence for the application that has registered to the service. It will then grant the detection of failures in the system as well as provide an alternative to the recovery mechanism to handle the failure in variety of ways. The application that registered to the service will be indexed in the Index Server in order to monitor the application, the criteria that needed to report if any failure occurs as well as the information of the report itself. The service architecture consists of three types of entities: Heartbeat Monitor (HM), Application Register (AR) and Index Server (IS).

2.1   Integrating Index Server with Extended Heartbeat Mechanism

The EHM will detect the failure occurrence for the application that has registered with AR. It will then grant the detection of failures in the system as well as provide an alternative to the recovery mechanism to handle the failure in variety of ways. The application that registers to the service will be indexed in the Index Server in order to monitors the application, the criteria that needed to report if any failure occur as well as the information of the report itself. Figure 1 illustrate the flow of the proposed methodology.

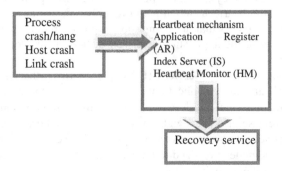

Fig. 1. The Approach Overview

The intention of the index server is to tolerate a variety of failures. The architecture of this service is illustrated in the figure 2 .The diagram depicts the relationships between the components of the FDSM. It comprises of three main components that are Heartbeat Monitor (HM), Application Register (AR) and Index Server (IS). The node that running in the grid is represented by the rectangle labeled with P_n.

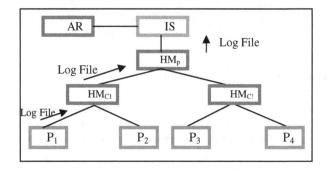

Fig. 2. Fault Detection Service Methodology Architecture

Application Register (AR)

In order to use the extended heartbeat mechanism (EHM), the each participated node needs to register with AR. AR provide the method to register the node to the EHM by taking the required information to be monitored. Once the node registered, the information provided by the node will be added and indexed in the Index Server (IS). The IS will be notified when the node is added to the index or changed since last indexed.

Index Server (IS)

The EHM is designed to be used in grid environment. It relies on heartbeat and event listener to detect failure components during the execution on the grid nodes. The Index Server (IS) is an entity that interested in the aliveness of application and its components. It can interpret message(s) to determine the state of the application such as 'inactive', 'active', 'done', 'failed', 'exception' and others that submitted to the EHM. The IS maintains all the state associated with node. The IS automatically creates the index of the registered node that recorded at the AR. The IS will be notified each time the AR register new node or change the node information since last indexed.

Heartbeat Monitor (HM)
HM is responsible for monitoring the state of the registered nodes. In the case of they differs from their usual state, it will notify the IS for necessary actions to be taken. Each node is periodically send a message indicating that it aliveness to the HM. This message is considered as heartbeat message in the form of log file. This log file will then send to the Index Server for updating the current status of the node.

2.2 Utilising Ping Service with Extended Heartbeat Mechanism

In detecting a failure node, the HMs uses the ping and heartbeat mechanism. The application will periodically send message in the form of log file which consider as heartbeat in a fixed time interval. If the HM does not receive the message within the time interval, the node is considered as having fault or might have fail. The HM will ping the nodes as the nodes is considered as having a problem. If the nodes do not reply to the pinging send by the HM with ping timeout , the nodes is considered as being failed and the status of the node will be updated in the Index Server and proper recovery action will be undertaken.

3 The Performance

In heartbeat performance, the most crucial aspect is monitoring the accuracy of the heartbeat reports that is the time taken to detect a failure as well as the number of false report received. In a normal heartbeat operation, the heartbeat monitors send heartbeat messages to the nodes at regular intervals. The equation of a normal heartbeat operation that is without having any failure is given by:

$$\sum T_n = T_{HM} + T_i$$

where,

i. The number of nodes in a grid environment, n.
ii. The interval between each message sent to the heartbeat monitor, T_i.
iii. Time taken for a message to arrived at heartbeat monitor, T_{HM}.

The T_{HM} and T_i parameter set to constant while the number of nodes in the grid environment, n is manipulated to measure the mechanism effectiveness in detecting fault.

3.1 The FDS Performance

The FDS performance and architecture for failure detection is illustrated in shown in Fig. 4.

From Fig. 4 The application periodically send heartbeat message to HM. If the HM does not receive the message within the time interval, the application is considered as having problem. The HM will wait for next interval. If the HM had received

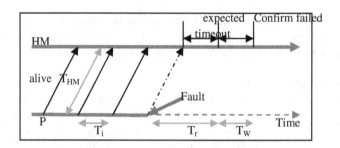

Fig. 4. Existing Heartbeat Mechanism

the message for the next interval, the Index Server will be updated with the new status of the monitored node .But if the HMs do not received the message after the second time interval, the application is declared as being failed. This will take a longer time to detect failures and to confirm that the node being faulty. The equation of FDS to detect a failure is given by:

$$\sum T_n = T_{HM} + T_i + T_r + T_w$$

where,

i. The number of nodes in a grid environment, n.
ii. The interval between each message sent to the heartbeat monitor, T_i.
iii. The waiting time of the heartbeat monitor before declaring that the node has dead, T_w.
iv. Time taken for a message to arrived at heartbeat monitor, T_{HM}.
v. The timeout when the heartbeat monitor realized that it have not received the message from the node, T_r.
vi. The time taken by heartbeat monitor to declare a node has dead, $\sum T_n$.

Table 1 shows the time taken for declaring the failed nodes using the existing heartbeat mechanism. Table 2 shows the overall time taken to detect the failed nodes under the grid environment where the number of nodes available varies from 100 to 1000. We assume that 10% from the numbers of nodes available are failed.

Table 1. The time taken for detecting the failed nodes using FDS mechanism

	T_{HM}	T_i	T_w	T_r	$\sum T$
Time (ms-1)	30	100	100	20	250

Table 2. The value of n Nodes and the time taken to detect fault using the FDS

n	100	200	500	600	700	1000
10% failure	10	20	50	60	70	100
$\sum T$(ms-1)	25000	50000	125000	150000	175000	250000

3.2   The Performance of the Proposed Model

Fig 5., shows the proposed mechanism called extended heartbeat mechanism (EHM) that integrates the heartbeat mechanism with the ping mechanism in order to shorten the time taken to detect failure node(s).

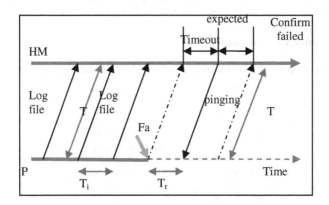

Fig. 5. Proposed Heartbeat Mechanism

The equation of the proposed model is given by:

$$\sum T_n = T_{HM} + T_i + T_r + T_P$$

where ,

i. The interval between each message sent to the heartbeat monitor, T_i.
ii. Time taken for a message to arrived at heartbeat monitor, T_{HM}.
iii. The timeout when the heartbeat monitor realized that it have not received the message from the node, T_r.
iv. The time taken by heartbeat monitor to ping out the suspected node, T_p.
v. The time taken by heartbeat monitor to declare a node has dead, $\sum T_n$.

Table 3 shows the time taken for declaring the failure nodes using EHM. Table 4 shows the overall time taken to detect the failed nodes under the grid environment where the number of nodes available varies from 100 to 1000. We assume that 10% from the numbers of nodes available are failed.

Table 3. The time taken for detecting the failed nodes using the Proposed Mechanism

	T_{HM}	T_i	T_W	T_r	$\sum T$
Time (ms^{-1})	30	100	20	24	174

Table 4. The value of n Nodes and time taken to detect fault using the EHM

n	100	200	500	600	700	1000
10% failure	10	20	50	60	70	100
$\sum$ T(ms-1)	17400	34800	87000	104400	121800	174000

3.3 Performance Comparison

The comparison between the existing mechanism and the proposed mechanism has been made as shown in the Fig. 6.

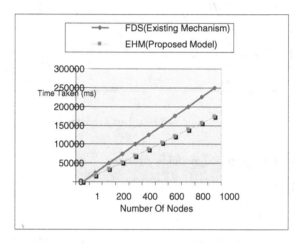

Fig. 6. The time taken for the EHM and the FDS mechanisms to detect 10% failed nodes versus number of nodes available

From Fig. 6., when the number of nodes increases, the time taken to detect the failure nodes are increased. However, EHM required less time taken as compared to FDS because for each suspected failure node EHM do not wait for next interval. Instead EHM ping the node to force the node to response. While the methodology used by FDS mechanism need to wait for the second interval for failure confirmation. For example from Fig. 6., when the number of nodes is 700, EHM model needs only 121800ms of processing time while FDS model needs 175000ms. It showed that EHM model provides an efficient approach up to approximately 30% as compared to FDS model.

4 Research Findings

The proposed fault detection mechanism is designed to monitor the grid resources, middleware, application and process simultaneously. The model integrates the heartbeat monitor with ping in which it will never affect the grid node protocols and policy in order to avoid future problems. The proposed fault detection methodology has been simulate in mathematical model. The overall finding as follow:

i. The proposed model capable in cut down the communication overhead by reducing time taken in detecting a fault as well as cut down the number of false failures.

ii. The indexing of the application that register to the service allow the construction of reliable recovery mechanism as the Index Server will provide the necessary information needed to run the application specific recovery service.

5 Conclusion

This paper demonstrates a methodology in detecting fault for a grid computing environment as a basis in providing a scalable, high availability and reliability grid environment. The model has proved by a simulation that it is capable in detecting fault and also reducing communication overhead as well as providing a source for a customizable recovery action to be taken.

This model is also able to detect large variety of failures such as process crash/hang failure, host crash and link crash. It also has a minimal perturbation to the application structure and do not affect the grid node by changing their protocols and policy. The fault detection service also has a minimal impact on the machine that runs this service.

In detecting fault, the most important things is to detect the failure nodes immediately as delaying the detection may cause delaying the recovery thus the system may be down for a considerable period of time. The proposed fault detection service may cut down the time taken to detect fault as well as providing a basis for a recovery action to be taken as it stores all the nodes information in an index form stored in an index server.

References

1. Nemeth, Z., Sunderam, V.: Introduction. In: Characterizing Grids: Attributes, Definitions and Formalisms, pp. 9–11 (2003)
2. Stelling, P., Foster, I., Kesselman, C., Lee, C., Laszewski, G.: A Fault Detection Service for Wide Area Distributed Computations. In: Proceedings of HPDC, pp. 268–278 (1998)
3. Soonwook, H.: A Generic Failure Detection Service for the Grid, Ph.D. thesis, institution =. University of Southern California (2003)
4. Renesse, R., Minsky, Y., Hayden, M.: A Gossip-Style Failure Detection Service,Technical Report, TR98-1687 (1998)
5. Abawajy, J.H., Dandamudi, S.P.: A Reconfigurable Multi-Layered Grid Scheduling Infrastructure. In: Proceedings of PDPTA 2003, pp. 138–144 (2003)
6. Foster, I.: The Need for a Clear Definition. What is the Grid? A Three Point Checklist (2002)
7. Abawajy, J.H.: Introduction. In: Fault Detection Service Architecture for Grid Computing Systems, pp. 107–108 (2004)

Trust-Oriented Multi-objective Workflow Scheduling in Grids

Amit Agarwal and Padam Kumar

Department of Electronics and Computer Engineering
Indian Institute of Technology Roorkee, India
{aamitdec,padamfec}@iitr.ernet.in

Abstract. Trust is a major concern of resource users and owners in the grid environment with uncountable and at times unreliable nodes. An intelligent scheduling mechanism is essential for executing tasks on highly dynamic and heterogeneous grid environment which may require several different criteria to be considered simultaneously when evaluating the quality of solution or a schedule. Two important criteria frequently used are the execution time and the economic cost. In addition, due to the dynamism of the grid, security and reliability are major issues in scheduling. This paper presents a *Trust-oriented Multi-objective Scheduling (Trust-MOS)* algorithm in grid environment based on a *sliding constraint*. The theoretical analysis and simulation results show that our approach generates good quality schedules and reduces task failure exertion and hence can be best suited for executing tasks in a secure manner.

Keywords: trust model; grid computing; multi-objective scheduling; economic cost; makespan; directed acyclic graph; trustworthiness; workflow scheduling.

1 Introduction

Trust has been recognized as an important factor for task scheduling in grid environments. Managing trust is crucial in a dynamic grid environment where grid nodes and users keep joining and leaving the system. The Grid is a unified computing platform which consists of heterogeneous resources (e.g. processors, storages, catalogs, network resources and sensors etc) over large geographical region. Considering trust in comparatively open structures like grids is a very relevant topic. Although, all computational grids and their toolboxes include certain secure techniques such as GSI [1] in Globus which supports single-sign credentials and the collaboration between local secure strategy and that of whole system, there is a need to obtain a trustworthy resource as the resources in grid are inevitably unreliable and unsafe. Therefore, there must be a mechanism to evaluate and manage the trust levels of grid nodes while scheduling the tasks. In this paper, we use the terms node and resource interchangeably in the grid environment. Security considerations may increase the cost of executing applications in grid. The objective of the current security solutions is to provide the grid system participants with certain degree of trust so that their resource provider nodes or user programs will be secure.

D. Ślęzak et al. (Eds.): GDC 2009, CCIS 63, pp. 96–107, 2009.
© Springer-Verlag Berlin Heidelberg 2009

The resource sharing in grid may lead to the illegal users acquiring much higher trust level to access the resources that they have no right to access. These illegal users may destroy certain resources and their information for ever. This paper addresses the *Grid Trust Model* to get solutions for these problems. A reliable trust mechanism is applied for management of dynamic trust level of resources based on a trust function. This trust model is integrated with *Grid Resource Management and Scheduling Model* to obtain more realistic schedule. Scheduling of tasks in grid with the characteristics of dynamism, heterogeneity, distribution, openness, voluntariness, uncertainty and deception, is a complex optimization problem and several different criteria are needed to be considered simultaneously to obtain a realistic schedule. Usually, execution time is applied as the most important criterion [2]. In current economic market models (especially in commercial Grids), economic cost (cost of executing a task on grid resource) is considered as another important criterion [3].

A majority of problems in the literature address a single criterion scheduling [2] [4]. Considering multiple criteria with trust-oriented scheduling enables the decision maker to propose a better solution. Users in the areas such as in national intelligent analysis, banking and financial data analysis etc will be greatly benefitted by trust oriented management and scheduling of resources in a grid. Traditionally, to cope up with these security issues, several methods such as to encrypt the data of execution and analysis, or isolate them from the Internet, and then schedule them on local resources have been used. Therefore, an efficient scheduling algorithm is needed to execute tasks on trustworthy resources while assuring the high speed of communication, reduce the task execution time and economic cost, lower the ratio of task failure execution, and improves the security of important data execution.

2 Related Work

In literature, the problem of multi-objective scheduling considers the execution time (or makespan) and the economic cost as two independent criteria [5]. But, very few research efforts have been done towards trust-oriented approach in multi-objective workflow scheduling. Existing scheduling algorithms largely ignore the security induced risks involved in dispatching tasks to remote sites. In [5], a bi-criterion scheduling algorithm (DCA) based on sliding constraints has been introduced for workflow applications in grid environments. But, it does not address the trust-oriented issues of grid resources. In [6], Zhu et al. proposed a grid economic model in which they presented two scheduling algorithms for independent tasks: *trust-aware time optimization scheduling algorithm within budget constraints*, and *trust-aware cost optimization scheduling algorithm within deadline constraints*. But, they do not address the scheduling for workflows. In [7], a trust-aware model between the resource producers and consumers has been proposed. In [8], a model based on experience and reputation for supporting trust has been proposed. This model allows entities to decide which other entities are trustworthy. Song et al. [4] enhanced the Min-min and Sufferage heuristics and proposed a novel *space-time genetic algorithm* for trusted job scheduling. Abawajy [9] presented a *distributed fault-tolerant scheduling* (DFTS) algorithm to provide fault-tolerance to task execution in grid systems. But, they do not focus on multi-criteria approach in scheduling.

This paper presents a trust based multi-criteria optimization model for task scheduling in grid environment. Three criteria namely *execution time, economic cost* and *trustworthiness* are evaluated to compute the quality of the schedule for workflow applications. Trustworthiness is an indicator of the quality of the resource's services. It is often used to predict the future behavior of the resource. Intuitively, if a resource is trustworthy, it is likely that it will provide good services in future transactions too. The scheduler must carefully evaluate the compromise involved in considering multiple criteria in scheduling applications. In this paper, a new hybrid multi-objective scheduling strategy is used to evaluate the trust-oriented time and cost optimized schedule in grid. The important issue for executing an application in grid is how to obtain trustworthy resource for the task to be executed over it. A trust-based decision in a specific domain is a multi-stage process. The first stage consists of identifying and selecting the proper input data, i.e. the trust evidences. In general, these are domain-specific and they result from an analysis conducted over the application involved. In the next stage, a computation is performed over evidences to produce trust values i.e. the estimation of the trustworthiness of resources in that particular domain. The selection of evidences and the subsequent trust computation are informed by a notion of *trust*, defined in the *grid trust model* (see Section 3). Finally, the trust decision is taken by considering the computed values and exogenous factors, like disposition or risk assessments.

3 Grid Trust Model

As definition [6] [10] [14]: *"Trust is the firm belief in the competence of an entity to act as expected such that this firm belief is not a fixed value associated with the entity but rather it is subject to the entity's behavior and applies only within a specific context at a given time".* Trust value of any resource is computed on past experiences of resources in a specific context. There are several issues that arise in a real grid environment. First, malicious nodes, which may damage resources or act against a protocol and try to attack the grid system, can degrade the performance of system drastically [10]. Second, selfish nodes or free riders, which may consume but do not contribute resources, have been a serious issue [11].

The trust life cycle is composed of three different phases: *trust formation phase, trust negotiation phase,* and *trust evaluation phase.* The formation phase is done before any trusted group is formed. It contains mechanism to develop trust functions and policies. The negotiation phase is activated when a new untrusted system joins the current distributed system. The trust evaluation phase reevaluates and updates the trust values based on transactions performed in the system. In this work, a trust model based on *Eigen Trust Model* [12] [14] is used to distinguish trustable nodes from malicious nodes in the grid environment. In grid, local trust values of nodes are assigned by other nodes after each transaction. For example, when resource i executes a task from resource j, it may rate the transaction as successful $x_{ij} = 1$, or ful $x_{ij} = -1$. The *local trust value* (ltv_{ij}) can be defined as the sum of the ratings of each transaction that node i has executed tasks from node j.

$$ltv_{ij} = \sum x_{ij} \qquad (1)$$

The system should select a very few number of pre-trusted nodes. In order to aggregate local trust values, it is essential to normalize them. Otherwise, malicious nodes may obtain arbitrarily high local trust values from other malicious nodes, and assign arbitrarily low local trust values to good quality nodes, easily subverting the system. We can define a *normalized local trust value* c_{ij} , as follows:

$$c_{ij} = \begin{cases} \frac{\max(ltv_{ij},0)}{\sum_j \max(ltv_{ij},0)} & , if \ \sum_j \max(ltv_{ij},0) \neq 0 \\ r_j & , otherwise \end{cases} \qquad (2)$$

Here, r_j can be defined as

$$r_j = \begin{cases} \frac{1}{|R|} & , j \in R \\ 0 & , otherwise \end{cases} \qquad (3)$$

where R is a set containing pre-trusted nodes. Now, we wish to aggregate the normalized local trust values. In grid, node i could get recommendations from its acquaintances about other nodes:

$$t_{ij} = \sum_k c_{ik} c_{kj} \qquad (4)$$

where t_{ij} represents the trust that node i places on node j based on asking its friends. If we write equation (4) in matrix notation, then we obtain a trust vector $\vec{t}_i = C^T \vec{c}_i$, where C represents the matrix $[c_{ij}]$, $\vec{c}_i = [c_{i1}, c_{i2}, \dots . c_{in}]^T$ contains c_{ij}, and $\vec{t}_i = [t_{i1}, t_{i2}, \dots . t_{in}]^T$ contains t_{ij}. To gain a wider view, node i may wish to ask its friends' friends, then $\vec{t}_i = (C^T)^2 \vec{c}_i$. If node i continues in this manner ($\vec{t}_i = (C^T)^n \vec{c}_i$), where C is irreducible and aperiodic, it will have a complete view of the global grid environment after n large iterations. In grid environment, there is a potential for malicious collectives to form. A malicious collective is a group of malicious nodes who know each other, who give each other high local trust values and give other nodes low local trust values in order to subvert the system order and acquire high global trust values. This problem can be resolved by taking:

$$\vec{t}^{(k+1)} = (1 - \varphi) \, C^T \, \vec{t}^{(k)} + \varphi \, \vec{r} \qquad (5)$$

where φ is a constant between 0 and 1. This is a way to break collective by having each node place at least some trust on the accessible nodes in grid that are not the parts of collective. Here, it is important that no pre-trusted node should be a member of malicious collective. In a grid environment, C and $\vec{t}$ are stored in each node and node i can compute its own global trust value t_i as:

$$t_i^{(k+1)} = (1 - \varphi) \, (c_{1i} t_1^{(k)} + c_{2i} t_2^{(k)} \dots + c_{ni} t_n^{(k)}) + \varphi \, r_i \qquad (6)$$

The global trust value (t_i) of each resource is computed using equation (6) and updated dynamically. The algorithm to compute t_i is shown as follows:

Algorithm 1. EigenTrust

Initial: r_i : *the initial trust value of node i*

EigenTrust()
1. for each node i do {
2.   for all nodes j,   where $j \neq i$, $t_i^{(0)} = r_j$
3.   repeat
4.   compute $t_i^{(k+1)} = (1 - \varphi)(c_{1i}t_1^{(k)} + \cdots + c_{ni}t_n^{(k)}) + \varphi\, r_i$
5.   send $c_{ij}t_i^{(k+1)}$ to all nodes
6.   wait for all nodes return $c_{ji}t_i^{(k+1)}$
7.   until $|t_i^{(k+1)} - t_i^{(k)}| < \epsilon$
8.   endfor
9. endfor

We define a probability ϵ, known as the *teleport probability* (the probability of visiting random nodes) for historical reasons, which measures how much trust the pre-trusted nodes receive due to their pre-trusted status. The default value of ϵ is 0.15.

4   Trust-Oriented Multi-objective Scheduling Problem

4.1   Workflow Application Model (WAM)

In the context of *Grid Computing*, there exist several applications such as bioinformatics, financial analysis etc which can be constructed as workflows. A scheduling problem can be defined as the assignment of different grid services to different workflow tasks. Every workflow, modeled as directed acyclic graph or DAG, can be represented by $W = (N, E, T, V)$, where N is a set of n computational tasks, T is a set of task computation volumes (i.e., one unit of computation volume is one million instructions), E is a set of communication arcs or edges that shows precedence constraint among the tasks and V is the set of communication data from parent tasks to child tasks (i.e., one unit of communication data is one Kbyte). The value of $\tau_i \in T$ is the computation volume for the task $n_i \in N$. The value of $v_{ij} \in V$ is the communication data transferring along the edge e_{ij}, $e_{ij} \in E$ from task n_i to task n_j, for $n_i, n_j \in N$. A task node without any parent node is called *entry node*, and a task node without any child node is called *exit node*. In our model, task executions are assumed to be non-preemptive and intra-processor communication cost between two tasks scheduled on the same resource is considered as zero.

4.2   Grid Resource Model (GRM)

A grid resource model can be represented by undirected weighted graph $G = (P, Q, A, B)$ where $P = \{ p_i \mid p_i \in P, \; i = 1, 2, \ldots, p\}$ is the set of p available resources, $A = \{\alpha(p_i) \mid \alpha(p_i) \in A, \; i = 1, 2, \ldots |P|\}$ is the set of execution rates, where $\alpha(p_i)$ is the execution rate for resource p_i (i.e., the unit is instruction counts/time, such as one million instructions/second), $Q = \{q(p_i, p_j) \mid q(p_i, p_j) \in Q,\ and\ i, j = 1, 2, \ldots. |P|\}$ is the set of communication links connecting pairs of distinct resources, $q(p_i, p_j)$ is the communication link between p_i and p_j, and $B = \{\beta(p_i, p_j) \mid \beta(p_i, p_j) \in B\ and\ i, j = 1, 2, \ldots, |P|\}$ is the set of data transfer rates, where $\beta(p_i, p_j)$ is the data transfer rate between resource p_i and p_j (i.e., the unit is volume/time, such as Kbytes/sec). In this model, we neglect the startup costs of resources and intra-processor communication cost is negligible.

4.3 Performance Criteria

In this paper, a fairly static methodology has been used for defining the weights of the computational tasks and communicating edges in the DAG. In scheduling, a workflow of tasks is submitted to the grid meta-scheduler where tasks are queued in non-decreasing order of their b-levels. The *b-level (bottom level)* of task n_i can be defined as the longest directed path including execution time and communication time from task n_i to the exit task in the given DAG. It can be computed recursively as:

$$b_i = \tilde{\omega}_i + max\ \{b_j + \tilde{\varepsilon}_{ij}\}\ \ \forall\ n_j \in succ(n_i) \tag{7}$$

where $\tilde{\omega}_i$ and $\tilde{\varepsilon}_{ij}$ is the mean computation cost of task n_i and mean communication cost between task n_i and task n_j respectively. The $succ(n_i)$ denotes a set of child nodes of node n_i. The communication cost between task n_i scheduled on resource p_m and task n_j scheduled on resource p_n can be computed as:

$$\varepsilon_{ij} = \frac{v_{ij}}{\beta(p_m, p_n)} \tag{8}$$

In this study, we define the *makespan* as the total execution time between the finish time of the exit task and start time of the entry task in the given DAG. Similarly, the *economic cost (EC)* is the summation of the economic costs of all workflow tasks scheduled on different resources which can be computed as:

$$EC = \sum_{i=1}^{n} D_{ij} \tag{9}$$

where D_{ij} is the economic cost of executing task n_i onto trusted resource p_j.

$$D_{ij} = M_j\ x\ \omega_{ij} \tag{10}$$

where M_j is the per unit time cost (in grid dollar) of executing task n_i on resource p_j and ω_{ij} is the execution time that task n_i takes to run on resource p_j. In this paper, *trustworthiness* [13] of grid resources has been used as performance metrics for comparing trust-oriented multi-objective scheduling heuristic (Trust-MOS) with DCA algorithm. It is an average of the global trust values of the resources used in scheduling a workflow. The simulated analysis and results reveal that trust oriented approach strengths the multi-objective scheduling problems yielding better make span and reducing the economic cost. Another performance metrics is *trust cost overhead* which is described in section 5. It can be computed using equation (12) for the tasks scheduled on different resources in grid. It is found that Trust-MOS generates less trust cost overhead as compared to DCA algorithm and reduces the execution time and economic cost overhead subsequently in multi-objective optimization process. It reflects that the resources with higher global trust values reduces the ratio of task failure exertion and produces the good quality schedules with lesser economic cost.

5 Trust-Oriented Multi-objective Scheduling Algorithm

This paper proposed an intelligent scheduling algorithm called trust-oriented multi-objective scheduling algorithm (Trust-MOS) to address the multi-objective optimization problem. The pseudo code of the proposed algorithm is described in Algorithm 2 and 3. It is divided into two major phases: (1) Primary Scheduling – Optimization for the primary criterion considering trust (2) Secondary Scheduling – Optimization for the secondary criterion while keeping the primary criterion within the defined sliding constraint. The total execution time (makespan) is selected as a primary criterion while the economic cost is selected as a secondary criterion. An efficient list-based scheduling heuristic [2] has been applied for execution time optimization. A cost optimization algorithm such as GreedyCost [3] has been used for selecting the cheapest resources for scheduling. In this paper, we apply an efficient sliding constraint method to define the user requirements [5]. The user is expected to define "sliding constraint" for the primary criterion, i.e. how much the final solution may differ from the best solution found for the primary criterion.

5.1 Primary Scheduling

The objective of primary scheduling is to obtain the optimal schedule of workflow for the primary criterion (i.e. makespan) only while considering the trustworthiness of resources. It generates a preliminary solution with the total costs of the primary and the secondary criterion which can be are denoted as c_1^{prel} and c_2^{prel} respectively. The task n_i is scheduled on to the resource p_j which minimizes the trust-based finish time (TFT_{ij}) for the primary criterion. It can be computed as:

$$TFT_{ij} = TC_{ij} + EFT_{ij} \qquad (11)$$

where TC_{ij} is the *trust cost overhead* of assigning task n_i on resource p_j and EFT_{ij} is the *expected finish time* of task n_i on resource p_j. The trust cost overhead (TC) for scheduling task n_i on resource p_j can be computed as:

$$TC_{ij} = (1 - t_j) \; x \; \omega_{ij} \qquad (12)$$

where ω_{ij} is the execution time of task n_i on resource p_j.

Algorithm 2. Primary Scheduling

1. *Compute global trust value t_j for each resource p_j using **EigenTrust** Algorithm*
2. *Construct a priority based task sequence ξ based on higher b-level using Eq. (7)*
3. *for (each unscheduled task n_i in task sequence ξ)*
4.   *for (each trusted resource p_j in grid)*
5.   *Compute trust cost overhead (TC_{ij}) using eq. (12)*
6.   *Compute trust based finish time (TFT_{ij}) using eq. (11)*
7.   *endfor*
8.   *Assign task n_i on resource p_j which minimizes TFT_{ij}*
9. *endfor*
10. *Calculate execution time c_1^{prel} using Eq. (14) and economic cost c_2^{prel} using Eq. (9).*

The pseudo code of the algorithm 2 presents the primary scheduling based on trust oriented approach for primary criterion only. First, we compute the global trust values of available resources in grid using the grid trust model as described in section 3. These values are periodically updated. Then, we generate a priority based task sequence based on b-levels using equation (7). Further, we compute the trust based finish time of each task on every resource and schedule task on to the resource which minimizes trust based finish time. Finally, we compute the total execution time (c_1^{prel}) and total economic cost (c_2^{prel}) of the schedule generated for the primary criterion.

5.2 Secondary Scheduling

The secondary scheduling optimizes primary solution for the secondary criterion (i.e. economic cost) while keeping the primary criterion within defined sliding constraint. It produces the best possible solution with the total costs of primary and secondary criteria which can be denoted as c_1^{final} and c_2^{final}. The sliding constraint is equal to L_T such that the primary criterion cost can be increased from c_1^{prel} to $c_1^{prel} + L_T$ in respect of reducing the secondary criteria cost in secondary scheduling. We assume that the maximum allowable execution time T_{Greedy} of workflow with cheapest economic cost C_{Greedy} can be computed using cost optimization algorithm such as GreedyCost [3]. Similarly, maximum allowable economic cost C_{Heft} of workflow with shortest execution time T_{Heft} can be computed using time optimization algorithm such as HEFT [2]. Thus, the sliding constraint for makespan can be computed as:

$$L_T^k = k \; x \; (T_{Greedy} - T_{Heft}) \qquad (13)$$

where k is the *sliding constant*. The value of k varies from 0.1 to 1.0 to provide us the sliding constraints that lie in ten equally distanced points for the makespan. In general, HEFT generated schedule contains shorter makespan as compared to GreedyCost algorithm. The makespan for the schedule may be computed as:

$$makespan = \max \; (TFT_{ij}) \qquad \forall \; 1 \leq i \leq n \; and \; 1 \leq j \leq p \qquad (14)$$

Algorithm 3. Secondary Scheduling

1. *Set Sliding constraint L_T using equation (13)*
2. *for (each task n_i in ξ scheduled on resource p_j in the schedule of primary scheduling)*
3.   *Set $net_{profit} = 0, cost_{profit}=0,\ time_{loss}=0,\ optimal\_node = 0$*
4.   *Compute set of alternative cheaper resources p' in grid*
5.   *for (each resource p'_j in p')*
6.   *Compute $D_{ij'}$ from eq. (10) and compute c_1^{temp} (new makespan)using eq. (14)*
7.   *if $D_{ij'} < D_{ij}$ and $c_1^{temp} \leq |c_1^{prel} + L_T|$*
8.   *$cost_{profit} = |D_{ij} - D_{ij'}|$ and $time_{loss} = |c_1^{temp} - c_1^{prel}|$*
9.   *$net_{profit} = cost_{profit}/time_{loss}$*
10.   *endif*
11.   *endfor*
12.   *optimal_node = p'_j that maximizes net_{profit}*
13.   *Migrate task n_i from resource p_j to p'_j for optimal_node > 0*
14. *endfor*
15. *Re-calculate execution time c_1^{final} using eq. (14) and economic cost c_2^{final} using eq. (9).*

The algorithm 3 presents secondary scheduling which optimizes both primary and secondary criteria. First, we compute the sliding constraints using equation (13) that lie in ten equally distanced points for total execution time. This algorithm finds the alternative services (resources) for rescheduling already scheduled task such that makespan should not increase beyond the maximum allowable execution time limit ($c_1^{prel} + L_T$) and economic cost is lesser on these services. The task is rescheduled on to the resource which maximizes net_{profit} as specified in algorithm 3. Finally, total execution time c_1^{final} and total economic cost c_2^{final} is estimated for optimized schedule re-generated for both criteria considering trustworthiness of grid resources.

6   Simulation and Experimental Results

The algorithm shown in section 5 has been evaluated and validated using simulated experiments on a variety of random workflows. We have implemented the scheduling algorithm and compared the schedules produced for different random DAGs on grids of different sizes. The specification layout for simulation is given in Table 1. The

Table 1. Grid Environment Layouts

Number of grid resources	[20, 100]
Resource Bandwidth	[100 Mbps, 1 Gbps]
Number of tasks	[100,500]
Computation cost of tasks	[5 msec, 200 msec]
Data Transfer Size	[20 Kbytes, 2 Mbytes]
Resource Capability (MIPS)	[220, 580]
Execution Cost (Per MIPS)	[1-5 grid dollar per MIPS]
Sliding Constant	[0.1 – 1.0]

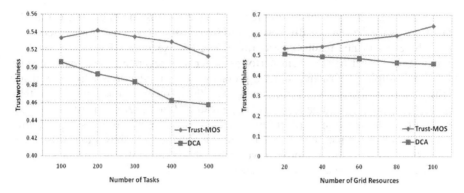

Fig. 1. Comparison of trustworthiness with respect to (a) number of tasks (workflow size) (b) number of grid resources

proposed algorithm (Trust-MOS) has been executed and compared with bi-criteria scheduling algorithm i.e. Dynamic Constraint Algorithm (DCA) [5] for different workflows in grids of different sizes. The DCA algorithm does not focus on trust related issues of resources in grid. Both the algorithms have been run under the same conditions for fair comparison i.e. for each workflow, each algorithm is run to find best possible second criteria cost while keeping the primary criterion within the defined sliding constraint in the same grid environment.

The algorithm 2 has been run for primary scheduling for both the criteria (i.e. makespan and economic cost) to find the best and worst solution (assumed) for primary criterion (T_{Heft} and T_{Greedy}) which yield the maximum sliding constraint i.e. the difference $|T_{Greedy} - T_{Heft}|$. The algorithm 3 is run for ten equally spaced different sliding constraint values to obtain the optimized execution time and economic cost. In fig. 1(a) and Fig. 1(b), Trust-MOS algorithm excels the DCA algorithm in terms of trustworthiness of grid resources used in executing the given workflow. Trustworthiness of both algorithms has been compared on workflows of different sizes (100, 200, 300, 400 and 500) as depicted in fig. 1(a) and in grids of different sizes (20, 40, 60, 80 and 100) as depicted in fig. 1(b). In fig. 2(a), the comparison has been illustrated for

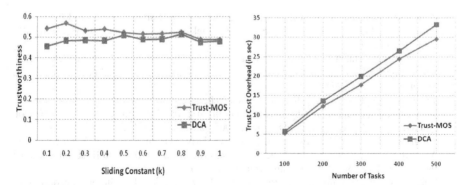

Fig. 2. (a) Comparison of trustworthiness for different sliding constants (b) Comparison of trust cost overhead with respect to number of tasks (workflow size)

trustworthiness with respect to different sliding constants ranging from 0.1 to 1.0 which produces the ten equally spaced sliding constraints for the primary criterion cost. The experimental results clearly reveal that the execution of workflow applications in trusted grid environment performs better and generates more realistic solutions for multiple performance criteria problems. The simulation results show that a higher trustworthiness can be achieved with the proposed scheduling algorithm. Another performance comparison has been illustrated in fig. 2(b) for trust cost overhead on random task graphs of different sizes. It transparently reflects that the trust cost overhead is comparatively very less in our approach. It shows that trust based multi-objective scheduling approach will generate good quality of schedules and reduce the execution time and economic cost.

7 Conclusions

The paper addresses the notion of trust in selecting hopefully trustworthy resources and executing tasks on these resources in grid computing environment. The trust criterion has been combined with other criterion like cost and execution time for considering such a multi-criteria scheme for grid scheduling algorithms. In this paper, an intelligent trust-based multi-objective workflow scheduling approach has been presented and analyzed. To the best of our knowledge, this is the first trust-based multi-criteria algorithm for workflow scheduling in grid environment. The algorithm has been implemented to schedule different random DAGs onto the grids of different sizes. Different variants of the algorithm were modeled and evaluated. We have presented a novel scheduling algorithm called Trust-oriented Multi-objective Scheduling algorithm (Trust-MOS) which optimizes both the makespan and economic cost of the schedule while maximizing the total trust (or reliability) of grid resources for executing applications. Our approach remarkably lessens the risks in task scheduling while considering multiple criteria and reduces the ratio of task failure exertion that can be best suited for executing tasks in a secure manner in grids.

References

1. Butt, A.R., Adabala, S., Kapadia, N.H., Figueiredo, R.J., Fortes, J.A.B.: Grid-Computing Portals and Security Issues. Journal of Parallel and Distributed Computing 63(10), 1006–1014 (2003)
2. Topcuoglu, H., Hariri, S., Wu, M.-Y.: Performance-Effective and Low-Complexity Task Scheduling for Heterogeneous Computing. IEEE Transactions on Parallel and Distributed Systems 13(3), 260–274 (2002)
3. Yu, J., Buyya, R., Tham, C.K.: Cost-based Scheduling of Scientific Workflow Applications on Utility Grids. In: Proceedings of the 1st IEEE International Conference on e-Science and Grid Computing, December 2005, pp. 140–147 (2005)
4. Song, S., Kwok, Y.K., Hwang, K.: Security-Driven Heuristics and A Fast Genetic Algorithm for Trusted Grid Job Scheduling. In: Proceedings of the 19th IEEE International Parallel and Distributed Processing Symposium (2005)
5. Wieczorek, M., Podlipnig, S., Prodan, R., Fahringer, T.: Bi-criteria Scheduling of Scientific Workflows for the Grid. In: Eighth IEEE International Symposium on Cluster Computing and the Grid, May 2008, pp. 9–16 (2008)

6. Zhu, C., Tang, X., Li, K., Han, X., Zhu, X., Qi, X.: Integrating Trust into Grid Economic Model Scheduling Algorithm. In: Meersman, R., Tari, Z. (eds.) OTM 2006. LNCS, vol. 4276, pp. 1263–1272. Springer, Heidelberg (2006)
7. Azzedin, F., Maheswaran, M.: Integrating trust into Grid Resource Management Systems. In: Proceedings of the 2002 International Conference on Parallel Processing (ICPP 2002), pp. 47–54. IEEE Press, Canada (2002)
8. Abdul-Rahman, A., Hailes, S.: Supporting Trust in Virtual Communities. In: Proceedings of the 33rd Hawaii Int'l Conference on System Sciences (January 2000)
9. Abawajy, J.H.: Fault-Tolerant Scheduling Policy for Grid Computing Systems. In: Proceedings of IEEE Int'l. Parallel and Distributed Symposium (April 2004)
10. DaSilva, L., Srivastava, V.: Node Participation in Ad Hoc and Peer-to-Peer Networks: A Game-Theoretic Formulation. In: Workshop on Games and Emergent Behavior in Distributed Computing Environments, Birmingham (2004)
11. Adar, E., Huberman, B.: Free Riding on Gnutella. First Monday 5(10) (2000)
12. Kamvar, S.D., Schlosser, M.T., Garcia-Molina, H.: The Eigentrust Algorithm for Reputation Management in P2P Networks. In: Proceedings of the 12th Int'l. Conference on World Wide Web, pp. 640–651 (2003)
13. Bertino, E., Crispo, B., Mazzoleni, P.: Supporting Multi-Dimensional Trustworthiness for Grid Workflows. In: DELOS Workshop: Digital Library Architectures, pp. 195–204 (2004)
14. Sun, M., Zeng, G., Yuan, L., Wang, W.: A Trust-Oriented Heuristic Scheduling Algorithm for Grid Computing. In: Malyshkin, V.E. (ed.) PaCT 2007. LNCS, vol. 4671, pp. 608–614. Springer, Heidelberg (2007)

Empirical Comparison of Race Detection Tools for OpenMP Programs*

Ok-Kyoon Ha[1], Young-Joo Kim[2], Mun-Hye Kang[1], and Yong-Kee Jun[1,**]

[1] Department of Informatics, Gyongsang National University,
Jinju 660-701, South Korea
[2] School of Engineering KAIST, Daejeon 305-732, South Korea
jassmin@gnu.ac.kr, yjkim73@kaist.ac.kr, {kmh,jun}@gnu.ac.kr

Abstract. Data races or races which occur in parallel programs such as OpenMP programs must be detected, because they may lead to unpredictable results of program executions. There are three representative tools which detect races which can occur in OpenMP programs: Thread Analyzer of Sun Inc., Thread Checker of Intel Corporation, and RaceStand of GNU. Two of these tools, Thread Checker and RaceStand, are known with their power for race detection through empirical analysis. But Thread Analyzer has not been analyzed empirically about its power for race detection and we cannot know exactly its race verification capability as well as its efficiency. This paper empirically analyzes the verification capability of Thread Analyzer using a set of synthetic programs which has nested parallelism or inter-thread coordination, and compares three race detection tools in an aspect of efficiency through OpenMP Micro-benchmarks of EPCC that measures loop scheduling and array operations. We predicted that Thread Analyzer verifies the existence of races in most OpenMP programs. And we found that Thread Analyzer is faster than Thread Checker about 5 times and 2 times slower than RaceStand in arraybench of EPCC. Also, it shows similar time variation with Thread Checker and is about 20 times slower than RaceStand in schedbench of EPCC.

Keywords: OpenMP programs, races, race detection tools, verification, efficiency, parallel loop programs.

1 Introduction

Data races or *races* [8] in parallel programs occurs when two parallel threads access a shared variable without proper inter-thread coordination and at least

---

* "This research was supported by the MKE (The Ministry of Knowledge Economy), Korea, under the ITRC (Information Technology Research Center) support program supervised by the IITA (Institute for Information Technology Advancement)" (IITA-2009-C1090-0904-0001).
** Corresponding author: In Gyeongsang National University, he is also involved in the Research Institute of Computer and Information Communication (RICIC).

D. Ślęzak et al. (Eds.): GDC 2009, CCIS 63, pp. 108–116, 2009.

one of these accesses is a write. It has become increasingly necessary to detect races for debugging effectively parallel programs such as OpenMP programs [9], because the races may lead to unpredictable results of the program executions.

Representative race detection tools such as *Thread Analyzer* [13, 14] of Sun Inc., *Thread Checker* [1, 11] of Intel Corporation, and *RaceStand* [5] of GNU (Gyongsang National University) have been developed to detect races to occur in OpenMP programs. Two of these tools, Thread Checker and RaceStand, are known for their power of race detection through an empirical analysis. The projection technique of Thread Checker does not verify the existence of races in programs with nested parallelism and inter-thread coordination [5,6]. RaceStand uses a labeling scheme [4,10] to generate an unique identifier for each thread and a pair of protocol schemes [3,7] to detect races checking concurrency of accesses. It has been developed for verifying the existence of races by GNU. Thread Analyzer [13,14] is a well-known tool that detects races in OpenMP programs, but it has not been analyzed empirically on its power for race detection and we cannot know exactly its race verification capability as well as its efficiency.

This paper empirically analyzes the verification capability of Thread Analyzer with a set of synthetic programs with nested parallelism or inter-thread coordination, and compares the three race detection tools in an aspect of efficiency through OpenMP Microbenchmarks from EPCC (Edinburgh Parallel Computing Centre) [2] that measures the efficiency of loop scheduling and array operations. As an empirical result of the verification capability of the tools, we predicted that Thread Analyzer can verify the existence of races in most OpenMP programs, because it detects at least one race in the synthetic programs which deliberately include races in OpenMP programs of various patterns considering nested parallelism and inter-thread coordination. For the efficiency of array operations, Thread Analyzer is faster than Thread Checker about 5 times and 2 times slower than RaceStand in arraybench of EPCC. For the efficiency of loop scheduling, Thread Analyzer shows similar time variation with Thread Checker and is about 20 times slower than RaceStand in schedbench of EPCC.

Section 2 illustrates the notion of races, and introduces the detection tools for OpenMP programs. Section 3 presents our synthetic programs to experiment the verification capability of the three tools, and designs experiments to compare their efficiencies using benchmarks. Section 4 analyzes the result of the experimentation. The last section provides our conclusion.

2 Background

A race in parallel program occurs when two threads access a shared variable without appropriate inter-thread coordination, and at least one of these accesses is a write. In this section, we illustrate the notion of races and detection tools for OpenMP programs which include Sun Thread Analyzer, Intel Thread Checker, and RaceStand.

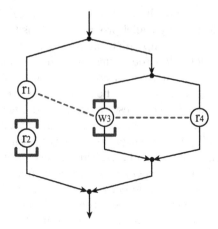

Fig. 1. A POEG for a Program with Nested Parallelism and Critical Sections

2.1   The Races in OpenMP Programs

The OpenMP [9] is an industry-standard model for shared memory parallel programs written in C/C++ and Fortran 77/99. Sequential programs can be transformed easily into parallel programs, if it is inserted with compiler directives for the OpenMP. These directives consist of parallel directives, work-sharing directives, data-environment directives, and synchronization directives.

Fig. 1 represents an execution of parallel program with nested parallelism and inter-thread coordination through a directed acyclic graph called POEG [3] (Partial Order Execution Graph). In this graph, a vertex means a fork or a join operation for parallel threads, and an arc started from a vertex represents a thread started from the vertex. The accesses r and w drawn in small disks upon the arcs name a read and a write access to a shared variable respectively. The numbers attached to accesses names indicate an observed order, and an arc segment delimited by symbol $\sqcap$ and $\sqcup$ means a region of thread protected by the same lock variable.

Using such a graph, we can easily figure out happens-before relationship between any pair of accesses. For example, $r1$ is ordered with $r2$ in Fig. 1, because a path exists between these accesses. An access $r1$ is concurrent with $w3$ and $r4$, because any path does not exist between any pair of accesses. There exists a race, if any pair of concurrent accesses e_i, e_j includes at least one write without proper inter-thread coordination. We denote the race e_i-e_j. Thus, Fig. 1 has two races: $r1$-$w3$, $w3$-$r4$ as indicated with two dashed lines. But, $r2$ and $w3$ does not consist of a race even if they are concurrent, because they are protected by a lock.

2.2   Race Detection Tools

It has become increasingly necessary to detect races effectively for debugging parallel programs such as OpenMP programs, because races may lead to unpredictable results of the program executions. To detect races in OpenMP programs, we have three tools: Sun Thread Analyzer [13, 14], Intel Thread Checker [1, 11], and GNU RaceStand [5] that we have been developing.

Thread Checker detects races by the projection technique [11]. This technology is applied to the relaxed sequential programs that are defined as parallelized only with OpenMP directives. A compiler for Thread Checker transforms such an OpenMP program into an instrumented source program using special compiler options. Thread Checker reports races by analyzing the traced information on shared variables and checking data dependency during an emulated sequential execution to project a trace of parallel threads. Unfortunately, the projection technology does not verify the existence of races in an execution of programs with nested parallelism and inter-thread coordination [5, 6].

RaceStand uses on-the-fly detection technique which checks mutual concurrency of accesses to each shared variable. This tool verifies the existence of races by applying a labeling scheme [4, 10] and a pair of protocol schemes [3, 7]. The labeling scheme generates a unique identifier which helps to compare the logical concurrency of two threads occurred in an execution of the program. Whenever an access occurs, the protocol schemes detect races by checking the mutual concurrency between current access and the previous accesses. Although RaceStand verifies the existence of races occurred in a parallel execution of a program, this tool consumes a large amount of space for maintaining the thread labels.

Thread Analyzer detects races by referencing the information such as the shared variables and the OpenMP directives. This tool generates an instrumented program during compilation, and it records performance data and shared variables by collecting the directives, shared variables, and input data. Thread Analyzer finally reports races by examining the collected information. We did not find any evidence for this tool not to verify the existence of races in an execution of program.

Terboven [14] illustrates errors such as races that can occur in OpenMP programs and describes races detected using Thread Checker and Thread Analyzer, and then compares the efficiency of them. According to this work, the memory consumption and the execution time of programs increase dramatically when applying the two tools. The result of race detection with Thread Analyzer depends on the number of threads used. If Thread Analyzer uses only two threads, it detects at least one race but some races can be missing, although these races might have been detected if it uses enough number of threads as many as the maximum parallelism. However, Thread Analyzer has not been analyzed empirically about its races verification capability as well as efficiency.

3   Experimentation

For empirical analysis of the three race detection tools, this section presents criteria of a set of synthetic programs, and designs a fair environment for the experimentation on the three tools including Thread Analyzer.

3.1   Design of Synthetic Programs

OpenMP programs with directives based on C language have a parallel computing program model and an activity management program model based on parallel threads [6, 12]. Parallel computing program divides single computation job into several parallel jobs and these jobs have the same kind of data structures and variables. Activity management program creates parent and child threads that have the allocated jobs in a program and these jobs have different kind of data structures which may be shared. Using these kinds of synthetic programs, we evaluate the verification capability of tools to analyze its accuracy.

To measure the accuracy, we observe whether the tools can verify the existence of races, and try to know the tool's principle of detecting races because its access maintenance policy can be comprehended. So we need to synthesize programs that consist of inter-thread coordination, nesting depth, and maximum parallelism. We classify synthetic programs for analyzing the tool's accuracy into twenty program models using the four criteria: at most one lock variable, the nesting depth of one or two, the maximum parallelism of two or three, and the number of total accesses. These synthetic programs have at least one access in each thread, because it makes to understand the maintenance policy of accesses for race detection in each tool. The synthetic programs are named according to the usage identifier, the number of lock variables, nesting depth, and maximum parallelism. Through the synthetic programs, we can experiment on most cases of OpenMP programs written by programmer.

3.2   Experimentation Methods

Our experiments are carried on a system with two Intel Xeon CPUs and 2GB of memory under the Linux operating system. We installed two kinds of C/C++ compilers for OpenMP programs on the system. One compiler is for Thread Checker, and the other is for Thread Analyzer. We installed Thread Checker 3.1 for Linux release 2, and Sun Studio 12 that includes Thread Analyzer. Race-Stand is implemented with run-time libraries written in C language which are inserted into the target program. Then, we compile and execute the instrumented program for the race detection.

We perform the following two steps for Thread Checker: instrumentation and execution. We use the projection technology of Thread Checker in Thread Count Independent (TCI) analysis mode, because this mode is effective on OpenMP programs. Thus, we transform a source program into an instrumented program by applying an Intel compiler with '-tcheck' option. Race information is reported by running of Thread Checker using the 'tcheck_cl' command. Thread Analyzer requires three steps to detect races: instrumentation, collection, and examination. We instrument OpenMP programs using Sun C/C++ compiler with '-xinstrument=datarace' option. Then, we perform the 'collect' command with '-r race' flag. Lastly, we examine the collected information using 'er_print' utility.

To experiment the verification capability of the three tools, we develop these synthetic programs considering nested parallelism and inter-thread coordination.

We analyze the verification capability of the three tools by comparing the results produced by the tools with the races created deliberately in the synthetic programs. We compare the efficiency of the three tools using the OpenMP Microbenchmarks [2] of EPCC which measures the efficiency of OpenMP programs. We measure the efficiency of array operations using an arraybench program which changes the array size, and the efficiency of loop scheduling by a schedbench program which changes loop scheduling options. For a fair experiment, we apply both Intel compiler and Sun compiler to experiment RaceStand.

4 Analysis of Results

This section analyzes the verification capability and efficiency of three tools based on the results of experimentation using the synthetic programs and benchmarks.

4.1 Verification Capability

We can understand the working principle of Thread Analyzer by analyzing the pattern of races detected in the synthetic programs written for the verification capability analysis. To understand this tool's working principle, we must grasp the maintenance policy of accesses. The policy is as followed through our experimentation using synthetic programs. If the current read access r_j is ordered with the previous read access r_i in the same thread, r_j is ignored by r_i that had maintained. Also, if the current write access w_j is ordered with the previous write access w_i in the same thread, w_j is ignored by w_i. And, if the current write access w_j is ordered with the previous read access r_i in the same thread, r_i is ignored and w_j is maintained for the thread.

Fig. 2 shows the maintenance policy of the accesses in the program. To maintain accesses in the thread, Thread Analyzer has priority of accesses in which an increasing order from the write access, the synchronized write or read access, to read access such as (a). In the figure, the rectangle which uses solid line is maintained access by a thread or a code block. The rectangle which uses dashed line is deleted access occurred by high priority access, but these accesses involved in race

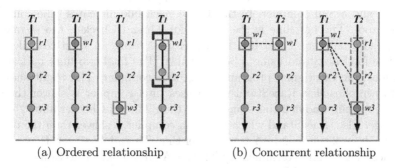

(a) Ordered relationship   (b) Concurrent relationship

Fig. 2. Access Management Policy in Thread Analyzer

Table 1. The Detected Races

	Synthetics			Thread Checker	Thread Analyzer	RaceStand
1	$r1$ $r2$	$w3$ $w4$	$r5$ $r6$	$r2$-$w3$, $r2$-$w4$ $w4$-$r5$, $w4$-$r6$	$r1$-$w3$ $w3$-$r5$	$r1$-$w3$, $r1$-$w4$ $w4$-$r5$, $w4$-$r6$
2	$r1$ $r2$	$w3$	$r4$	$r2$-$w3$	$r1$-$w3$, $w3$-$r4$	$r1$-$w3$, $w3$-$r4$
3	$r1$ [$r2$]	[$w3$]	$r4$	----	$r1$-$w3$, $w3$-$r4$	$r1$-$w3$, $w3$-$r4$

detection with a maintained access in the other thread such as (b). The accesses without any rectangle indicate ignored accesses by a maintained access.

Table 1 shows a part of the test results from the synthetic programs using the three tools. These programs are representative of the synthetic programs. The first program invokes three parallel threads represented by three columns, and the next two types of programs invoke two parallel threads of which the second thread forks two child-threads. In this result, although all tools detect some races occurred in first and second synthetic programs, Thread Checker does not detect the races between the two child-threads in the second program. Other than Thread Checker, Thread Analyzer and RaceStand detect the races occurred in the third program with inter-thread coordination. We predicted that Thread Analyzer can verify the existence of races in most OpenMP programs, because it detects at least one race in the synthetic programs which deliberately include races in OpenMP programs with most kinds of nested parallelism and inter-thread coordination.

4.2   Efficiency

Fig. 3 shows the result of measurement of the required time for race detection with the benchmark of EPCC. Fig. 3(a) compares three tools using an Intel compiler and a Sun compiler. In this figure, each line indicates time consumed by each tool. The first line is the results for Thread Checker, the second line for Thread Analyzer, Third line for RaceStand using an Intel compiler, and forth line for RaceStand using a Sun compiler. The final two lines indicate the execution time of original program using both compiler. The result shown in Fig. 3(a) implies that RaceStand which uses Intel compiler is slower than the original program about 2 times and faster than Thread Checker about 5 times in average. Also, RaceStand which uses Sun compiler is slower than the original program about 2 times and is 2 times faster than Thread Analyzer. However, the difference of the time consumed by Thread Analyzer and RaceStand is small, about 1 second.

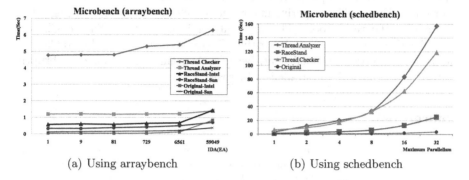

Fig. 3. The Required Time Measured for Race Detection

We measure the time variation with a schedbench program using options for parallel loop scheduling such as `static`, `dynamic`, `staticn`, and `guided`, increasing the maximum parallelism by multiple of two. We cannot measure RaceStand without modifying the program because of the memory overflow when the maximum parallelism of logical threads is over 500,000. Neither Thread Checker could be measured when the maximum parallelism is over 1,200,000. But we have not found that Thread Analyzer lacks memory space. So, this makes the efficiency be compared only with the same memory space that executes all of the three tools. In Fig. 3(b), Thread Analyzer is slower than RaceStand about 20 times in average, and it shows similar results with Thread Checker. Moreover, if the maximum parallelism increases, the time consumed by Thread Analyzer and Thread Checker abruptly increases.

From Fig. 3(a)-(b), we find that Thread Analyzer is more efficient than Thread Checker for the two cases of benchmarks, but its efficiency depends on cases of benchmarks with RaceStand. Both of Thread Checker and Thread Analyzer are inefficient because the time consumption abruptly increases as the maximum parallel is increase.

5   Conclusion

Data races or races are notoriously difficult to detect in parallel programs. Representative race detection tools such as Thread Analyzer, Thread Checker, and GNU RaceStand have been developed to detect races to occur in OpenMP programs. Sun Thread Analyzer is an important tool for race detection, but it has not been compared with respect to the verification capability of the races and its efficiency with Thread Checker or RaceStand we have developed. We analyzed the verification capability of the three tools with a set of synthetic programs with nested parallelism and inter-thread coordination, and we compared the efficiency of the tools with a set of benchmarks which measures the efficiency of array operations and loop scheduling.

For the verification capability, Thread Analyzer verifies the existence of races according to the result of experiments by the set of synthetic program. Regarding efficiency of the three tools, Thread Analyzer is faster than Thread Checker about five times, but is 2 time slower than RaceStand. However, Thread Checker and Thread Analyzer are inefficient, because their time overheads can abruptly increase as the maximum parallelism increase.

References

1. Banerjee, U., Bliss, B., Ma, Z., Petersen, P.: A Theory of Data Race Detection. In: The 2006 Workshop on Parallel and Distributed Systems: Testing and Debugging (PADTAD), pp. 69–78. ACM Press, New York (2006)
2. Bull, J.M.: Measuring Synchronization and Scheduling Overheads in OpenMP. In: European Workshop on OpenMP (EWOMP), pp. 99–105 (1999)
3. Dinning, A., Schonberg, E.: Detecting Access Anomalies in Programs with Critical Sections. In: The ACM/ONR Workshop on Parallel and Distributed Debugging, pp. 85–96. ACM Press, New York (1991)
4. Jun, Y., Koh, K.: On-the-fly Detection of Access Anomalies in Nested Parallel Loops. In: 3rd ACM/ONR Workshop on Parallel and Distributed Debugging, pp. 107–117. ACM Press, New York (1993)
5. Kim, Y., Kang, M., Ha, O., Jun, Y.: Efficient Race Verification for Debugging Programs with OpenMP Directives. In: Malyshkin, V.E. (ed.) PaCT 2007. LNCS, vol. 4671, pp. 230–239. Springer, Heidelberg (2007)
6. Kim, Y., Kim, D., Jun, Y.: An Empirical Analysis of Intel Thread Checker for Detecting Races in OpenMP Programs. In: IEEE International Conference on Computer and Information Science, pp. 409–414. IEEE Press, New York (2008)
7. Mellor-Crummey, J.M.: On-the-fly Detection of Data Races for Programs with Nested Fork-Join Parallelism. In: The ACM/IEEE conference on Supercomputing, pp. 24–33. ACM/IEEE, New York (1991)
8. Netzer, R.H.B., Miller, B.P.: What Are Race Conditions? Some Issues and Formalizations. ACM Lett. Program. Lang. Syst. 1(1), 74–88 (1992)
9. The OpenMP API specification for parallel programming, http://www.openmp.org
10. Park, S., Park, M., Jun, Y.: A Comparison of Scalable Labeling Schemes for Detecting Races in OpneMP Programs. In: Eigenmann, R., Voss, M.J. (eds.) WOMPAT 2001. LNCS, vol. 2104, pp. 68–80. Springer, Heidelberg (2001)
11. Petersen, P., Shah, S.: OpenMP Support in the Intel Thread Checker. In: Voss, M.J. (ed.) WOMPAT 2003. LNCS, vol. 2716, pp. 1–12. Springer, Heidelberg (2003)
12. Rinard, M.: Analysis of Multithreaded Programs. In: Cousot, P. (ed.) SAS 2001. LNCS, vol. 2126, pp. 1–19. Springer, Heidelberg (2001)
13. SUN Microsystems, Inc.: Sun Studio 12: Thread Analyzer User's Guide (2007)
14. Terboven, C.: Comparing Intel Thread Checker and Sun Thread Analyzer. In: Minisymp. on Scalability and Usability of HPC Prog. Tools Workshop, Parallel Computing (ParCo), NIC, NIC Series, Juelich, vol. 38, pp. 669–676 (2007)

Efficient Service Recommendation System for Cloud Computing Market

Seung-Min Han[1], Mohammad Mehedi Hassan[1], Chang-Woo Yoon[2],
Hyun-Woo Lee[2], and Eui-Nam Huh[1]

[1] Department of Computer Engineering
Kyunghee University, Global Campus, South Korea
[2] Electronics and Telecommunications Research Institute (ETRI)
{han905,hassan,johnhuh}@khu.ac.kr, {cwyoon,hwlee}@etri.re.kr

Abstract. In recent years, Cloud computing is gaining much popularity as it can efficiently utilize the computing resources and hence can contribute to the issue of Green IT to save energy. So to make the Cloud services commercialized, Cloud markets are necessary and are being developed. As the increasing numbers of various Cloud services are rapidly evolving in the Cloud market, how to select the best and optimal services will be a great challenge. In this paper we present a Cloud service selection framework in the Cloud market that uses a recommender system (RS) which helps a user to select the best services from different Cloud providers (CP) that matches user requirements. The RS recommends a service based on the network QoS and Virtual Machine (VM) platform factors of difference CPs. The experimental results show that our Cloud service recommender system (CSRS) can effectively recommend a good combination of Cloud services to consumers.

Keywords: Cloud Service, Cloud Market, Service Selection, Recommendation System.

1 Introduction

In today's world the emerging Cloud computing offers a new computing model where resources such as computing power, storage, online applications and networking infrastructures can be shared as 'services' over the internet [1]. Cloud computing is actually virtual services, which have many important aspects such as dynamic, weight, low cost, transparent, reliable and secure. In recent years, efficient energy IT framework also called Green IT is being undertaken seriously so Cloud computing can contribute to the energy issue as it can efficiently utilizes the computing resources. In order to make the Cloud services commercialize, Cloud markets will be one of candidate approaches and studied being studied and developed now a days by several researcher and organizations.

In near future there will be many Cloud services available in the Cloud market and the increase of available services may present a significant problem if consumers want to find relevant best or optimal services among many different type of services. So selection of optimal Cloud service will be a great challenge.

D. Ślęzak et al. (Eds.): GDC 2009, CCIS 63, pp. 117–124, 2009.
© Springer-Verlag Berlin Heidelberg 2009

Recommendation systems (RS) are one the computer-based intelligent techniques to deal with the problem of finding appropriate services or products from a large no. of available services or products. They can be utilized to efficiently provide personalized services in most e-business domains, benefiting both the consumer and the provider. Recommender Systems will benefit the consumer by making to him suggestions on services or product. and this is advantaged what user need a service or finding a product. At the same time, the business will be benefited by the increase of sales which will normally occur when the consumer is presented with more items and services user would likely find appealing [2, 3].

In this paper, we present a Cloud service selection framework in the Cloud market that uses a recommendation system (RS) which helps a user to select the optimal services from different Cloud providers (CP) that matches requirements of the user. The RS creates ranks of different services with providers and present to the user so that they can select the appropriate or optimal services.

The rest of this paper is organized as follows: Section 2 presents the related works in the literature. Section 3 describes the architecture of Cloud resource recommendation system. Section 4 describes a case study of how the RS works in the Cloud market. We conclude our work by presenting summary and future directions in Section 5.

2 Related Work

There are very few literatures using a recommendation system in the Cloud market, while some papers have recently published regarding Cloud market. So here we just briefly present the basic concept of a recommendation system and the Cloud market.

2.1 Recommendation System

(1) Demographic Recommender Systems [4]
It uses user's attributes, shared rating based on data of user statistics and then recommends. In other words, it provides needed information analyzed by user attributes based on population statistical calculations. It is easy to apply in a system relatively, because it recommends by user attributes and do not need to analyze many users' log.

(2) Collaborative Recommender Systems [4-6]
Collaborative filtering (CF) is the most mature and most widely used for recommend system. It relies only on opinions explicitly delivered by the users on items. The system recommends to the targeted customer products (or people), which have been evaluated in plus by another people, whose ratings are similar to the ratings of the targeted user. This mean that similar tendencies (hobbies, interests, interests, etc.) with the category of users based on the existing users of the assessment to the current user will be referred to the information we want, but this filtering has problem of "Cold-Start" [6] and "Data Sparseness" [7]. Cold-Start is problems with new users.

(3) Hybrid Recommender Systems [5, 6]
The hybrid approach to recommendation system combines the Content–based and Collaborative filtering. There are many different ways to combine the Content–based

and Collaborative filtering. The best known are: implement both methods separately and combine the outputs of these methods, add some of the collaborative characteristics to the Content–based filtering and add some of the Content–based characteristics to the Collaborative filtering.

2.2 Cloud Computing Market

Recently, Cloud computing is becoming a hot research topic after it was initially proposed by Weiss [8] in 2007. It now enables Cloud providers to provide platform as well as share resources such as computing power, storage, applications, networking infrastructures etc. as services. In [9], authors present a vision of 21st century computing, describe some representative platforms for Cloud computing covering the state-of-the-art and provide the architecture for creating market-oriented Clouds for resource management. As defined in [10], a cloud-based infrastructure contains cloud-based storage service, cloud-based data services and cloud-based computing services. Many practical cases of Cloud computing can be found, like Google Docs, Photoshop Express, Microsoft. Live Service, Salesforce.com, IBM Blue Cloud, Amazon S3 storage cloud, EC2, etc. Through web browsers or other fixed or mobile terminals, users can access those services running on remote servers. Since Cloud computing is growing rapidly, the number of available Cloud services dramatically increases. To find appropriate Cloud service for each individual user, it requires an effective recommendation system [11].

So we use a Cloud service recommender system that also uses collaborative filtering to effectively recommend the services to user.

3 Architecture Recommendation System Based Cloud Market

Our Cloud service RS (CSRS) recommends to user the effective resources from the Cloud market using QoS and service rank analysis of resources provided by Cloud providers (CPs). QoS includes max execution time, average execution time, max response time, average response time etc. of Cloud services. Service-rank(S-Rank) considers the quality of virtualization hypervisors used by different Cloud service platform, user feedback and cost of services to provide better services. The proposed RS for Cloud services will contribute to the research model for Green IT and a use to manage the resources efficiently.

3.1 Cloud Resource Recommendation System

The proposed architecture of Cloud service RS (CSRS) is shown in Fig. 1. The main components of the CSRS include web portal, request manager, resource register, resource manager, application specific service, resource monitoring and provisional manager.

Web portal is used by the CPs to register their resources/services to the CSRS system. Also user can submit their requirements of Cloud services and get the recommendation results through the web portal.

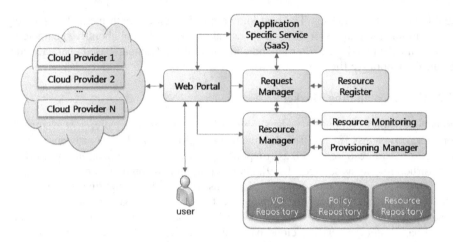

Fig. 1. Cloud Resource Recommendation System

Resource Manager as a core module of the system controls the market system and manages various resources of CPs. It stores meta-data that is the logical organization of the resources distributed by the VO (Virtual Organization) in VO repository and the cost of the market and measured performance in Policy repository. It has a role to set up the virtual environment in the CPs via *Provisioning Manager.* It also monitors the status of the resources through the *Resource Monitoring* and sends the S-Rank update request to the *Resource Register.*

Application Specific Service is used to provide the software services to user directly.

3.2 Resource Register to the Cloud Market

Hardware and software are registered separately in the Cloud market using a registry module as shown in Fig. 3 HaaS (Hardware-as-a-services) are classified into Storage, Computing and Network services and includes PaaS (Platform-as-a-Service) provided by CPs. And in case of SaaS (Software-as-a-Service) it is classified into software and online applications. Each module function is in Table 1.

Table 1. Resource registration process

Step	Service	HaaS, PaaS	SaaS
1	Importer	Progress with hardware Cloud provider offered	Progress with hardware Cloud provider offered
2	Validate Module	Check the agreement of the XML-based contracts offered and service	Check the agreement the XML-based contracts offered and service
3	QoS Analysis	QoS analysis for the hardware efficiency and the network efficiency	QoS analysis for the network efficiency
4	Rank Analysis	Rank analysis by the QoS and price offered	Rank analysis by the QoS and price offered

3.3 Resource Rank Analysis

3.3.1 QoS Analysis

The most important thing is to analyze the QoS of each service to register resources to cloud market. QoS is divided into SaaS and HaaS, QoS of SaaS is given by

$$QoS_{SaaS} = \sum [QoS_{network}] \tag{1}$$

In the second phase, QoS, HaaS including PaaS is calculated as follows:

$$QoS_{[HaaS, PaaS]} = \sum [QoS_{network}] + \sum_{n} SP[Sn, Cn, Mn] \tag{2}$$

Cloud service is a web-based service, so QoS of network is very important. We can use a variety of variables like max execution time, average execution time, max response time, average response time etc. Specification of HaaS and PaaS is measured by QoS with network property and SP (Service Performance) such as CPU, memory and storage. In case of SaaS, network QoS is considered only.

3.3.2 Performance Testing of Virtual Machine

VM is a middleware which is performed in hardware. So, it has an important role to provide the desired service by user having VM factor. The experiments were performed on Inter Core-2 6300 CPU PC with 2GB RAM under windows XP using Visual C++ 6.0 software. We installed three VMs (Virtual PC, Xen and VMware) on same hardware and conducted benchmarking tests regarding only CPU performance.

We rename the VM software as follows: virtual PC as VM1, Xen as VM2 and VMware as VM3. the benchmarking tests just consider about CPU and memory interface performances using 12 performance functions of CPU and Memory.

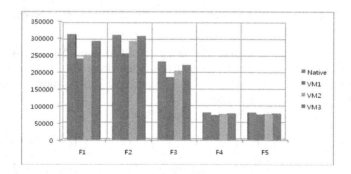

Fig. 2. Fixed-point benchmark chart

Fig. 2 shows the experiment for fixed-point operator in each VMs, of course, native environment is the most faster.

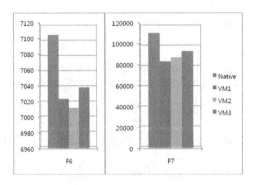

Fig. 3. Memory benchmark chart

Fig. 3 shows the results for memory tests in our benchmark. we expect both virtualization hypervisors to score close to native and memory results compared to native, higher values are better.

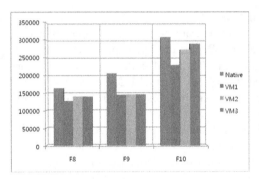

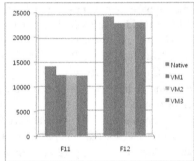

Fig. 4. Floating-point benchmark chart1   **Fig. 5.** Floating-point benchmark chart2

Fig. 4 and 5 are the benchmarks of floating point functions. The results, as shown in Table 3, illustrate a slowdown over native ranging from 10–20 percent and each hypervisor in VMs an average slowdown of 15 percent. Table 2 shows relative score to native, higher is better performance.

The average VM factor can be obtained as follows:

$$VMn_{factor} = (\frac{VM_n \sum f(I)}{Native \sum f(I)} + \frac{VM_n \sum f(M)}{Native \sum f(M)} + \frac{VM_n \sum f(F)}{Native \sum f(F)})/3 \tag{3}$$

From the equation 3, we can see that it has three parts; the first part calculates fixedpoint operation functions, the second part calculates memory operation functions and last part is calculation of floating point operation functions.

Table 2. Values of Benchmarking score

Function		VM			
		Native	VM1	VM2	VM3
Fixed-point	function1	1.0000	0.7692	0.8031	0.9361
	function2	1.0000	0.8232	0.9434	0.9896
	function3	1.0000	0.7988	0.8826	0.9544
	function4	1.0000	0.9032	0.9395	0.9676
	function5	1.0000	0.9300	0.9460	0.9671
Memory	function6	1.0000	0.9884	0.9867	0.9905
	function7	1.0000	0.7524	0.7875	0.8415
Floating-point	function8	1.0000	0.7702	0.8513	0.8516
	function9	1.0000	0.7026	0.7061	0.7083
	function10	1.0000	0.7425	0.8844	0.9380
	function11	1.0000	0.8748	0.8712	0.8654
	function12	1.0000	0.9420	0.9468	0.9496

The requirements for datacenter adoption are demanding and far beyond single-server virtualization. We can predict performance of hypervisor if some system provides virtualization method using VM factor.

3.3.3 Rank Analysis

In Cloud service, one of the important factors is the cost of the service even though QoS is very important. Users generally choose the low cost services. Furthermore, user will willingly select a service that is higher quality among the same price services tagged. At first when a CP registers its services, it submits the including service and resource capacity parameters. And our proposed RS system makes S-Rank value. This rank continually is updated through user feedbacks (Uf).

When users search for a service, system uses S-Rank, at time it is a primary role like as a DBMS. User can change α and β according to their service requirement for instance some users may prefer to consider the VM factor other than QoS.

In general RS system employs variable user's feedbacks. Thus we also add Uf on calculation of the improve S-Rank like equation 4

$$S - Rank_{final} = \alpha * e^{VM_{factor}} + \beta * e^{QoS} + \gamma * Uf \qquad (4)$$

where α, β and γ are constants and their summation is 1

4 Conclusion

In this paper, we propose a Cloud service recommendation system in the Cloud market that helps a user to select the best combination of services from different Cloud providers that match his/her requirements. The RS creates ranks of different services and present to user. User can select the services based on his/her requirements. In future, we will improve the S-Rank with more benchmarking functions like storage performance and network I/O.

Acknowledgments

This work was supported by the IT R&D program of KCC/MKE/KEIT [2009-S-018-01, Development of Open-IPTV Platform Technologies for IPTV Convergence Service and Content Sharing].

References

1. Armbrust, M., et al.: Above the clouds: A berkeley view of cloud computing. Technical Report UCB/EECS-2009-28 (2009)
2. Boykin, P.O., Roychowdhury, V.P.: Leveraging social networks to fight spam. IEEE Computer (2005)
3. Jones, Q., Grandhi, S.A.: P3 systems: Putting the place back into social networks. IEEE Internet Computing (2005)
4. Cantador, I., Fernáandez, M., Castells, P.: A Collaborative Recommendation Framework for Ontology Evaluation and Reuse. Universidad Autóonoma de Madrid, Spain (2006)
5. Adomavicius, G., Tuzhilin, A.: Toward the Next Generation of Recommender Systems: A Survey of the State-of-the-Art and Possible Extensions. IEEE Educational Activities Department (2005)
6. Schafer, J.B., Frankowski, D., Herlocker, J., Sen, S.: Collaborative Filtering Recommender Systems. In: The Adaptive Web (2007)
7. Golbeck, J.: Computing with Trust: Definition, Properties, and Algorithms. In: Securecomm and Workshops (2006)
8. Weiss, A.: Computing in the Clouds. Net Worker 11(4), 16–25 (2007)
9. Buyya, R., Yeo, C.S., Venugopal, S.: Market-Oriented Cloud Computing: Vision, Hype, and Reality for Delivering IT Services as Computing Utilities. In: HPCC 2008 (September 2008)
10. Grossman, R.L., Gu, Y., Sabala, M., Zhang, W.: Compute and storage clouds using wide area high performance networks. Future Generation Computer Systems 25(2), 179–183 (2009)
11. Hayes, B.: Cloud computing. Commun. ACM 51(7), 9–11 (2008)

Scalable Cooperative Positioning System in Wireless Sensor Networks

Cheolsu Son[1], Wonjung Kim[1], Hyun Sim[1], and Hyeong-Ok Lee[2]

[1] Department of Computer Science, Sunchon National University, Sunchon, Chonnam,
540-742, Korea
[2] Department of Computer Computer Education, Sunchon National University, Sunchon,
Chonnam, 540-742, Korea
{mrbr,kwj,simhyun,oklee}@sunchon.ac.kr

Abstract. Locations of positioned nodes as well as gathered data from nodes are very important because generally multiple nodes are deployed randomly and data are gathered in wireless sensor network. Since the nodes composing wireless sensor network are low cost and low performance devices, it is very difficult to add specially designed devices for positioning into the nodes. Therefore in wireless sensor network, technology positioning nodes precisely using low cost is very important and valuable. This research proposes Cooperative Positioning System, which raises accuracy of location positioning and also can find positions on multiple sensors within limited times. And this research verifies this technology is excellent in terms of performance, accuracy, and scalability through simulation.

Keywords: Cooperative Positioning, Wireless Sensor Network, RSSI.

1 Introduction

Wireless Sensor Networks (WSN) are composed of multiple low power and low performance sensor nodes. In WSN, sensor nodes measure and gather data such as temperature, humidity, pressure, slope, and strength and then send them to sink nods through wireless network. It is very important to know position of each sensor node as well as gathered data.

For example, when multiple sensor nodes are deployed to detect a forest fire, it is very important to find out position of the sensor node generating fire detection event.

Methods of node positioning are very diverse based on which equipment and which technology are implemented. Positioning systems such as GPS, Active Badge, Active Bats, MotionStar implement radio, infrared light, ultrasonic waves, and video devices.

The technologies utilized to the above positioning system are proximity, ToA(time of arrival), TDoA(time difference of arrival), AoA(angle of arrival), signal strength of radio frequency, and scene analysis, etc. Most of positioning systems use specially designed equipment to get location of nodes. These equipment need lots of costs in order to install and operate and so recently many researches are performed to find out methods of low cost positioning utilizing existing wireless network infrastructure [2, 3, 4].

D. Ślęzak et al. (Eds.): GDC 2009, CCIS 63, pp. 125–132, 2009.

RADAR[1] does not use dedicated positioning equipment but utilizes existing wireless local area network infrastructure environments and obtains RSSI(received signal strength indicator) from wireless devices such as wireless LAN card and AP(access point) and finds out locations by converting RSSI into distance. The strength of radio signal has certain character and it becomes weaker as distance becomes far away. This character can be used to measure distance. However it includes lots of errors when converting RSSI into distance because of the characteristic of radio signal such as interference phenomenon and multi-path phenomenon occurred while receiving radio signal. Therefore, reducing the errors included in the distance obtained by converting RSSI is a task to be solved in positioning system using RSSI.

Every positioning system should provide accuracy enough to use for specific purpose application. And also under the circumstances of restricted available resources and limited given time, performance as much as accuracy becomes another important goal to be accomplished in positioning system. It requires scalability to perform positioning efficiently to multiple nodes since calculations are needed more as number of nodes increases like general wireless sensor network. The purpose of this research is to propose a positioning system that improves accuracy, performance, and scalability in wireless sensor network composed of multiple nodes.

2 Relative Studies

There are two methods to calculate positioning of a sensor node. One is beacon-based positioning method that location is determined by measuring distances between beacon nodes of locations known. Other is cooperative positioning system that location is determined by measuring distances between nodes including location of nodes not determined [5, 6].

In beacon-based positioning system, power consumption is needed more because signals of radio waves should be strong and performance of each node should be excellent. In cooperative positioning system, it is effective in multi-hop environments since only part of nodes can communicate with beacon and the rest of nodes communicate with neighbor nodes to measure distances and thus costs and energy consumption are less.

In cooperative positioning system, an algorithm of 2W (WiPS[5] and WiCOPS[6]) using nonlinear programming to measure locations is introduced and defects are analyzed in this chapter. Problem of the existing 2W studies is that *location convergence adjustment factor* α, which is used to move each node repeatedly in order to reach specified error range, is decided not by calculation but by heuristic. Since the value is fixed, performance is not good when number of nodes is increased and it is not converged to location but diverged if number of nodes is over certain number.

In order to solve the above problem of WiPS [5], WiCOPS [6] decides *location convergence adjustment factor* α by calculation using *acceleration factor* β and number of related nodes which affects to location convergence process of nodes. This solves the problem of divergence and performance is better than WiPS. The notations of expression in this paper can be referred in [6].

$$\alpha_i = \beta \frac{1}{n(G_i) + n(N_i)} \tag{1}$$

However, acceleration factor β of WiCOPS is decided not by calculation but heuristic and so it has problems in expansion and performance.

3 SCOPS

This research proposes cooperative positioning system SCOPS which improves accuracy, performance, and scalability in wireless sensor network composed of multiple nodes. SCOPS utilizes nonlinear programming for calculation.

3.1 Improved Positioning Convergence Adjustment Factor

Both WiPS [5] and WiCOPS [6] use (2) to decide $k+1th$ locations to first node in positioning.

$$p_i^{(k+1)} = p_i^{(k)} + \alpha \nabla(i) \tag{2}$$

Modification of location of a node affects positioning of that node and neighboring node. On the other hand, location of certain node affects positioning of neighboring nodes in previous step.

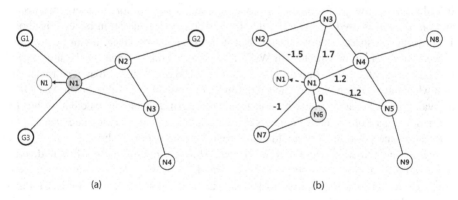

(a)   (b)

Fig. 1. Affection relation between nodes and Actual affection relation between nodes

In (a) of Fig. 1, G1, G2 and G3 are beacon nodes and N1, N2, N3 and N4 are nodes that have to be positioned. Location movement of from N1 to N'1 is decided by neighboring nodes G1, G2, N2 and N3. Also, if N1 moves to N'1, it affects positioning of N2 and N3. Therefore, there are co-relationship between convergence adjustment factor and number of nodes which affect positioning. Number of nodes which affects ith nodes can be obtained by (3).

When location of one node is decided, if location is decided by only moving value of $\nabla(i)$, it is not converged but diverged or vibrated. Thus, the value of convergence adjustment factor α of (1) should be decided appropriately. If value of α is above 1, probability of divergence is higher than that of convergence. Therefore, value of α should be above 0 and below 1. Thus, value of stable convergence adjustment factor in probability is (1).

$$impactNumber(i) = n(G_i) + n(N_i)$$ (3)

However, (3) calculates number of nodes affecting positioning of certain node by simply number of that node and neighboring nodes. (b) of Fig. 1 shows certain step that has been adjusted repeatedly to locate a node. Node N1 neighbors on N2, N3, N4, N5, N6, and N7. Differences between estimated distance and measured distance of each node are assumed -1.5, 1.7, 1.2, 1.2, 0, and -1, number of nodes neighboring N1 is 6 but actual affecting nodes is 5, because difference between estimated distance and measured distance of N1 and N6 is 0.

Therefore, convergence speed can be high by only considering number of nodes that give affection actually in iteration like (4). (4) is convergence adjustment factor applying number of nodes that give effects to *ith* nodes actually in *kth* iteration.

$$\alpha_k = \frac{1}{n'(G_i) + n'(N_i)}$$ (4)

3.2 Convergence Acceleration Factor

In order to improve performance by reducing number of iteration, convergence acceleration factor β is used like (1). If value of convergence acceleration factor β is above 1, convergence speed becomes faster. But if the value is too large, it can be not converged but diverged or vibrated. In WiCOPS, value of convergence acceleration factor β is set to 1, 2, and 3 and simulation is performed. The result shows that performance is best when value of convergence acceleration factor β is set to 2. Like this, in WiCOPS, the value of convergence acceleration factor is determined not by calculation but by heuristics. Therefore, value of convergence acceleration factor β can be determined by calculation and performance should be improved while keeping stability.

Fig. 2 is a simulation result of WiCOPS and shows a moving path of first node during location convergence process. In this simulation, number of location-known beacon nodes is set to 4 and number of location-unknown nodes is set to 50. Location is converged after about 80 iterations.

Initialized location is (14.97, 113.55) and converged location is (18.62, 107.27) respectively. Location is converged to almost same direction from the stabilization stage after 5 times iterations. Like this, after the stabilization stage, moving direction is almost constant but convergence speed is quite low.

AS we see from Fig. 2, direction is changed significantly until stabilization stage but degree of direction change is very low after stabilization stage. Therefore if value of convergence acceleration factor β is increased dynamically after stabilization stage, then convergence speed will be improved. In order to change the value of convergence acceleration factor β, the following two factors should be determined.

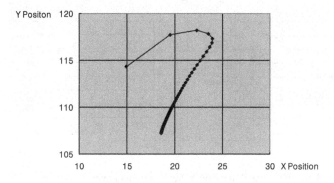

Fig. 2. Location modification path of first node

Decision of stability phase to change convergence acceleration factor

```
IF previousUnitVector     45 and currentUnitVector     45
    bStableFlag ← True
Else
    bStableFlag ← False
End if
```

Determination of convergence acceleration factor

```
IF bStableFlag = True
    iAccelatorFactor++
Else
    iAccelatorFactor =1
End if
```

Criteria for decision of stability phase are defined to iteration count, progress of moving distance, and progress of direction. But it is difficult to decide by iteration count simply because stability phases are different based on number of nodes and distribution of nodes. Therefore, progress of moving direction is used to decide stability phase in this research

As shown in the decision of stability phase, if changes of moving direction are below 45 unit vector twice consecutively, it is considered as stability phase. If changes of direction do not meet the criteria, it is considered as non stability phase. As shown in the determination of convergence acceleration factor, value of convergence acceleration factor is increased in stability phase case and the value is initialized in non stability phase case.

4 Simulation and Results

In the existing WiPS and WiCOPS, values of convergence adjustment factor or convergence acceleration factor are determined heuristically to measure locations. In this

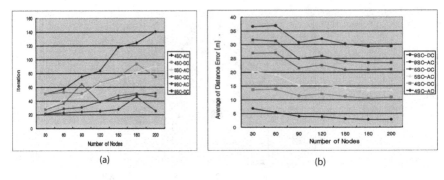

Fig. 3. Scalability and iteration & Scalability and average of distance error

research, determination methods of dynamic convergence adjustment factor based on number of nodes affecting actually and of dynamic convergence acceleration factor based on progress of moving direction are proposed. Simulation is performed to prove that this proposed method is superior to existing research 2W in terms of performance and stability.

Simulation is performed on the square plane that width is 200 m and length is 200m. Wireless telecommunication distance is set to 100m based on ZigBee that is mainly used to compose wireless sensor network. Number of fixed beacon, whose location is known itself, is 4, 5, or 9 and these are deployed. Number of nodes is increased by 5 from 5 to 100. If 4, 5 and 9 nodes of beacon are deployed on certain square plane to normalize deployment of beacon nodes, distances between beacon nodes are approximately 200m, 141m, 100m.

4*, 5*, and 9* are simulation results for 4, 5, and 9 of number of nodes respectively in (1) Fig. 3. If *SC-AC and *SC-DC are compared with in terms of number of beacon nodes, we can see that iteration count of SC-DC applied to divide and conquer method is about 50 % lower than SC-AC.

In (b) of Fig. 3, as number of node is increased, averages of distance error are compared. Since SC-DC, applied divide and conquer method, uses only 30 nodes for positioning and SC-AC uses every node cooperatively, SC-DC has bigger average error than SC-AC.

In Fig. 4, as number of node is increased, variations of complexity are compared. Complexity is a very important factor when it is applied actually since complexity indicates actual total execution time of algorithm even though iteration speed indicates execution time too. As we see in Fig. 4, complexity is increased exponentially in SC-AC but it is increased linearly in extended SCOPS applied Divide and Conquer algorithm. Therefore, it is possible to predict execution time on increasing number of nodes when SC-DC is applied.

SCOPS is similar to WiCOPS in terms of stability and accuracy but SCOPS shows better results than WiCOPS in terms of performance and scalability. Design goal of SCOPS is verified through simulation as below.

Accuracy: In SCOPS, accuracy means that locations of original nodes are converged within expected error scope when performing positioning algorithm. As we see the simulation results, SCOPS guarantees accuracy by occurring errors within certain limits in every case.

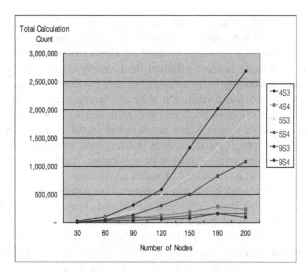

Fig. 4. Scalability and Complexity

Performance: In SCOPS, performance means time until finishing positioning within desired errors. SCOPS shows better performance than previous WiPS and WiCOPS.

Scalability: Positioning system should measure locations within desired time and desired error even under the environments of multiple nodes congested. Simulation results show that SCOPS can predict accuracy based on size of group and complexity is increased not exponentially but linearly even number of nodes is increased. It is assured that SCOPS has scalability in positioning locations for numerous nodes.

Even though accuracy becomes high if positioning is performed simultaneously for all nodes cooperatively, reducing time complexity is more important in order to apply practically. Since accuracy and time complexity have anti-relationship, it is desired to set proper size of group based on desired accuracy and time complexity when implements actually.

5 Conclusions

In this research, distance-based positioning system to measure locations of nodes is studied. This system uses only RSSI obtained from wireless telecommunication device equipped basically to every node, without using separate additional positioning purpose-only device, under wireless sensor network environments. Common goals of location positioning system are to measure exact location of node and to solve restraint of short telecommunication distance that is one of characteristics in wireless sensor network. In order to reach these goals, cooperative positioning system, using RSSI together from neighboring nodes as well as from beacon nodes that locations are already known, is set to a research object.

In order to develop scalable positioning system under wireless sensor network environments composed of numerous nodes, problems of WiPS and WiCOPS, one of existing cooperative positioning system, are analyzed and solutions are found as below. First, in cooperative positioning system, it analyzes and verifies that deciding value of convergence adjustment factor based on number of nodes which give effects to location change of node is more efficient than simply considering connectivity in terms of affection relationship between nodes during positioning. Second, In order to improve performance of positioning algorithm, convergence acceleration factor is used to reduce iteration count of nonlinear programming and speed of convergence is improved. When value of convergence acceleration factor is determined, it is more effective by analyzing progress of location convergence and assigning dynamically than by simply assigning certain constant heuristically. Third, under wireless sensor network environments, when locations of nodes are measured, errors are decreased as number of nodes is increased but it has problems that complexity is increased exponentially. In order to solve these problems, divide and conquer method dividing mass nodes into several groups is proposed and this is confirmed as effective.

Simulator used in this research implements Microsoft Visual Basic 6.0 and can be downloaded from http://selab.scnu.ac.kr/pub/ps/SCOPS and used. Results of simulation can be seen on screen and also be saved to file to analyze.

Acknowledgments. This work was supported in part by MKE & IITA (09-Infra, Industrial original technology development project).

References

1. Bahl, P., Padmanabhan, V.N.: Radar: An in-building RF-based User Location and Tracking System. In: Proceedings of the IEEE Infocom 2000, vol. 2, pp. 775–784 (2000)
2. Bulusu, N., Heidemann, J., Estrin, D.: GPS-less Low Cost Outdoor Localization For Very Small Devices. IEEE Personal Communications Magazine 7(5), 28–34 (2000)
3. Albowicz, J., Chen, A., Zhang, L.: Recursive Position Estimation in Sensor Networks. In: Proceedings of the IEEE Internation Conference on Network Protocols, pp. 35–41 (2001)
4. Savvides, A., Han, C.-C., Strivastava, M.B.: Dynamic Fine-Grained Localization in Ad-Hoc Networks of Sensors. In: MOBICOM 2001, pp. 166–179 (2001)
5. Kitasuka, T., Nakanishi, T., Fukuda, A.: Wireless LAN Based Indoor Positioning System WiPS and Its Simulation. In: Proceedings of the IEEE PACRIM 2003, vol. 1, pp. 272–275 (2003)
6. Son, C., Yoo, N., Kim, W.: Positioning System using Dynamic Location-convergence Adjustment Factor for Wireless LAN Infrastructures. In: Sixth IEEE International Conference on Computer and Information Technology (CIT 2006), p. 233 (2006)

One-to-One Embedding between Hyper Petersen and Petersen-Torus Networks

Jung-Hyun Seo[1,*], Moon-Suk Jang[1], EungKon Kim[1], Kyeong-Jin Ban[1], NamHoon Ryu[1], and HyeongOk Lee[2]

[1] Dept. Of Computer Eng., [2] Dept. Of Computer Edu.,
National Univ. of Sunchon,
Maegok 315, Sunchon, Jeonnam, South Korea
{jhseo,jang,kek,multiwave}@scnu.ac.kr, kmpi9560@hanmail.net,
oklee@scnu.ac.kr

Abstract. Once a designed network is embedded into a newly designed network, a developed algorithm in the designed network is reusable in a newly designed network. Petersen-Torus has been designed recently, and Hyper Petersen has already been designed as a well-known interconnection network. In this study, it was proven that Hyper Petersen network whose degree increases with the increased number of nodes can be embedded into a Petersen-Torus network having fixed degree. Hyper Petersen $HP_{\log_2 n^2+3}$ was embedded into Petersen-Torus $PT(n,n)$ with expansion 1, dilation 1.5n+2, and congestion 5n. The embedding algorithm was designed for expansion 1, and congestion and dilation are in proportion to $O(n)$ owing to the aspect of Hyper Petersen that the degree increases.

Keywords: Parallel Processing, Interconnection Network, Petersen-Torus, Hyper Petersen, Embedding.

1 Introduction

In parallel processing, a shared memory model is called a multiprocessor system whose processor uses common memory. The local memory model is called a multicomputer system whose each processor has local memory. If a communication link between processors for data exchange is fixed, it is called a static network, while if it is not fixed, it is called a dynamic network. In general, a network where a communication link between processors is fixed is called interconnection network. Interconnection network consists of a set of processors, local memory, and a communication link between processors for data transfer. An interconnection network for a multicomputer system is divided into a static network and a dynamic network. A static network is divided into the tree class, the mesh class, the hypercube class and the star graph class according to the composition of nodes and edges to compose the network. An interconnection network can be modeled in a graph $G=(V,E)$. Each processor P_i is

* This research was supported by MKE(The Ministry of Knowledge Economy), Korea, under the ITRC(Information Technology Research Center) support program supervised by the NIPA(National IT Industry Promotion Agency)" (NIPA-2009-C1090-0902-0001).

D. Ślęzak et al. (Eds.): GDC 2009, CCIS 63, pp. 133–139, 2009.
© Springer-Verlag Berlin Heidelberg 2009

an element of a node set V, and two processors P_i and P_j are connected by a communication links (P_i, P_j). If an interconnection network is modeled in a graph, a processor is mapped into a node and a communication link into an edge. The number of nodes adjacent to node P_i is defined as degree of the node.

Given a guest graph G and a host graph H, embedding of G into H is described by an ordered pair (Φ, Ψ), where Φ maps each node of G to a node of H and Ψ maps each edge (u, v) of G to a path of H from nodes $\Phi(u)$ to $\Phi(v)$(hereafter referred to as Ψ-path). *Dilation* of the edge (u, v) is length of the Ψ-path in H, and *dilation* of the embedding (Φ, Ψ) is the largest value among dilations for all edges of G. *Congestion* of the edge of H is Ψ-paths traversing an edge of H, and *congestion* of the embedding (Φ, Ψ) is the largest value among congestions for all edges of H. *Expansion* of the embedding (Φ, Ψ) is a ratio of the number of nodes of G to that of H. The measures to evaluate the embedding algorithm are *dilation*, *congestion* and *expansion*. The closer the values are to 1, the better the embedding algorithm is[1].

The d-dimensional Hyper Petersen having $10 \times 2^{d-3}$ nodes in various algorithms for parallel processing has a simple solution that it has time complexity $O(d)$. In terms of network scalability, since the mesh class adds and expands a few processors by linking the adjacent processor and the hypercube class adds the exactly same number of nodes and links each processor, it is readily scalable. Therefore it is meaningful that the hypercube class having a good parallel algorithm is embedded in the mesh class which can be commonly used by virtue of its high scalability[2,3]. As Torus has degree 4 and Hypercube has more degree with increased dimensions, when Hypercube(in excess of degree 4) above 5 dimensions is embedded into Torus, congestion and dilation gradually increase in excess of 1[3]. In study [4], 6-dimensional Hypercube was embedded into 8×8 mesh at dilation 11, congestion 2, and expansion 1. In study [2], 11-dimensional Hypercube was embedded into 32×64 mesh at dilation 32 and congestion 57, and smaller Hypercube and meshes were embedded. In these two studies, Hypercube of the limited size was embedded in mesh, and the embedding scale was constant. In study [3], the result was generalized without limitation to previous studies. The d-dimensional Hypercube was embedded into mesh having the same number of nodes at dilation 2^d-2 and expansion 1.

The paper is organized as follows. Section 2 introduces the Petersen-Torus network and the Hyper Petersen network. Section 3 proposes an embedding algorithm of Hyper Petersen into Petersen-Torus network, and finally conclusion is given.

2 Related Work

The Petersen-Torus $PT(m,n)(m,n{\geq}2)$ sets a Petersen Graph(Fig. 1(b)) as a basic module, arranges m(x axis)×n(y axis) modules on grid points, and connects them under edge definition. The Petersen-Torus network $PT(m,n)=(V_{pt}, E_{pt})$. The node definition of Petersen-Torus $PT(m,n)$ is

$$V_{pt}=\{(x,y,p),\ 0{\leq}x<m,\ 0{\leq}y<n,\ 0{\leq}p{\leq}9\}$$

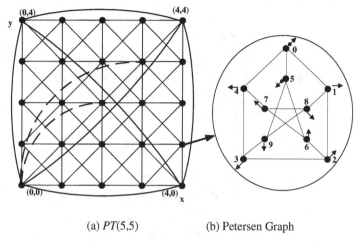

(a) $PT(5,5)$ (b) Petersen Graph

Fig. 1. Petersen-Torus $PT(5,5)$

The edge of $PT(m,n)$ is divided into internal edge and external edge. The edge connecting nodes belonging to the same module is called internal edge, and the edge of Petersen Graph is used as it is as internal edge. The edge connecting nodes in different modules is called external edge. Edges are defined in the following. The symbol '%' is remainder operator in the following equations. ① The longitudinal edge is $((x,y,6), (x,(y+1)\%n,9))$. ② The latitudinal edge is $((x,y,1), ((x+1)\%m,y,4))$. ③ The diagonal edge is $((x,y,2), ((x+1)\%m,(y+1)\%n,3))$. ④ The reverse diagonal edge is $((x,y,7), ((x-1+m)\%m,(y+1)\%n,8))$. ⑤ The diameter edge is $((x,y,0), ((x+\lfloor m/2\rfloor)\%m, (y+\lfloor n/2\rfloor)\%n,5))$. Edges are defined in[5].

The Hyper Petersen network is a Hypercube-like network and can be made by Cartesian Product of Petersen Graph and Hypercube. It is a regular graph where degree is same in all nodes. Also, it has high degree, high connectivity, and small diameter. j-dimension HP consists of $10\times2^{j-3}$ nodes and $5j\times2^{j-3}$ edges and is indicated in $HP_j=(V_{hp}, E_{hp})$. A set of peaks is composed of two tuples and defined as follows[6]:
$V_{hp}=\{[B(u),P(i)]|B(u)$ is j-3 binary bit string, $\{0\leq P(i)\leq9\}$.

Edge is divided into two:
Petersen-edge : In $([B(u),P(i)], [B(u),P(j)])$, $P(i)$ and $P(j)$ are linked in a Petersen graph.
Hypercube-edge : In $([B(u), P(i)], [B(v), P(i)])$, $B(u)$ and $B(v)$ are 1 bit different exactly.

HP_j is $Q_{j-3} \times P(j\geq3)$ and made by Cartesian product of Petersen Graph and j-3 dimensional Hypercube. That is, each node of Q_{j-3} Hypercube is replaced with a Petersen Graph. Fig. 2 shows 5-dimensional Hyper Petersen. The node address is a combination of $B(u)$ consisting of binary bit strings and $P(i)$ consisting of one-digit numbers. Petersen-edge is all indicated and to avoid complexity of the figure, Hypercube-edge is indicated only if $P(i)$ is 0, 3, and 8. Even if $P(i)$ is a number except 0, 3, and 8, edge exists between nodes where $B(u)$ is one bit different and $P(i)$ is same, as in the case of 0, 3, and 8. Hyper Petersen dimension is the number of bit strings for $B(u)$ + 3.

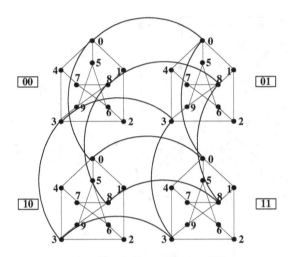

Fig. 2. Hyper Petersen HP_5

j-dimension Hyper Petersen has 1.25×2^j nodes, degree j, and diameter j-1. The nature of Hyper Petersen is very similar to that of Hypercube, and the number of nodes for Hyper Petersen is more than 1.25 times of Hypercube on condition that it has similar diameter and degree[6].

3 Embedding Hyper Petersen into Petersen-Torus

The basic embedding strategy is to map a Petersen Graph of HP into that of a PT basic module. Mapping the node address $B(u)$ of HP into the address of PT basic module (x,y). Ten nodes(Petersen Graph) having the same node address $B(u)$ among HP nodes are called a HP basic module.

Theorem 1. Hyper Petersen $HP_{log_2 n^2+3}$ is embedded into Petersen-Torus $PT(n,n)$ at expansion 1, dilation $1.5n+2$, and congestion $5n$ (n is a power of 2).

Proof: The number of nodes for Petersen-Torus $PT(n,n)$ and that for Hyper Petersen $HP_{log_2 n^2+3}$ is $10n^2$. Therefore expansion is 1. In $HP_{log_2 n^2+3}$ node $[B(u),P(k)]$, the bit in the place of i for $B(u)$ is set as $B(u)_i$. In $B(u)$, a combination of bits in the place of odd numbers by order from LSB is $xb(u)=B(u)_{log_2 n^2-1} \dots B(u)_{i+2}B(u)_iB(u)_{i-2} \dots B(u)_3B(u)_1$, and a combination of bits in the place of even numbers by order is $yb(u)=B(u)_{log_2 n^2} \dots B(u)_{i+3}B(u)_{i+1}B(u)_{i-1} \dots B(u)_4B(u)_2$($i$ is an odd number). The node $[B(u),P(k)]$ of $HP_{log_2 n^2+3}$ is mapped into the node $(xb(u)_{(10)}, yb(u)_{(10)}, P(k))$ of $PT(n,n)$.

Fig. 3 shows HP_7 and $PT(4,4)$. In the two graphs, one point is a basic module, and in mapping into a PT basic module from an HP basic module, the address of a Petersen Graph is mapped into the exactly same node. For example, xb of HP node [1001,5] is 01 and yb is 10, therefore it is mapped into the PT node (1,2,5).

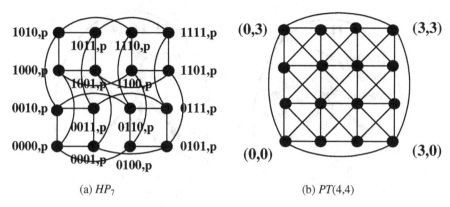

(a) HP_7 (b) $PT(4,4)$

Fig. 3. HP_7 embedding into $PT(4,4)$

HP edge is divided into Petersen-edge and Hypercube-edge. The edge ($[B(u),P(k)]$, $[B(v),P(k)]$) is Hypercube-edge having the same Petersen Graph address, while the edge ($[B(u),P(k)]$, $[B(u),P(o)]$) is Petersen-edge having the same Hypercube address. As Petersen-edge ($[B(u),P(k)],[B(u),P(o)]$) is mapped into (($xb(u)_{(10)},yb(u)_{(10)},P(k)$) and ($xb(u)_{(10)},yb(u)_{(10)},P(o)$), dilation is 1 and congestion is 1.

In Hypercube-edge ($[B(u),P(k)]$, $[B(v),P(k)]$) of HP, the HP node $[B(u),P(k)]$ is mapped into the PT node (($xb(u)_{(10)},yb(u)_{(10)},P(k)$) and the HP node $[B(v),P(k)]$ into the PT node($xb(v)_{(10)},yb(v)_{(10)},P(k)$)). $B(u)$ and $B(v)$ are exactly 1 bit different, and if the different bit is the bit in the place of an odd number from LSB, $xb(u)\neq xb(v)$ and $yb(u)=yb(v)$, while if the different bit is the bit in the place of an even number, $xb(u)=xb(v)$ and $yb(u)\neq yb(v)$. The bit in the place of t for $xb(u)$ is assumed as $xb(u)_t$, and the bit in the place of t for $yb(u)$ is assumed as $yb(u)_t(1\leq t\leq\log_2 n^2/2)$. If $xb(u)\neq xb(v)_t$ there is difference of 2^{t-1} between $xb(u)_{(10)}$ and $xb(v)_{(10)}$. When t is the largest value $\log_2(n/2)$, it is $n/2$, thus length of the external path for (($xb(u)_{(10)},yb(u)_{(10)},P(k)$), ($xb(v)_{(10)}',yb(v)_{(10)}',P(k)$)) is up to $n/2$ and that of the internal path is $(n/2+1)\times 2$. The sum of two path lengths is $1.5n+2$, and the value is dilation. The same is also applied to $yb(u)\neq yb(v)_t$.

In two PT nodes ($xb(u)_{(10)},yb(u)_{(10)},P(k)$) and ($xb(v)_{(10)},yb(v)_{(10)},P(k)$), two nodes u and v of the HP edge (u, v) are mapped. If $xb(u)\neq xb(v)_t$ two nodes are at a distance of $n/2$ in the x axis when y value is in the same basic module and at the farthest distance. Both the start basic module of the path and the $(n/2)-1$ middle passing basic module use the same external edge $((x,y,1), (x+1,y,4))$. If $yb(u)\neq yb(v)_t$ an external edge $((x,y,6), (x,y+1,9))$ is used. At this edge, congestion is $n/2\times 10$. Therefore embedding into dilation $1.5n+2$ and congestion $5n+2$ is possible.   □

For example, at the edges $[0000,4]$ and $[0100,4]$ of Fig. 4, the node $[0000,4]$ is mapped into $(0,0,4)$ and the node $[0100,4]$ into node $(2,0,4)$. The path between node $(0,0,4)$ and node$(2,0,4)$ is as follows: $(0,0,4)$, $(0,0,0)$, $(0,0,1)$, $(1,0,4)$, $(1,0,0)$, $(1,0,1)$.

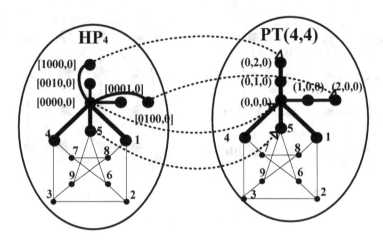

Fig. 4. HP_7 embedded into $PT(4,4)$

(2,0,1), (2,0,0), (2,0,4). The path has two external edges and 3×2 internal edges and the length is 8.

Theorem 2. Hyper Petersen $HP_{log_2 2n^2+3}$ is embedded into Petersen-Torus $PT(2n,n)$ at expansion 1, dilation $3n+2$, and congestion $10n+2$ (n is a power of 2).

Proof: The number of nodes for Petersen-Torus $PT(2n,n)$ and that for Hyper Petersen $HP_{log_2 2n^2+3}$ is $20n^2$. Therefore expansion is 1. Node mapping is as demonstrated in Theorem 1. This embedding just indicates that HP_j is made by Cartesian product of a Q_{j-3} graph and a Petersen Graph on condition that j-3 is an odd number, and in a PT graph, the x axis is exactly twice greater than the y axis. This embedding is same as that of $PT(2n,2n)$ into $HP_{log_2 4n^2+3}$. Length of the external path for $((xb(u)_{(10)},yb(u)_{(10)},p)$ and $(xb(v)_{(10)}',yb(v)_{(10)}',p))$ is up to n. Length of the internal path is $(n+1)×2$ and maximum length of the path is $3n+2$, thus it is embedded at dilation $3n+2$. As 10 nodes of a Petersen Graph having the edge $([B(u),P(k)], [B(v),P(k)])$ use the same external path, congestion at external path is $10n$. Congestion at the last node of the path is 2, therefore it is embedded at congestion $10n+2$. Thus embedding at dilation $3n+2$ and congestion $10n+2$ is possible.   □

4 Conclusion

Embedding between interconnection networks is meaningful in that the designed parallel algorithm is reusable. In this study, a Hyper Petersen network designed based on a Petersen Graph was embedded into a PT network. Hyper Petersen $HP_{log_2 n^2+3}$ was embedded into $PT(n,n)$ at expansion 1, dilation $1.5n+2$, and congestion $5n$. This result indicates that the algorithm designed in Hyper Petersen is effectively reusable in PT. Reversely, it is worth studying embedding of a PT network into other networks in order to use the algorithm developed in a PT network in another network.

References

1. Bettayeb, S., Cong, B., Girou, M., Sudborough, I.H.: Embedding Star Networks into Hypercubes. IEEE trans. comput. 45(2), 186–194 (1996)
2. Stricker, T.M.: Supporting the hypercube programming model on mesh architectures. In: Proc. of the fourth annual ACM symposium on Parallel algorithms and architectures, pp. 148–157 (1992)
3. Gonzalez, A., Garcia, V., Cerio, L.D.: Excuting Algorithm with Hypercube Topology on Torus Multicomputers. IEEE Transactions on Parallel and Distributed Systems 6(8), 803–814 (1995)
4. Matic, S.: Emulation of Hypercube Architecture on Nearest-Neighbor Mesh-Connected Prcessing Elements. IEEE Transaction on computer 39, 698–700 (1990)
5. Seo, J.H., Lee, H.O., Jang, M.S.: Petersen-Torus Networks for Multicomputer Systems. In: Proc. int'l Conf. of NCM 2008, September 2008, vol. 1, pp. 567–571 (2008)
6. Das, S.K., Banerjee, A.K.: Hyper Petersen network: Yet another hypercube-like topology. In: Proc. of the 4th Symp., on the Frontiers of Massively Parallel Computation, McLean, Virginia, USA, October 1992, pp. 270–277 (1992)

A Dynamic Mobile Grid System for 4G Networks

Manel Abdelkader and Mohamed Hamdi Noureddine Boudriga

Communication Networks and Security Research Lab., University of Carthage,
Tunisia
manel.abdelkader@gmail.com, mmh@supcom.rnu.tn, boudriga@csc.lsu.edu

Abstract. Future networks specially International Mobile Telecommu-
nications-advanced, better known as 4G, will come up with a panoply of
services so as to provide a comprehensive and secure IP-based solution
where facilities such as voice, data and stremed multimedia will be provided to users anywhere at anytime. This solution will also provide much
higher data rates compared to previous generations. More importantly,
the 4G architecture will strongly promote ubiquitous computing, which
involves many computational devices and systems simultaneously. Such
devices and systems can even be unaware that they are contributing to
computational process.

Grid systems have been known in traditional networks as an efficient
solution to provide distributed services. However, their applicability to
4G networks is not straightforward because of the intrinsic features of
serveral network categories. In this paper, we propose a new Grid architecture suitable with the characteristics of 4G networks. A particular
emphasis will be put on the provision of ubiquitous computational services in and across ad hoc environments. We define a new relational
model enabling Grid service composing.

1   Introduction

Mobile networks are witnessing a prominent development. They are changing
from being simple access means to value added service providers. In fact, considering the growing mobile population and the induced raw and unexploited
resources, important applications and services could be defined based on the infrastructure provided by mobile networks. The advent of 4G networks will prob-
ably promote the development of more sophisticated services. The architecture
of these networks, mainly their cooperative nature, will allow the implementation of ubiquitous computational frameworks. In fact, 4G networks build bridges
between traditionally heterogeneous networks (e.g., WLAN, UMTS, WSN) in a
manner that the shortcuts of a network are overcame by the strengthes of other
networks. For instance, the short range characterizing ad hoc networks can be
extended using mobile backbones (possibly constituted by cellular segments).
This allows taking benefit of the high transmission rates available through ad
hoc networks over long ranges.

Grid [1] is a distributed system composed of various, heterogeneous, autonomous and distributed resources such as processes, computing applications,

D. Ślęzak et al. (Eds.): GDC 2009, CCIS 63, pp. 140–147, 2009.

storage systems, network resources, protocols and services. Grid works on unifying and exploiting these resources to compose and conduct complex services in a seamless and transparent way for its users. Thus, Grid is responsible for identifying the available resources, ensuring their interworking and scheduling, and guaranteeing their security and accounting. To provide a service, Grid defines the composing subservices and tasks, assigns the latter to the suitable and available resources, monitors service and subservices progress, retrieves elementary outputs and composes the final service outputs. Hence, Grid systems would bring important contributions in providing pervasive services in 4G networks. However, their application to such networks is not straightforward, mainly because of the heterogeneity of resource distribution over the subnetworks and the frequent topology changes.

Particularly, ad hoc networks are known for their limited local resources, their changing topology and their operational limitations [2]. In spite of these restrictive constraints, ad hoc networks are increasingly needed for specific missions accomplishment or value added services provision. Indeed, they bring important provisions for different domains where it is difficult or impractical to set up an infrastructure-based network. An increasing demand is announced in various fields such as geography, military, health and communication [3, 4]. To respond to these requirements, mobile ad hoc networks should introduce new cooperation models ensuring nodes collaboration and resources sharing in dynamic, efficient and secure way. Grid presents an interesting solution for these networks.

Considering the aforementioned features of ad hoc networks, new challenges face the Grid system. While a conventional Grid system is based on static predefined resources with pre-established security profiles and accounting models, a Grid system for ad hoc networks should take into account resources variation and nodes dynamic behavior before and during service provision. In fact, since mobile nodes vary continuously, Grid system can not rely on their permanent presence nor on their long-term availability and provision of the required and agreed QoS. This integration becomes more challenging when the key management functions of the Grid are ensured by mobile ad hoc nodes.

Different works focused on the definition and the integration of Grid system models in mobile networks [3, 5, 6, 7, 8, 9, 11]. Two main approaches were defined. In the first, mobiles are defined as Grid users or resources. Thus, they are enabled to access fixed Grid system and exploit the pre-defined services [9] or used as mobile resources consolidating the fixed Grid system through performing submitted tasks [6, 7, 8]. For the second approach, all Grid system management functions are ensured by mobile ad hoc networks [3, 11]. The proposed solutions presented conceptual models of mobile Grid computing for resource aggregation and collaborative problem solving. Nevertheless, problems related to changing topology, dynamic scheduling, mobility, disconnection, QoS variation, security and accounting are not yet resolved [3].

In this work, we present solutions for dynamic service composition and assignment to mobile service nd resource providers. Our work presents a mathematical formalism is given to cope with the assignment of compound services to multiple providers. We rely on relational algebra to build a job assignment policy that takes into account the individual and the network resources.

The remaining of the paper is organized as follow. Section 2 presents the proposed service composition model for Grid systems in 4G networks. The job assignment policy is then introduced in section 3. In section 4 a potential extension is discussed. Section 5 concludes the paper.

2   Service Composition for Grid Systems in 4G Networks

In this section, we develop a service composition policy that adapts to the GRID-SAN architecture introduced in [10]. It allows the implementation of efficient job allocation policies by Grid provider nodes (GPNs). Our main concerns are:

- The service execution time should fulfill the requirements set by the requestor.
- The job(s) allocated to a SP should complies(y) with its energy and storage requirements.
- The radio channels that may be used by the allocated job must be available at the SP node.

In the following, we develop a set of service decomposition rules based on relational algebra. The associated assignment policy is discussed in the following section.

To model a situation where a Grid service is provided throughout a 4G mobile system, we consider a specification-based approach where the GPN is assumed to be able to build an abstract specification of the service. The *GPN* is then in charge of performing the following tasks:

1. The specification of the service is rewritten into a compound expression where multiple operators are used to express the interactions between the elementary specifications.
2. The requirements of the elementary services are identified and independence between the elementary specifications is enforced.
3. The elementary services are allocated to the available SPs in a way that the aforementioned constraints are respected.

We use relational specifications to express the abstract behaviour of a service S. Binary relations have been extensively used in the literature to capture the properties of software programs [12]. In fact, a specification can be represented by two states s and s', where s is the input state and s' is the output state. From the mathematical point of view, these states are characterized by a set of free unprimed variables, denoted by w, and a set of free primed variables, denoted by w'.

A binary relation R is therefore expressed as follows:

$$R = \{(s, s')|p[w \setminus s, w' \setminus s']\}, \tag{1}$$

where $p[.,.]$ is a predicate on the variables sets w and w'.

Informally speaking, a binary specification is interpreted as follows: if a computation starts in a state s for which the predicate p holds (i.e., there exists a state s' such that $p[w \setminus s, w' \setminus s'])$, then it must terminate in a state s' such that $p[w \setminus s, w' \setminus s']$ holds. If a computation starts in a state for which the predicate is not defined, then any result is acceptable (including non-termination).

One major advantage of using relational specifications is the support of composition operators defining relational algebras. In our context, specifications are mainly used to express service requirements. Therefore, the most relevant operators are given below.

A relation R on a set S is a subset of the Cartesian product $S \times S$. In other terms, a relation on S is a set of pairs of S. The basic operations on relations that will be used in the following are given in the following (R, R_1, and R_2 are relations on S):

- Intersection: $R_1 \cap R_2 = \{(s, s') \in S^2 | (s, s') \in R_1 \wedge (s, s') \in R_2\}$,
- Union: $R_1 \cup R_2 = \{(s, s') \in S^2 | (s, s') \in R_1 \vee (s, s') \in R_2\}$,
- Composition: $R_1 \circ R_2 = \{(s, s') \in S^2 | \exists z \in S : (s, z) \in R_1 \wedge (z, s') \in R_2\}$.

Moreover, several special relations should be highlighted at this level. Particularly, the universal relation $U = S \times S$, the empty set $\emptyset = \overline{U}$, and the identity relation $I = \{(s, s) \mid s \in S\}$ have a special interest as it will be shown below.

Given a relation R on S and an element $x \in S$, the image set of s by R is $s.R = \{y | (x, y) \in R\}$. In addition, a *domain* and an *image*, denoted respectively $dom(R)$ and $rng(R)$, will be associated to every relation R. These sets are defined as follows: $dom(R) = \{s \in S | \exists s' \in S : sRs'\}$, and $rng(R) = \{s \in S | \exists s' \in S : s'Rs\}$.

The first task to be performed by a GPN is to decompose the specification of a service S into a compound expression where elementary services, denoted by $S_1, .., S_n$, are involved. Since these elementary services can be potentially assigned to different service providers SPs, independence is a crucial need since it ensures that two distinct service providers SPs can execute two distinct services without mutually needing the outputs of each others.

Hereinafter, the specification of a service S is denoted by $[S]$. In the literature, the problem of computing the relational specification of a software program has been well-discussed. The interested reader would refer to [12] for a detailed description of such techniques. For the sake of parsimony, we only give the basic rules used to express a service using the operators cited above. Three rules are typically used:

1. **Sequence rule:**
   $[B_1] = R_1 \wedge [B_2] = R_2 \Rightarrow [B_1; B_2] = R_1 \circ R_2$.
2. **Conditional rule: (if/else statement)**
   $[B_1] = R_1 \wedge [B_2] = R_2 \Rightarrow [\text{if } c \text{ then } B_1 \text{ else } B_2] = R_1 \circ_{S \setminus \{c\}|} R_2$, where $_{X|}R = \{(s, s') \in R : x \in X\}$.
3. **Iteration rule:**
   $[B] = R \Rightarrow [\text{while } t \text{ do} B] \sqsupseteq (U \circ R) \circ I(\neg c)$, where $\sqsupseteq$ denotes the refinement operator defined in [8].

It is noteworthy that the iteration rule can be used to find an approximation for the relational specification of a loop-structured statement.

Unfortunately, the use of the aforementioned rules does not guarantee independence between the elementary specifications. Therefore, we develop a set of new operators that respect this condition.

Definition 1. *(Independent Operators) Let R_1 and R_2 be two relations expressed by:*

$$R_1 = \{(s, s')|p[w_1 \setminus s, w_1' \setminus s']\}$$
$$R_2 = \{(s, s')|p[w_2 \setminus s, w_2' \setminus s']\}$$

We introduce three operators, denoted by $\diamond, \sqcap, \sqcup$, representing independent composition, independent intersection, and independent union; respectively. These operators are defined as follows:

1. *Independent composition:* $R_1 \diamond R_2 = \{(s, s')|(s, s') \in R_1 \circ R_2 \wedge w_1' \notin w_2\}$,
2. *Independent intersection:* $R_1 \sqcap R_2 = \{(s, s')|(s, s') \in R_1 \cap R_2 \wedge w_1' \cap w_2 = \emptyset\}$,
3. *Independent union:* $R_1 \sqcup R_2 = \{(s, s')|(s, s') \in R_1 \cup R_2 \wedge w_1' \cap w_2 = \emptyset\}$.

To achieve a good granularity, the elementary specifications emanating from the decomposition should be as 'small' as possible. Therefore, we introduce the minimality concept defined in the following.

Definition 2. *(Minimal independent decomposition) Let S be a service for which an independent decomposition is expressed by:*

$$[S] = [S_1] \star_1 [S_2] ... \star_{n-1} [S_n],$$

where $\star_i \in \{\diamond, \sqcap, \sqcup\}$ for every $i \in \{1, .., n-1\}$.

This decomposition is said to be minimal if, and only if, for every $j \in \{1, .., n-1\}$, there is no specifications S_j^1 and S_j^2 such that S_j can be decomposed into $S_j^1 \star S_j^2$, where $\star \in \{\diamond, \sqcap, \sqcup\}$.

In the following, we show how minimal independent decompositions can be used for service assignment.

3   Service Assignment Policy for 4G Networks

Upon the reception of the different service providers responses, the GPN proceeds to service allocation according to a specific policy. The latter defines a set of rules allowing elementary services allocation according to user requirements and service provider capacities. Indeed, an elementary service S_i is allocated to a service provider SP_i if, and only if, the SP_i offored resources (built in and radio) could respond to the GPN and the user requirements. We distinguish four parameters used by the GPN for allocation decision making, which are service execution time, storage capacity, power resources, and radio resources.

These parameters are given in the following:

- τ is the function defining the service execution time provided by a service provider SP_i. τ is defined as:

$$\tau : \Sigma \times \{SP_i\} \to \quad \mathbb{R}_+^*$$
$$([S],\, SP_i) \mapsto \tau([S],\, SP_i)$$

where Σ is the set of service specification and $\{SP_i\}$ is the set of service providers offoring their resources to GPN.

- σ the function defining the storage space offored for service provision at an instant t. σ is defined as:

$$\sigma : \Sigma \times \mathbb{R}_+^* \to \quad \mathbb{R}_+^*$$
$$([S],\, t) \mapsto \sigma([S],\, t).$$

- π the function defining the power resources needed to perform a set of elementary services $[S]$ by SP_i at instant t.

$$\pi : \Sigma \times \{SP_i\} \times \mathbb{R}_+^* \to \quad \mathbb{R}_+^*$$
$$([S],\, SP_i, t) \mapsto \pi([S],\, SP_i, t).$$

- γ the function defining the radio channels needed to support a set of elementary service $[S]$ at a service provider SP_j at instant t.

$$\gamma : \Sigma \times \{SP_i\} \times \mathbb{R}_+^* \to \quad \mathbb{R}_+^*$$
$$([S],\, SP_i, t) \mapsto \gamma([S],\, SP_i, t)$$

Given a service S that can be decomposed into a set of elementary services is denoted by $[S] = [S_1] \star_1 [S_2] \ldots \star_{n-1} [S_n]$, the assignment of a set of the elementary services $S_1, \ldots, S_n$ to a service provider among $\{SP_j\}$ is governed by the assignment policy which defines a set of assignmant rules.

Let Φ be the assignment function defined as:

$$\Phi : \{S_i\} \to \quad \{SP_j\}$$
$$S_i \mapsto SP_j = \Phi(S_i)$$

where $\{S_i\}$ is the set of (elementary and compound) services.

Φ is used to define the assignment policy using the following rules:

Rule 1: A service S is assigned to $\{SP_i\}$ if $sup_i(\tau([S_i],\, \Phi(S_i)) < \tau_{max}$, where τ_{max} is determined from user requirements.

Rule 2: The average storage capacity required for service execution is less than the storage capacity offored by the service providers $\forall i \in \{1, \ldots, n\}, \sigma([S_i],\, t_0, t_1) < \sigma_c(\Phi(S_i)),\, t_0,\, t_0 + \sigma([S_i]_i,\, \Phi(S_i))$, where

$$\sigma_c : \Sigma \times \mathbb{R}_+^* \times \mathbb{R}_+^* \to \quad \mathbb{R}_+^*$$
$$([S],\, t_0, t_1) \mapsto \sigma([S],\, t_0, t_1)$$

is the average storage capacity over the execution interval $[t_0, t_1]$.

Rule 3: The initial power level available at the service provider is higher than the power required for service execution:$\pi(SP_i, t_0) - \pi(S_i, SP_i) > 0$.

Rule 4: The required radio channels required by the service are less than the available channels at instant t_0, $\Gamma(S_i, SP_i) \leq \Gamma_0(SP_i, t_0)$.

4   Towards a Service Continuity Model

Due to mobility and energy depletion, Grid topology may change more or less frequently during service provision and even before accomplishing assigned services. This obviously may have strong incidence on the assignment policy. A *GPN* should update the assignment policy accordingly. Two situations may be faced:

1. A *SP* node suddenly leaves the topology without providing an intermediate output for the incomplete service execution. In this case, the *GPN* has no alternative than re-assigning the entire job to another *SP*.
2. A *SP* node provides an intermediate output before leaving the topology and uses a special signalling message to inform the *GPN*. The latter assigns the residual job to another *SP*. This residual job is computed by solving the relational equation (in X):

$$\widetilde{[S]} \circ X = [S],$$

where $\widetilde{S}$ is the portion of the service executed by the *SP* and S is the initially assigned service. This equation has had a strong mathematical interest and has been solved in [13] where it has been shown that the least-defined solution can be expressed using the conjugate kernel operator.

5   Conclusion

In this work, we have proposed a service composition model for mobile Grid systems in 4G networks. By integrating Grid functionalities on ad-hoc network, we dynamically exploit ad hoc resources to offer available Grid services. Indeed, a job assignment policy has been proposed on the basis of the composition model. Some insights raised by the mobile topology have been discussed.

References

[1] Foster, I., Kesselman, C., Tuecke, S.: The Anatomy of the Grid, Enabling Scalable Virtual Organizations. International Journal of High Performance Computing Applications 15(3) (2001)

[2] Ramanathan, R., Redi, J.: A Brief Overview of ad hoc Networks: Challenges and Directions. IEEE Communications Magazine 40(5) (2002)

[3] Li, H., Sun, L., Ifeachor, E.C.: Challenges of Mobile ad-hoc Grids and their Applications in e-Healthcare. In: 2nd Int. Conf. on Computational Intelligence in Medicine and Healthcare (CIMED 2005), Portugal (2005)

[4] Waldburger, M., Stiller, B.: Toward the Mobile Grid: Service Provisioning in a Mobile Dynamic Virtual Organization. In: 4th ACS/IEEE Int. Conf. on Computer Systems and Applications (AICCSA 2006), UAE (2006)

[5] Litke, A., Skoutas, D., Varvarigou, T.: Changes and Challenges of Resource Management in a Mobile Grid Environment

[6] Katsaros, K., Polyzos, G.C.: Optimizing operation of a hierarchical campus-wide mobile Grid. In: Proc. of PIMRC 2007, Greece (2007)

[7] Katsaros, K., Polyzos, G.C.: Towards the Realization of a Mobile Grid. In: CoNEXT 2007, USA (December 2007)

[8] Akogrimo Consortium: Access to Knowledge through the Grid in a Mobile World; European FP6-IST Project (2007), http://www.mobilegrids.org

[9] Park, S.-M., Ko, Y.-B., Kim, J.-H.: Disconnected Operation Service in Mobile Grid Computing

[10] Abdelkader, M., Maalaoui, M.S., Boudriga, N.: GRIDSAN: an Available Dynamic Grid System for Ad hoc Networks. In: 3rd international workshop on Use of P2P, Grid and agents for the development of content networks table of contents (UPGRADE-CN08), jointly held with the ACM/IEEE International Symposium on High Performance Distributed Computing (HPDC), Boston, MA, USA (June 2008)

[11] Marinescu, D.C., Marinescu, G.M., Ji, Y., Bölöni, L., Siegel, H.J.: Ad hoc Grids: Communication and computing in a power constrained environment. In: Workshop on Energy-Efficient Wireless Communications and Networks (EWCN), Phoenix, USA (2003)

[12] Frappier, M., Mili, A., Desharnais, J.: A Relational Calculus for Program Construction by Parts. Sci. Comput. Program. 26(1-3), 237–254 (1996)

[13] Hamdi, M., Boudriga, N.: Towards a Relational Calculus for Security Library Management. In: GLOBECOM 2006, USA (2006)

Authorization Framework for Resource Sharing in Grid Environments

Jing Jin[1] and Gail-Joon Ahn[2]

[1] University of North Carolina at Charlotte
jjin@uncc.edu
[2] Arizona State University
gahn@asu.edu

Abstract. Grid data sharing services provide a unified platform for dynamic discovery, access and sharing of distributed data in Grid environments. A common authorization system is needed to provide access control for both Grid data sharing services as well as the data resources that are being shared through these services, accommodating different security requirements from the service providers and the data providers. In this paper, we present a flexible policy-driven authorization system, called RamarsAuthZ, for secure data sharing services in Grid environments. RamarsAuthZ adopts a flexible role-based approach with trust-aware feature to advocate originator control and provide unified access control both at the service level and at the data level.

1 Introduction

Data and resources in Grid environments are highly diverse in locations, types, structures, ownerships, naming conventions and access capabilities. The emergence of Grid data sharing services, such as the Globus Data Replication Service (DRS) [1], introduces a unified platform for data discovery, access and sharing transcending institutional boundaries. However, the data sharing facility provided to Grid clients requires more advanced access control mechanisms to accommodate various challenges ranging from the authorization model to the system architecture and deployment.

Firstly, Grid systems are usually composed of a number of dynamic and autonomous domains involving a large number of distributed users. An effective and manageable authorization scheme is necessary for the resource owners to control access and sharing of their resources. Attribute-based access control (ABAC), which makes access decisions relying on attributes of requesters and resources, has been widely adopted as a scalable and flexible authorization solution for highly distributed Grid environments [2]. In an attribute-based authorization system, the entity that manages user attributes is referred to as an Identity Provider (IdP). A user's attributes are normally collected by multiple IdPs in Grid environments. For example, a user is associated with a "home institution" which typically manages his employment status and affiliation attributes, while another IdP is associated with a Grid Virtual Organization (VO) that maintains attributes such as membership and role information within multiple domains. The authorization systems that

D. Ślęzak et al. (Eds.): GDC 2009, CCIS 63, pp. 148–155, 2009.

support ABAC in Grid environments eventually need to be seamlessly integrated with all related IdPs and delivers users' attributes in a secure and trusted manner. Secondly, from the system architecture and deployment perspectives, there are a number of dimensions to be considered for an attribute-based authorization system. In terms of the attribute collection process, the "push" strategy requires the clients to obtain and push their attributes to the Grid service at the initial request. The "pull" strategy, on the other hand, does not require the clients to submit any attribute. Instead, the authorization system is responsible for acquiring attributes from the client's IdPs. While the clients have more options to select the attributes being released for authorization in the "push" mode, the "pull" mode simplifies the overall interception by the clients. It is impossible to determine which mode is more suitable for dynamic Grid environments. However, it is highly desirable for authorization systems be flexible enough to cope with both options. In terms of system deployment, the reliance on statically configured modules to render an authorization decision such as policy and attribute management should be minimized, as the authorization systems may serve for various Grid services running within the infrastructure. Finally, the data resources being shared through the Grid data sharing service normally belong to different institutions. These institutions, as the owners of the data resources, should directly participate in defining authorization policies for their data sets, and their authorizations need to be efficiently conveyed and effectively enforced within the Grid data sharing service. Meanwhile, the access and invocation of Grid data sharing service itself apparently need to be well protected to accommodate security requirements of its service provider. Therefore, it is required for authorization systems to be flexible enough to synthesize both service level and data level controls accommodating security policies from different stakeholders such as the data resource providers and the service providers.

There are continuous attempts to develop a common attribute-based authorization framework for Grids. Shibboleth [3] is an attribute authority service developed by the Internet2 community. A Shibboleth IdP asserts attributes about a user's home institution, and the relying parties can make access decisions based on these attributes. In VOMS [4], every Grid VO manages its own members, and a Grid user can access the resources by obtaining and presenting a credential that contains his VO membership to the resource. In [5], Grimm et al. proposed a "push" mode authorization system where Grid users are able to collect attributes both from his home institution as maintained in Shibboleth IdP and the Grid VO as maintained in VOMS, so that authorization decisions can be made based on the attributes from both sources. The Akenti system [6] represents the authorization policies for a resource as a set of certificates digitally signed by multiple distributed stakeholders. These certificates express the attributes a user must have in order to get specific rights to a resource. Akenti allows the certificates to be stored in distributed remote repositories and provides mechanisms based on the "pull" architecture to ensure that all applicable usage conditions are combined when making an access control decision. PERMIS [7] leverages the role-based access control and it has been recently integrated with Shibboleth as a "pull" mode system to retrieve the role attribute of a user. These authorization systems, however, rely on static configurations of their own policies and attribute providers, and cannot support dynamic policies and attribute discoveries to accommodate the above-mentioned requirements. In this paper, we present a flexible policy-driven authorization system, called RamarsAuthZ, for secure data sharing services in Grid environments. RamarsAuthZ adopts a flexible role-based approach with trust-aware feature to advocate originator control, delegation and dissemination control. A case study based on Globus DRS service is presented to provide effective access control both at the service level and at the data level. The rest of this paper is organized as follows. In Section 2, we introduce our proposed authorization framework and discuss the integrated RamarsAuthZ system design. Section 3 describes the performance evaluation of our RamarsAuthZ system. We conclude our paper with future research directions in Section 4.

2   Injecting Ramars Framework to Grid Environments

Role-based Access Management for Ad-hoc Resource Sharing framework (RAMARS) has been proposed as a policy-driven role-based access management solution for resource sharing in ad-hoc collaborative environments [8,9]. In RAMARS, the owner of the resource, also called an *originator*, has the ultimate authority over the resource that is being shared within the collaboration. An originator does not rely on any established security services to maintain membership and privileges. Instead, the originator defines its own sharing control domain by specifying a collection of collaborator roles and delegating fine-grained data sharing capabilities to these roles. Remote users are dynamically included in the originator's sharing control domain and authorized with certain access privileges by being assigned to the collaborator roles. Unlike the traditional RBAC that users are identified and assigned based on their identities, RAMARS introduces another layer of abstraction, where users are assigned to roles based on their attributes. In particular, an originator defines a set of attributes that a user must possess for the user to be assigned to a particular collaborator role. Remote users should present credentials to claim the possession of required attributes, yet it is up to the originator's discretion to validate and determine the trustworthiness of these credentials, thereafter to decide whether the claimants of certain attributes can be accepted for the role assignment. As there is no centralized trust base available in RAMARS, the delegation of authority is considered as an important mechanism for an originator to manage the degree of trust with different attribute authorities. For instance, an originator may place a higher level of trust for the "citizenship" attribute when the user presents his passport issued by US Department of State rather than a driver's license issued by a local DMV office.

As a policy-driven approach, RAMARS introduces a collection of policy components using standard XACML policy language [10] to realize the proposed authorization scheme. The policy set consists of the following components.

- Role-based Originator Authorization policy set (ROA) maintains the core authorization and trust management policies for an originator to govern

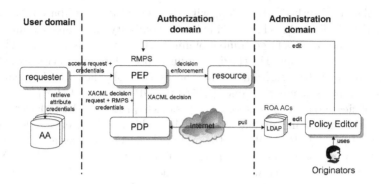

Fig. 1. RAMARS System Architecture

its control domain and delegate data sharing capabilities. The policy set contains the following subpolicies:

- Role Policy Set (RPS) defines a set of collaborator roles within an originator's control domain.
- Capability Policy Set (CPS) specifies the sharing capabilities assigned to each collaborator role.
- Role Assignment Policy Set (RAPS) defines the required attributes for a remote user to be assigned to a certain collaborator role.
- Trust Assessment Policy (TAP) defines internal policies to evaluate the trustworthiness of a user's attributes.

- Root Meta Policy Set (RMPS) is a light-weight top-level policy for an originator to declare the ownership of the data resource and specify the location of its ROA policy set. This enables the distributed policy deployment in RAMARS system as the authorization systems could dynamically locate and retrieve the ROA policies by utilizing the RMPS.

RAMARS system is designed to be deployed in distributed collaborative environments without assuming any centralized policy store. Different originators can edit and maintain their own ROA policies in their local administrative domains. The root RMPS for each respective data resource, however, should always be associated with the data resource for RAMARS system to locate its originator's ROA policies. Upon receiving a user's access request, RAMARS PEP invokes the PDP with a formulated XACML access decision request along with the root RMPS and the user's supportive credentials. RAMARS PDP then dynamically retrieves ROA policies from the originator's policy store based on the location reference specified in RMPS. The requester's credentials are evaluated against the originator's TAP policies where trusted attributes are derived. These trusted attributes are evaluated against RAPS policy to determine the user's roles. The access decision (e.g., *Permit* or *Deny*) is then determined based on the user's role. This access decision is sent back to PEP as an XACML response for decision enforcement. Figure 1 illustrates the architecture of RAMARS system.

The role-based authorization along with the trusted attribute-based role assignment method in RAMARS has provided great flexibility and manageability for an originator to authorize a large number of unknown users across domains. This feature could easily be adopted by the data resource providers and service providers in Grid environments to specify fine-grained access control policies. By implementing the unified policy scheme, the same RAMARS PDP engine could be used to evaluate the policies and make access control decisions to protect both the data resources and the Grid services in a unified manner. Meanwhile, as the user's credentials are pushed to the RAMARS PDP and the originator's ROA policies are dynamically pulled at runtime based on RMPS policy, a light-weight and portable RAMARS PDP could be implemented without having them configured with any centralized policy and credential stores to render an access decision. This increases the flexibility for RAMARS PDP to be coupled with existing Grid services (or loosely attached to the Grid infrastructure for authorization purposes).

2.1   Integrated RamarsAuthZ System

Figure 2 illustrates the system architecture for the integrated RamarsAuthZ system. Inside the Globus Container, a RAMARS Adaptor is introduced for the Grid service (e.g., DRS service) to communicate with the RamarsAuthZ service, which is essentially based on RAMARS PDP. The RamarsAuthZ service can be called out by RAMARS Adaptor through two mechanisms: a localized function call by API or a remote service invocation by standard OGSI SAML messages [11]. In terms of attribute acquisition, both "push" and "pull" modes are supported. A Grid client can retrieve his attribute assertions from various IdPs and "push" these assertions to the Grid service. Alternatively, the Grid client can embed the metadata information about his preferred IdPs in the credential so that RamarsAuthZ is able to dynamically locate and retrieve authorization attributes based on the metadata. We call this newly introduced credential with specialized extensions as a RamarsAuthZ proxy certificate [12]. By including these information in the legitimate extension fields of X.509 certificate, the RamarsAuthZ proxy certificate can be accepted and verified by the existing Grid GSI authentication module [13] without requiring any further changes. Since a proxy certificate is a self-issued certificate by the Grid user, all embedded attribute assertions and/or IdP's metadata must be signed by the issuing IdP and the metadata distributor, respectively. Any unsigned attribute assertions and IdP metadata without proper integrity protection are discarded and cannot be used by RamarsAuthZ for making authorization decisions.

The overall authorization flow for DRS service works as follows: the service provider of DRS first specifies and stores the ROA authorization policies in his administrative domain. The DRS service maintains the location reference of the ROA policies when the service is deployed in the Grid infrastructure. When a Grid client sends a RamarsAuthZ proxy certificate and his data replication request to the Grid DRS service, the client is authenticated through the Grid GSI module. Then RAMARS Adaptor is invoked to parse the extensions in the proxy certificate and prepare an authorization request for RamarsAuthZ service

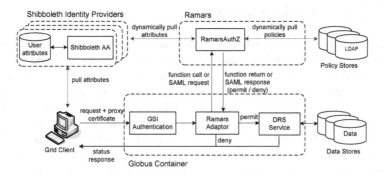

Fig. 2. Integrated RamarsAuthZ Authorization System

to check whether the Grid client is authorized to invoke the DRS service. The authorization request includes information on the requester's attributes and/or preferred IdPs passed by the proxy certificate, and the location reference of the service provider's ROA policies. Based on the authorization request, the RamarsAuthZ service can dynamically retrieve the service provider's ROA policies and the requester's attributes to make the authorization decision. The decision is sent back to RAMARS Adaptor and enforced accordingly by the DRS service.

2.2   Enhanced DRS for Access Control

As discussed in Section 1, data originators delegate the data sharing responsibilities to the DRS service, yet the DRS service is responsible to enforce the data originators' authorization policies on their behalf during each step of data sharing process. We demonstrate such capabilities by implementing an enhanced DRS service.

In the original DRS service, each data resource is identified by a unique *logical name*. A registry database is maintained where a *logical name–physical location* mapping is maintained for each data resource and its replicas. For instance, "*GeneSequence–gsiftp://abc.com/var/gseq.tar*" states an entry in the registry database. By querying the logical name "*GeneSequence*," a user could locate his desired data item at "*gsiftp://abc.com/var/gseq.tar*." After the physical location of the data item is successfully located, a file transfer component in DRS is invoked to copy the user's desired data item to the target location. We demonstrate how the invocation of DRS service can be protected by RamarsAuthZ. However, such configuration cannot further protect the actual data resources that are replicated through DRS. In order to enable the originator control for each individual data resource being shared through DRS, we introduce additional attributes with each registry entry to indicate the originator of the data item and its ROA policy information as *originator* and *roa_location*, respectively. With these two attributes being specified, the DRS service not only discovers the physical location of the data resource, but also collects the necessary ROA information for the RamarsAuthZ service to locate the data originator's policies. And these policies can be evaluated and enforced by RamarsAuthZ in the same manner as we discussed in Section 2.1.

3   Performance Evaluation

We conducted a series of experiments to evaluate how well the system scales along with the increased evaluation complexity and also analyzed the overhead of RamarsAuthZ authorization service over Globus DRS service. Figure 3 indicates the process time in miliseconds when we increase the number of user attributes involved in the authorization evaluation. The RamarsAuthZ policy evaluation time shows that with extreme complexity of evaluation when 80 attributes are involved, the overhead introduced by RamarsAuthZ authorization is 6.66% over the traditional GridMap authorization, which we believe is a promising outcome with respect to the performance of RamarsAuthZ authorization service. Same to our expectation, achieving a fine-grained authorization for stepwise data sharing involves considerable cost. However, considering the potential reduction of the administrative overhead against the practices of manually maintaining individual user accounts, RamarsAuthZ service still shows clear advantages both architecturally and technologically. Compared to the locally deployed authorization module, the overhead of SAML authorization messages cannot be neglected. Therefore, the usage of SAML for authorization in Grid envrionments needs to be limited for simple and optimized message assertion exchanges. Especially, instead of transferring a large number of attribute assertions as "push" mode, a reference to the Grid client's IdPs should be transferred within SAML message for RamarsAuthZ to operate under "pull" mode.

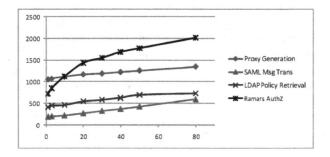

Fig. 3. RamarsAuthZ System Evaluation

4   Conclusion

In this paper, we have proposed an integrated framework that provides effective policy-driven role-based access control for Grid data sharing services. We also demonstrated that the RamarsAuthZ service does not rely on centralized policy stores and attribute authorities, which increases its scalability and portability, providing the authorization functionalities for various Grid services. As our future work, we currently attempt to explore policy cache and attribute negotiation mechanisms to further improve the performance of RamarsAuthZ system.

Acknowledgments

This work was partially supported by the grants from National Science Foundation (NSF-IIS-0242393) and Department of Energy Early Career Principal Investigator Award (DE-FG02-03ER25565).

References

1. Globus: GT 4.0: Data Replication Service (DRS),
   http://www.globus.org/toolkit/docs/4.0/techpreview/datarep/
2. Lang, B., Foster, I., Siebenlist, F., Ananthakrishnan, R., Freeman, T.: A Flexible Attribute Based Access Control Method for Grid Computing. Journal of Grid Computing 7(2) (2008)
3. Cantor, S.: Shibboleth Architecture: Protocols and Profiles (2005),
   http://shibboleth.internet2.edu/docs/internet2-mace-shibboleth-arch-protocols-200509.pdf
4. Alfieri, R., Cecchini, R., Ciaschini, V., dell'Agnello, L., Frohner, A., Gianoli, A., Lorentey, L., Spataro, F.: VOMS, an authorization system for virtual organizations. In: Proc. of 1st EuropeanAcross Grids Conferences (2003)
5. Groeper, R., Grimm, C., Piger, S., Wiebelitz, J.: An Architecture for Authorization in Grids using Shibboleth and VOMS. In: Proc. of 33rd EUROMICRO Conference on Software Engineering and Advanced Applications, pp. 367–374 (2007)
6. Thompson, M., Johnston, W., Mudumbai, S., Hoo, G., Jackson, K., Essiari, A.: Certificate-based Access Control for Widely Distributed Resources. In: Proc. of 8th Usenix Security Symposium (1999)
7. Chadwick, D.W., Otenko, A.: The PERMIS X.509 role based privilege management infrastructure. In: Proc.of the 7th ACM symposium on Access control models and technologies (SACMAT), pp. 135–140 (2002)
8. Jin, J., Ahn, G.J.: Role-based Access Management for Ad-hoc Collaborative Sharing. In: Proc. of 11th Symposium on Access Control Models and Technologies (SACMAT), pp. 200–209 (2006)
9. Jin, J., Ahn, G.J., Shehab, M., Hu, H.: Towards Trust-aware Access Management for Ad-hoc Collaborations. In: Proc. of 3rd IEEE International Conference on Collaborative Computing, pp. 41–48 (2007)
10. OASIS: XACML 2.0 core: extensible access control markup language (XACML) version 2.0 (2005),http://docs.oasisopen.org/xacml/2.0/access-control-xacml-2.0-core-spec-ospdf
11. Welch, V., Ananthakrishnan, R., Siebenlist, F., Chadwick, D., Meder, S., Pearlman, L.: Use of SAML for OGSI authorization (2005),
    https://forge.gridforum.org/projects/ogsa-authz/document/draft-ogsi-authz-saml-aug15-05.pdf/en/1
12. Tuecke, S., Welch, V., Engert, D., Pearlman, L., Thompson, M.: Internet X.509 Public Key Infrastructure (PKI) Proxy Certificate Profile (2004),
    http://rfc.net/rfc3820.html
13. Welch, V., Siebenlist, F., Foster, I., Bresnahan, J., Czajkowski, K., Gawor, J., Kesselman, C., Pearlman, S.M.L., Tuecke, S.: Security for Grid Services. In: Proc. of 12th IEEE International Symposium on High Performance Distributed Computing, pp. 48–57 (2003)

Design and Implementation of a SOA-Based Medical Grid Platform[*]

Chao-Tung Yang[**], Shih-Chi Yu, and Ting-Chih Hsiao

Department of Computer Science,
Tunghai University, Taichung City, 40704, Taiwan ROC
{ctyang,g97350064,g96350010}@thu.edu.tw

Abstract. As the evolution of information technology goes so quickly and the network technology spread so far, those healthcare scenarios only appeared in movies are coming toward us. With the E-hospital rapid growth, various types of information systems develop and use unceasingly. However, in the hospital information system of development methods under their own way, sharing of information between the systems is difficult day after day. In order to satisfy the hospital information system to the heterogeneity, interoperability, information sharing, and information integration, a kind of new software system architecture to came with the tide of fashion -- Service-Oriented Architecture (SOA) [1, 2, 5]. Our research take the SOA technology, combined with the grid based of the hospital for back-end platform—MedicalGrid [3, 6], provides a powerful computing capabilities, and fit with a Cross Grid Information Service (CGIS) [3] that enables Resource Brokers [8, 9, 10, 11] to get information from cross grid environments for other components. It can also provide medical care after discharge from hospital and health monitoring.

Keywords: Information Technology, Service Oriented Architecture, Cross grid, Resource Broker.

1 Introduction

Face in the quality of medical care services more and more better and cost considerations, complete patient care and enhance the quality of medical be taken seriously. In order to achieve personalized health management and maintenance the rights of the people to know. This paper develops a grid-based medical resources sharing platform, which provide medical services to the populace. Aims at separately by the home viewpoint (patients) and the hospital viewpoint (doctors) provide the different service.

To the home point of view, provide a standard platform (middleware) to integrate the health care services when the patient being out of hospital. In order to achieves the goal of health management, which can help patients take the follow-up treatment. To the hospital point of view, this paper use SOA technology to integrate

---

[*] This paper is supported in part by National Science Council, Taiwan R.O.C., under grants no. NSC 96-2221-E-029-019-MY3 and NSC 97-3114-E-007-001-.

[**] Corresponding author.

D. Ślęzak et al. (Eds.): GDC 2009, CCIS 63, pp. 156–163, 2009.

Grid & Medical (MedicalGrid) systems, to provide physicians and patients interactive with each other. The health care services which can provide originally the hospital extended to individuals and families. In the process, we discuss with a number of attending physicians, nurses and related medical experts many times. The collection of clinical practice and views on professional advice, to sum up the views of staff to the general public demand for health services management as a major research direction will be produced after the system prototype design and development system.

Our paper was use the Service Oriented Architecture (SOA) and grid technologies come to develop a basic Healthcare Service Grid Infrastructure. It contains one of the main Grid Resource Management and Information Service, service platform and the entrance of health information user interface (Service Portal), Health Level Seven [7] Data Management System, Health Services API, and Data Replica and Parallel Download Management parts. We also propose a SOA solution to present a number of incompatible information systems, so that the services can be integrated and combined to each other. We implement a web portal to provide healthcare services and WSDL related documentations. We provide access right control mechanism to provide user more secure.

2 System Design and Implement

2.1 Architecture

The system software stack includes three layers constructed using a bottom-up methodology as shown in Fig. 1. The layers are described below:

- Bottom Layer: principally consists of Nodes. The layer contains two main blocks: the Information Provider, which uses Ganglia to gather machine information on Nodes, such as number of processors/cores, processor loading, total/free memory, and disk usage, and Network Weather Service (NWS), which gathers essential network information such as bandwidth and latency. The second block contains Grid Middleware, used to join Grid Nodes together, and the MPICH-G2 required for running parallel applications on the Grid.
- Middle Layer: we use SOA technology to build a middleware, combined with Resource Broker, MedicalGrid and P2P network. User can invoke services and resources that MedicalGrid and P2P network provided.
- Top Layer: when user login to SOA web portal, it will accord your privilege what services you can apply.

2.2 Resource Broker

The main layers of our system architecture include SOA web portal, Services, Grid portal, Resource broker, Grid nodes.

We use a Resource Broker for Computational Grids. It discovers and evaluates Grid resources, and makes job submission decisions by comparing job requirements

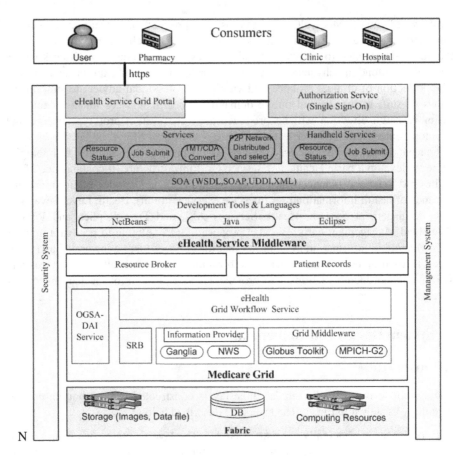

Fig. 1. System Architecture

with Grid resources. The Resource Broker system architecture and the relationships among components are shown in Fig. 2. Each rectangle represents a discrete system component.

The Resource Broker's primary task is to compare user requests and resource information provided by the Information Service. After an appropriate assignment scheme is chosen, Grid resources are assigned and the Scheduler submits the job for execution. The results are then collected and returned to the Resource Broker, which records them in the Information Center database via the Information Service Agent. Users can view the results through the Grid portal.

The system architecture includes five layers: SOA web portal, Service, Grid portal, Resource broker, Grid nodes. The following sections will be described in detail.

2.3   SOA Web Portal

We propose access right control mechanism into our portal to provide user more secure way to utilize our healthcare system. Unauthorized user is only capable of seeing

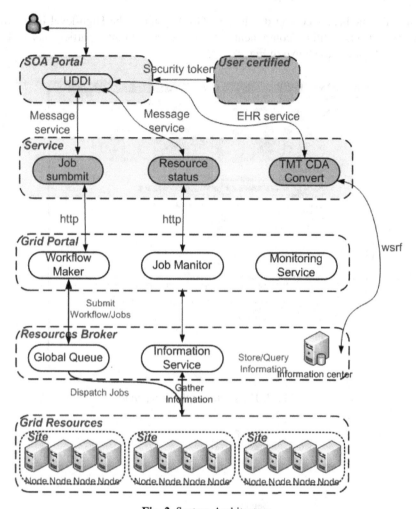

Fig. 2. System Architecture

the service information and health and medical information without service invoke. Our web portal lists the WSDL documents shown in Fig. 3.

2.4 SOA Technology Combination Resource Broker

SOA combination of elements typically include: software components, services and flow. When the hospital or enterprises face an external request, the external flow is responsible for the definition of the requirements of treatment steps; Services of specific steps, including all program components and software components are responsible for the implementation of programs. We use the characteristics of SOA, and resource brokers (Resource Broker) for the combination of resource brokers go through the medical access grid (MedicareGrid) system. The High-level interactions between various entities, components, resources, and human participants and the channels of control as shown in Fig. 4.

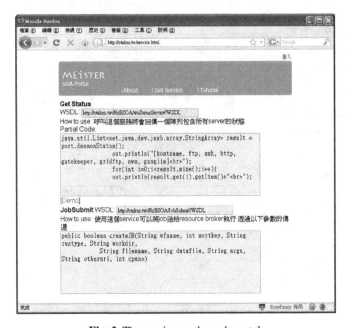

Fig. 3. The service on the web portal

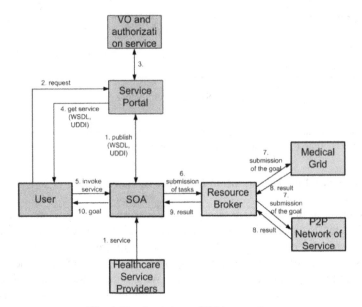

Fig. 4. The flow chart of SOA operation

1. SOA components will be imported from time to time updates on web services, the service's Web Services Description Language (WSDL) to release to be published on the SOA web portal for users to search.
2. User initiates session with portal by selecting modeling resources required and 'planning' experiment with the resources. .On the SOA web portal, the user can search for suitable services and resources.
3. User obtains authorization through VO and authorization service.
4. User to get the service of WSDL document.
5. WSDL of the service allows users to be connected to the Internet through the SOA components, and will invoke service.
6. SOA portal through the SOA technology contacts Resource Broker to request resources (remote/local services or database). MedicalGrid and P2P network. SOA component will take submission of tasks to resource broker.
7. Resource broker submitted the tasks to MedicalGrid or P2P network in order to achieve the goal.
8-10. Results are visualized on the users' desktop through the Web browser.

2.5 Services

We identify the following modules in our paper:

1. Resource Status: The main function was provided users to view the machines status when user create job, then they can choose the correct machines. The user chooses one or more nodes and sends a request to the Information Service, which finds the information and returns it in a sorted list. Information type include hostname and machine status.
2. Job Submit: The users can submit job into the Workflow Engine by the SOA middleware, and then will be allocated to the grid environment for computing machines by the resource broker (RB).
3. TMT/CDA Convert: the general public of the personal health record information, because of differences in medical situations may be scattered in a variety of medical institutions; to make the information on to the network for the exchange and integration, we need the same information in a standard format will be edited. We use international standards as the Health Level 7 as the exchange of information integration.
4. Handset service: We use SOAP protocol as intermediate. The kSOAP library is a SOAP web service that can connect with handset devices.

3 Experiment Results

We calculate the latency time of job submission in personal computer (PC) and handset device. The latency time is denote by a job submit to the resource broker until it return "true" message to user. We can see the result in **Fig. 5**. The latency time of handset device is higher than PC about 3 times. Because the handset devices use wireless network and android system use SOAP protocol. It spent more time to use XML parser to explain the SOAP message. The SOAP encoding rules include some type of

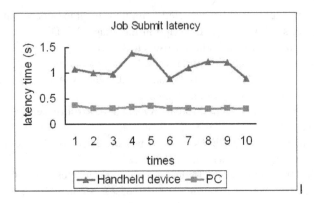

Fig. 5. Job submit latency comparison

additional information. It will take up some storage space and increase system encoding and decoding of the additional processing time. But the highest latency time of handset device is close to 1.5 seconds. The time can be ignored for user.

4   Conclusion and Future Work

The paper provided an analysis of use of the SOA paradigm in the context of an e-health Web-based system. We design and implementation a SOA web portal. The web portal provides the services that combine resource broker. The resource broker enables users to submit job, monitoring grid nodes and viewing patient records, etc. via a SOA web portal. So, user will be able to take care of their own will be more convenient. Our feature work will focus on handset device API and the service from hospital. We hope the patient records can follow user all the time. Whenever the user got sick, they can be anywhere for medical treatment.

References

Chu, X., Lonie, A., Harris, P., Thomas, S.R., Buyya, R.: A service-oriented Grid environment for integration of distributed kidney models and resources. Middleware for Grid Computing: Future Trends 20, 1095–1111 (2008)

Andrzejak, C., Mastroianni, P., Fragopoulou, D., Kondo, P., Malecot, A., Reinefeld, F., Schintke, T., Schütt, G.-C., Silaghi, L.M., Silva, P., Trunfio, D., Zeinalipour-Yazti, E., Zimeo, E.: Grid Architectural Issues: State-of-the-art and Future Trends, Project no. FP6-00426 (2008)

Yang, C.-T., Chen, T.-T., Chou, K.-Y., Chu, W.C.: Design and Implementation of an Information Service for Cross-Grid Computing Environments. In: 12th IEEE International Workshop on Future Trends of Distributed Computing Systems, pp. 99–105 (2008)

Cheng, T.-M.: Taiwan's New National Health Insurance Program: Genesis And Experience So. Far. Health Affairs 3, 61–76 (2003)

Grit, L.E.: Broker Architectures for Service-oriented Systems (2005)

Krefting, D., Bart, J., Beronov, K., Dzhimova, O., Falkner, J., Hartung, M., Hoheisel, A., Knochf, T.A., Lingner, T., Mohammed, Y., Peter, K., Rahm, E., Sax, U., Sommerfeld, D., Steinke, T., Tolxdorff, T., Vossberg, M., Viezens, F., Weisbecker, A.: MediGRID: Towards a user friendly secured grid infrastructure. Future Generation Computer Systems 25, 326–336 (2009)

Blazona, B., Koncar, M.: HL7 and DICOM based integration of radiology departments with healthcare enterprise information systems. International Journal of Medical Informatics 76, 425–432 (2007)

Aloisio, G., Cafaro, M.: Web-based access to the Grid using the Grid Resource Broker portal. Concurrency Computation: Practice and Experience 14, 1145–1160 (2002)

Krauter, K., Buyya, R., Maheswaran, M.: A taxonomy and survey of grid resource management systems for distributed computing. Software Practice and Experience 32, 135–164 (2002)

Yang, C.T., Lin, C.F., Chen, S.Y.: A Workflow-based Computational Resource Broker with Information Monitoring in Grids. In: Fifth International Conference on Grid and Cooperative Computing (GCC 2006), pp. 199–206 (2006)

Yang, C.T., Chen, S.Y., Chen, T.T.: A Grid Resource Broker with Network Bandwidth-Aware Job Scheduling for Computational Grids. In: Cérin, C., Li, K.-C. (eds.) GPC 2007. LNCS, vol. 4459, pp. 1–12. Springer, Heidelberg (2007)

Foster, I., Kesselman, C.: Globus: A Metacomputing Infrastructure Toolkit. International Journal of Supercomputer Applications 11(2), 115–128 (1997)

RFID-Based Onion Skin Location Estimation Technique in Indoor Environment

Gihong Kim and BongHee Hong

Dept. of Computer Engineering, Pusan National University,
Busan, Republic of Korea
{buglist,bhhong}@pusan.ac.kr

Abstract. There are Location Based Service (LBS) localization techniques such as Global Positioning System (GPS), Angle of Arrival (AOA) and Time Difference of Arrival (TDOA). To use these methods it should be guaranteed that received signals propagate through a Line-of-Sight (LoS) path. Fingerprinting methods have appeared to perform better in None Line-of-Sight (NLoS) environment. But these also have a problem in the dynamic environment where moving obstructions disrupt the signal propagation. To solve these problems we propose a method and algorithm. Tags are mapped to geographical coordinates and deployed on the ceiling with grid spacing. RFID reader is equipped on the target moving object and obtains the information from the tags on the ceiling. And it sends to location engine. The location engine can determine the location of the target object via the collected tags set with proposed Onion Skin Location Determination (OSLE) algorithm.

Keywords: RFID, location determination, geo-location, location based services, wireless indoor localization.

1 Introduction

Location based service (LBS) has recently emerged as an important research issue. LBS is geographic information service with mobile device through the wireless network [1][2]. Key questions of LBS are as follows.

- Where am I? – localization
- How do I get there? – navigation
- Where is the nearest gas station? – surrounding information

LBS have 4 basic components: mobile device, localization, communication network, service provider [1]. Localization is key components of LBS because all the services are on the assumption of positional accuracy.

There are localization techniques such as mobile based, network based and mobile assistant method [1]. The representative technology of mobile based is Global Positioning System (GPS) [3][4]. The signal is received from the satellite by the mobile device to calculate the position of the mobile devices using the geometric trilateral rules. For calculating position at least three satellites information is needed but more

D. Ślęzak et al. (Eds.): GDC 2009, CCIS 63, pp. 164–175, 2009.
© Springer-Verlag Berlin Heidelberg 2009

than three satellite is used for precisely calculate the position of the devices. But this technology is not appropriate to the indoor environment.

Angle of arrival (AOA) [5][6] is a network-based positioning technology which computes the angle of arrival of the mobile device from two different access points. It uses the directional antenna and simple geometric rules to calculate the distance from the angle measurements. So by calculating the straight line from two different access points and taking the intersection of the two lines we can calculate the accurate position of the particular mobile device. This type of positioning system is mainly used in areas of sparse cell site density, or where cell are arrange linearly such as along a stretch of highway. This technology needs extra antenna or array of antenna at the base station and also need LoS condition. For its scattering characteristics and multi path signals hinder the performance and it is not good to use in indoor environment.

Third technology is mobile assistant method [5][7][8]. Time of Arrival (TOA) is a trilateral positioning technique which uses the time of arrival of a signal from the sender to the receiver to calculate the position of the mobile devices. The stations have to synchronize the clock and calculate the time of arrival of the signal and comparing the time of arrival (TOA) of the signal it can find the position of the mobile device accurately.

The above described location determination technologies require Line-of Sight (LoS) propagation. It is assumed that the received signals propagate through a LoS path. However, violation of this assumption causes inaccurate localization data [9][10][11]. Fingerprinting methods have appeared to perform better in environment with NLoS [12]. NLoS means there is no LoS between the transmitter and receiver in radio propagation. Fingerprinting method [10][12] is a pattern matching technique. In the radio signal collecting phase it maps unique characteristics of radio signal to geographical coordinates. Then in the location determination phase, it finds most similar to input radio signal data in the pre-calculated or pre-measured reference data. It determines the location as the geographical coordinate mapped to result reference data. Each geographical coordinate has its unique data characteristic, therefore this method is called fingerprinting method. This method is appropriate to the static environment where obstructions don't change their position.

However, in the most real environment, there are not only blocking obstructions but also moving obstructions. The former causes NLoS and the latter causes the error in the fingerprinting methods. Because the key concept of fingerprinting is static information of environment, it is not robust method in the dynamic environment.

In this paper, to solve above problem we propose a method and algorithm. Tags are deployed to the ceiling with grid spacing and RFID reader is equipped on the target moving object. The reader equipped to the target object obtains the information from the tags on the ceiling and sends to location engine. The location engine can determine the location of the target object via the collected tags set with proposed Onion Skin Location Estimation (OSLE) algorithm, because the ID of tag is mapped to geographic coordinate. This method minimizes the probability which obstructions are located in the Fresnel zone [13] and as a result, it reduces the location error.

Paper is organized as follows. Second section shows related work and third section defines the target environment and problem. In the section 4, solutions will be described specifically with location determination algorithm. Last chapter of this paper concludes the research and brings up future studies.

2 Related Work

Many efforts have been made to provide location determination method. Methods can be divided into two categories: Line-of-Sight (LoS) based and Non Line-of-Sight (NLOS) based [1][9]. In the LoS localization techniques, there are mobile based, network based and mobile assistant method.

The representative technology of mobile based is Global Positioning system (GPS) [3][4] where the signal is received from the satellite by the mobile device to calculate the position of the mobile device. Each satellite above the earth continuously transmits the message containing the time of the message sent by the mobile device, precise orbit information. The receiver measures the transit time of each message and computes the distance of each satellite and finds the position of the device using the geometric trilateral rules. The position is displayed with a moving map or latitude and longitude. To calculate position at least three satellites information is needed but more than three satellites information is used for precisely calculating the position of the devices. But this technology is not appropriate to the indoor environment.

Angle of arrival (AOA) [5][6] is a network-based positioning technology which computes the angle of arrival of the mobile device from two different access points using the directional antenna and simple geometric rules to calculate the distance from the angle measurements. It is possible to calculate the position by measuring the signal strength, time of arrival, and phase at the access point. So by calculating the straight line from two different access points and taking the intersection of the two lines we can calculate the accurate position of the particular mobile device. The accuracy of the AOA decreases with increasing distance between mobile station and base station due to the scattering environment. This type of positioning system is mainly used in areas of sparse cell site density, or where cell are arrange linearly such as along a stretch of highway. This technology can gain 99% accuracy in determining position of a mobile device and does not require a mobile device upgrade to operate. But it needs extra antenna or array of antenna at the base station and also need LoS condition. For its scattering characteristics and multi path signals hinder the performance and it is not good to use in indoor environment.

Next three technologies are mobile-assisted or hybrid methods. Time of Arrival (TOA) [5][7][8] is a trilateral positioning technique which uses the time of arrival of a signal from the sender to the receiver to calculate the position of the mobile devices. For this technology, at least three access points are needed to calculate the arrival of the signal from the sender to efficiently calculate the position of the mobile devices. The stations have to synchronize the clock and calculate the time of arrival of the signal and comparing the time of arrival (TOA) of the signal it can find the position of the mobile device accurately.

Time Difference of Arrival [14] (TDOA) is also a mobile-assisted or hybrid-based trilateral technology which uses the time difference of a signal from the sender to the receiver to calculate the position of the mobile devices. And like TOA, it also needs at least three base stations to accurately calculate the position of the mobile device but the clock synchronization is not needed. The major concerns with both the TDOA and TOA are the preciseness of time measurement, and unlike other techniques, the error factor decrease as the distance between mobile station and the base station increases. As the time delay to be measured in microcellular technologies is very small, technology like Bluetooth do not easily support this type of technique.

Receive Signal Strength Indication (RSSI) [15][16] is a metric of measuring power presented in a received radio signal. RSSI is very important in various fields. RSSI value can be used to determine the distance between two communicating nodes. As radio signal strength attenuates as a function of distance, the greater the distance the smaller the perceived RSSI value. The RSSI value can also be used to estimate the distance between the nodes. But RSSI value is affected by some interference from other signal, reflection, diffraction and presence of obstacles on the path.

Fingerprinting methods [10][12] can find the position even in the None Line-of-Sight (NLOS) environment where obstacles are present in between the access points and objects. They have appeared to perform better in environment with NLoS [9][12]. NLoS means that there is no LoS between the transmitter and receiver in radio propagation. The fingerprint technique uses network characteristics such as RSS, from the access points and this can be taken as fingerprint of those locations. This technology works in two modes where in learning mode it collects unique RSS value of all the grid points and stored it in the database which is known as radio map. Then in the location determination phase, for finding the location of target device, the instant network characteristics of that device are examined with respect to radio map and most likely location is determined. Each grid point (geographical coordinate) has its unique data characteristic, therefore this method is called fingerprinting method. This method is appropriate for the static environment where obstructions don't change their position. Using only existing WLAN, fingerprint technique can be deployed without the need of special hardware.

3 Target Environment and Problem Definition

3.1 Target Environment

In this chapter, it will be described that the characteristics of our target environment.

First characteristic is not outdoor but indoor environment. For outdoor environment Global Positioning System (GPS) is a very effective solution to determine location of objects. But in indoor environments there're no effective solutions like GPS. Second there're obstacles disturbing the radio frequency propagation.

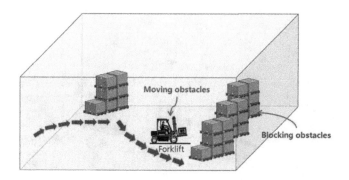

Fig. 1. Warehouse environment with moving obstacles and blocking obstacles

For example, Fig. 1 shows warehouse environment where forklift heaps up the loads moving this way and that. In this environment, the aim of system is tracking the moving objects. The radio wave to trace the moving objects is heavily disturbed by moving forklift and blocking obstacles.

In the next chapter, the problem will be described and the reason of problem will be analyzed specifically.

3.2 Problem Definition

This chapter describes the problem of existing technologies and the cause of the problem.

Fig. 2 shows the situation that a radio wave is disturbed by moving obstacles and blocking obstacles which are in the Fresnel zone [13]. Location determination technologies such as Time of Arrival (TOA), Time Difference of Arrival (TDOA) or Received Signal Strength Indication (RSSI) measures the arrival time of radio signal, its time difference or signal strength attenuation respectively to determine the location of target objects. These location determination technologies have some problems.

As described in the previous chapter, there are two factors disturbing the measurement of location.

First is jamming by blocking obstacles that block the radio wave and cause the reflection. In the Fig. 2 the burdens heaped up block the radio signal. The signal cannot be reached to the reader therefore it is impossible to determine the location of target objects. Line-of-Sight (LoS) propagation technologies have this problem.

Second factor is jamming by moving obstacles that cause a degree of diffraction of radio signal around the obstructions. This occurs in the dynamic environment where people walk around or objects position is updated frequently. As is well known, existing technologies relatively works well in the static environment, but not in the dynamic environment. In the Fig. 2 shows moving forklift disturbing the signal. The signal makes a detour by obstacles. Signal strength will be attenuated and arrival time of signal will be delayed. Therefore the location determination has error and becomes inaccurate. RSSI, TDOA or TOA commonly have this problem. NLoS propagation technologies such as fingerprint methods also have this problem.

Let us now examine the cause of problem. To begin with, I would like to define some terms such as *Distance*, *Height*, *Width* and α in the Fig. 2 and Fig. 3.

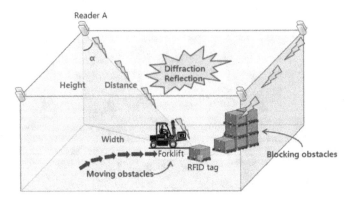

Fig. 2. Warehouse environment with jamming

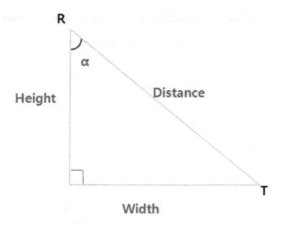

Fig. 3. *Distance*, tangential component *Width*, normal component *Height* and α

As illustrated in Fig. 2, we will use the *Distance* to refer to line between reader A and target object attaching RFID tag. Tangential component of *Distance* is *Width* and normal component of *Distance* is *Height*. The angle between *Distance* and *Height* is α. You can understand more clearly by Fig. 3.

If target object is moving, normal component *Height* is constant but tangential component *Width* and α is variable. At this stage, tangential component *Width* is closely linked to *P_noise* that is the probability of moving obstacles disturbing the radio signal. For example, in proportion to the increase of *Width* obstacles could be existed frequently between Reader A and target object. As a result, *P_noise* increases. *P_noise* varies directly as *Width* and *Width* varies directly as α. It is represented by the formula below.

$$\alpha \propto Width \propto P\_noise \tag{1}$$

Main cause of *P_noise* is α which is the angle between R (Reader A) and T (target object) in the Fig. 3.

In summary, in indoor environment where movements of object frequently occur and blocking obstacles are located, existing location determination technologies have a problem of location error. This is caused by α which is the angle between reader and target object. As α increases, *P_noise* that is likelihood of jamming also increases.

4 Model and Algorithm

4.1 Location Estimation Model

In this chapter we will explain installation of H/W and S/W. Essentially our approach in this paper is based on the concept of decreasing the angle α between transmitter (passive RFID tag) and receiver (RFID reader).

Fig. 4 shows detailed illustration of our system installation. System is composed by transmitter (passive RFID tag), receiver (RFID reader), wireless AP and location engine.

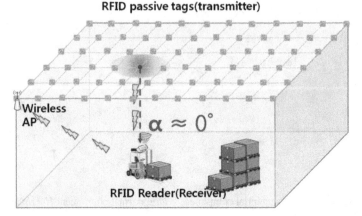

Fig. 4. Installation of transmitters (RFID tags) and receiver (RFID reader)

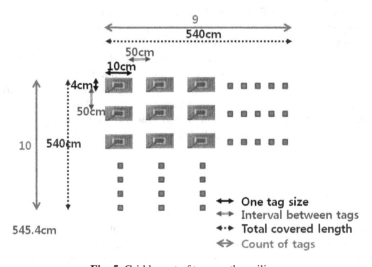

Fig. 5. Grid layout of tags on the ceiling

First, tags are attached on the ceiling with grid spacing. Fig. 5 shows the grid layout of tag arrangement. It is possible to get physical location of tags attached on the ceiling, because grid ID information in EPC code means geographical coordinates (x, y) of the ceiling. Second reader is attached to the target object to estimate the physical location and collects tag information through a directional antenna. After collecting tag information, reader transmits the tag information to wireless AP. Third wireless AP transmits tag information, which is collected from reader, to the location engine via wired network. At last, location engine estimates the location of target objects using tag information obtained from wireless AP. Location estimation algorithm is presented in the next chapter. Our system is installed at the (a) of Fig. 6, and (b) of Fig. 6 illustrates real installation of RFID passive tags on the ceiling.

Fig. 6. a) RFID test center environment in Pusan national university (b) real installation of RFID passive tags on the ceiling

4.2 Onion Skin Location Estimation (OSLE) Algorithm

In this chapter location estimation algorithm will be described. Basic variables are illustrated in the Fig. 7 for explaining the algorithm. Background of Fig. 7 is ceiling. Let u be total tag set, t be detected tag set, o be the outlier tag set, CT be the center of t and z be the set of tag, whose distance from CT belongs to same interval. z is like a onion skin. The key concept of proposed algorithm is to find outlier by peeling away each layer of an onion skin one by one.

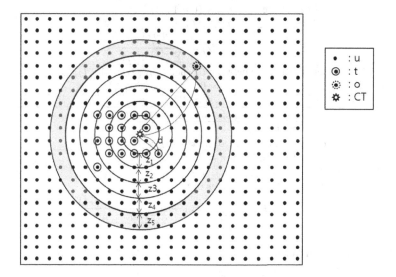

Fig. 7. Basic variable description (u: total tag set, t: detected tag set, o: outlier tag set, CT: center of t, z: onion skin)

Table 1 shows mathematical definition of variables which will be used to explain the OSLE algorithm.

Table 1. Variables Description

Name	Description
u	set of total tags on the ceiling $u = \{u_1, u_2, .. u_k, ... u_n\}$, $u_k = (x_k, y_k)$
t	set of detected all tags $t = \{t_1, t_2, .. t_k, ... t_n\}$, $t_k = (x_k, y_k)$
n	number of elements in t, $n(t)$
CT	center of t, average value of all elements of t $$CT = \frac{\sum_{k=1}^{n} t_k}{n} = \left(\frac{\sum_{k=1}^{n} t_k(x)}{n}, \frac{\sum_{k=1}^{n} t_k(y)}{n} \right)$$
d	set of Euclidian distance between CT and each element of t $(k = 1 ... n)$ $d = \{d_1, d_2, .. d_k, ... d_n\}$, $$d_k = |CT(x,y) - t_k(x_k, y_k)| = \sqrt{(x_k - x)^2 + (y_k - y)^2}$$
p	set which has elements as pairs of t_k and d_k, $(k = 1 ... n)$ $p = \{p_1, p_2, ... p_k, ... p_n\}$, $p_k = \{t_k, d_k\}$
z	set which has elements as set of p_k, where $i < d_k < i+1$, $(i = 1 ... l, k = 1 ... n)$ $z = \{z_1, z_2, ... z_i, ... z_l\}$, $z_i = \{p_k | i < d_k < i+1\}$
l	number of elements in z, $n(z)$
CZ	set which has elements as average value of d in z, where $z_1 \sim z_{l-i+1}$ $(i = 1 ... l)$ $CZ = \{CZ_1, CZ_2, ... CZ_i, ... CZ_l\}$, $$CZ_i = \frac{\sum_{i=1}^{l-i+1} z_i}{\sum_{i=1}^{l-i+1} n(z_i)}$$
s	set of difference between CZ_i and CZ_{i+1} $(i = 1 ... l)$ $s = \{s_1, s_2, ... s_i, ... s_{l-1}\}$ $s_i = CZ_{i+1} - CZ_i$
θ	minimum threshold of s (user defined value)
o	set of outliers tags $o = \{o_1, o_2, .. o_k, ... o_n\}$, $o_k = (x_k, y_k)$
r	set of remaining tags $r = t - o$ $r = \{r_1, r_2, .. r_k, ... r_n\}$, $r_k = (x_k, y_k)$
CR	center of r, average value of $r(x, y)$ $$CR = \frac{\sum_{k=1}^{n} r_k}{n(r)} = \left(\frac{\sum_{k=1}^{n} r_k(x)}{n(r)}, \frac{\sum_{k=1}^{n} r_k(y)}{n(r)} \right)$$

Rough flow of algorithm is as follows.

  i.   Find o, the outlier tag set
 ii.   Find r, the remaining tag set ($r = t - o$)
iii.   Determine the estimated location by averaging position of r which is remaining tag set.

In the next paragraph an overview will be described to help understanding of algorithm and then more specific algorithm will be proposed.

Briefly speaking, the algorithm is finding geographical center of tags. But practical characteristics of radio frequency causes error by outliers as illustrated in the Fig. 7.

Define outliers to be tag set that is numerically distant from the rest of the tags. Therefore outliers cause a little center shift of tags, which causes the error of location estimation.

Above all things, finding outliers is essential for OSLE algorithm. First step is very similar to peel away each layer of an onion skin one by one. Particularly in the Fig. 7, detected tag set t is divided to z which has uniform interval like layers of an onion. First step examines that which layer z has a bad influence on s the center shift which is varia-tion of average, peeling layer of onion one by one from outer skin, until s the variation

Table 2. Onion Skin Location Estimation (OSLE) Algorithm

CS1: Find o, the outlier tag set

① Compute CT, the center(average) of detected tags

$$CT(x,y) = \frac{\sum_{k=1}^{n} t_k}{n} = \left(\frac{\sum_{k=1}^{n} t_k(x)}{n}, \frac{\sum_{k=1}^{n} t_k(y)}{n} \right)$$

② Compute d_k, the distance between CT and t_k, for each t_k ($k = 1 \dots n$)

$$d_k = |CT(x,y) - t_k(x_k, y_k)| = \sqrt{(x_k - x)^2 + (y_k - y)^2}$$

③ Make p_k which is pair of t_k and d_k ($k = 1 \dots n$)

$$p_k = (t_k, d_k)$$

④ Classify all the p_k into z_i if d_k, the element of p_k, is in the same range where $i < d_k < i+1$ ($i = 1 \dots l, k = 1 \dots n$)

$$z_i = \{p_k | i < d_k < i+1\}$$

⑤ Compute CZ_i, the center(average) of $z_1 \sim z_i$ ($i = 1 \dots l$)

$$CZ_i = \frac{\sum_{i=1}^{l-i+1} z_i}{\sum_{i=1}^{l-i+1} n(z_i)}$$

⑥ Compute s_i, adjacent difference of CZ_{i+1} and CZ_i ($i = 1 \dots l-1$)

$$s_i = CZ_{i+1} - CZ_i$$

⑦ Compute o, the outliers of detected tag set

$i = l$

while ($\theta < s_i$) do

$i = i - 1$

end while

$$o = \sum_{k=1}^{i} z_k$$

CS2: Find r, the remaining tag set

$r = t - o$

CS3: Determine CR, the estimated location using r

$$CR(x,y) = \frac{\sum_{k=1}^{n} r_k}{n(r)} = \left(\frac{\sum_{k=1}^{n} r_k(x)}{n(r)}, \frac{\sum_{k=1}^{n} r_k(y)}{n(r)} \right)$$

of average is smaller than given threshold θ. Then all the elements of peeled-off layers are outliers. Mathematical representation is presented in the Table 2.

Second and third steps are very simple. The second step eliminates the outliers tag set from the detected tag set, and the result is the remaining tag set. And finally, we can determine the estimated location by averaging the remaining tag set in the last step.

5 Conclusion and Future Work

In this paper, we propose a location determination system and its algorithm in dynamic indoor environment. Global Positioning System (GPS) is very famous for positioning but not appropriate for indoor environment. There are some technologies such as Time of Arrival (TOA), Time Difference of Arrival (TDOA), Angle of Arrival (AOA) and Received Signal Strength Indication (RSSI). The above described location determination technologies require LoS (Line-of Sight) propagation. It is assumed that the received signals propagate through a LoS path. However, violation of this assumption causes inaccurate localization data. Fingerprint methods have appeared to perform better in environment with None Line-of-Sight (NLoS). However, in the most real environment, there are not only blocking obstructions but also moving obstructions which cause the error in the fingerprinting methods.

To solve above this problem, this paper has shown the problem, and proposed a system and its algorithm. The cause of problem is that the probability of moving obstacles disturbing the radio signal increases as the angle between transmitter and receiver increases. Our approach in this paper is based on the concept of decreasing the angle between transmitters (RFID tags) and receiver (RFID reader). This method minimizes the probability which obstructions are located in the Fresnel zone and as a result, it reduces the location error. Transmitters (RFID tags) are deployed to the ceiling with grid spacing and receiver (RFID reader) is equipped on the target moving object. The reader equipped to the target object obtains the information from the tags on the ceiling and sends to location engine. The location engine can determine the location of the target object via the collected tags set with proposed location determination algorithm. This algorithm deletes the outliers from the data set and extracts the centroid which is location of target object by calculating the mean value of remained data set.

The paper concludes by mentioning some of the further research. First we will consider hardware settings such as adjusting interval between tags, changing antenna type or adjusting power level of reader to improve accuracy of location determination. Next we will modify location determination algorithm according to the shape of the ceiling. Also by experimental comparison with existing techniques, we will show the improvement of our work.

Acknowledgments. This work was supported by the grant of the Korean Ministry of Education, Science and Technology. (The Regional Core Research Program/Institute of Logistics Information Technology).

References

1. Shu, W., Min, J., Yi, B.: Location Based Services for Mobiles: Technologies and Standards. In: IEEE International Conference on Communication (ICC) 2008, Beijing, China (2008)
2. Bellavista, P., Küpper, A., Helal, S.: Location-Based Services: Back to the Future. Journal of IEEE Pervasive Computing 7(2), 85–89 (2008)
3. Farrell, J., Barth, M.: The global positioning system and inertial navigation. McGraw-Hill Professional, New York (1999)
4. Tsui, J.B.: Fundamentals of global positioning system receivers. John Wiley and Sons, Chichester (2004)
5. Kolodziej, K.W., Hjelm, J.: Local Positioning System: LBS application and service. CRC Taylor & Francis Press, Boca Raton (2006)
6. Niculescu, D., Nath, B.: Ad hoc positioning system (APS) using AoA. In: Twenty-Second Annual Joint Conference of the IEEE Computer and Communications Societies (IEEE INFOCOM), April 2003, pp. 1734–1743 (2003)
7. Hightower, J., Borriello, G.: A Survey and Taxonomy of Location Systems for Ubiquitous Computing. IEEE Computer 34(8), 57–66 (2001)
8. Ward, A., Jones, A., Hopper, A.: A new location technique for the active office. In: IEEE Personnel Communications 1997, pp. 42–47 (1997)
9. Venkatraman, S., Caffery, J.: Statistical approach to non-line-of-sight BS identification. In: The 5th International Symposium on Wireless Personal Multimedia Communications, October 2002, vol. 1, pp. 296–300 (2002)
10. Nerguizian, C., Despins, C., Affes, S.: Indoor Geolocation with received Signal Strengths Fingerprinting Technique and Neural Networks. ICT, Putten (2004) (presented at)
11. Kriegl, J.: Location in cellular networks, Diploma Thesis, Institute for Applied Information. In: Processing and Communications. University of Technology Graz, Austria (2000)
12. Kaemarungsi, K.: Design of indoor positioning systems based on location fingerprinting technique, PhD. Dissertation, University of Pittsburgh, Pittsburgh, USA (2005)
13. Wireless - Fresnel Zones and their Effect,
    http://www.zytrax.com/tech/wireless/fresnel.htm
14. Savvides, A., Han, C., Strivastava, M.B.: Dynamic fine-grained localization in ad-hoc networks of sensors. In: Proceedings of the 7th annual international conference on Mobile computing and networking, pp. 166–179. ACM Press, New York (2001)
15. Bahl, P., Padmanabhan, V.N.: RADAR: An in-building RF-based user location and tracking system. In: INFOCOM 2000, pp. 775–784 (2000)
16. Priyantha, N.B., Chakraborty, A., Balakrishnan, H.: The cricket location-support system. In: 6th ACM International Conference on Mobile Computing and Networking (ACM MOBICOM), pp. 32–43 (2000)

Harmonized Media Service Middleware
Using to Emotional Knowledge

Jihye Lee and Yong-Ik Yoon

Dept of Multimedia Science, Sookmyung Women's University,
Seoul, 140-742, Korea
{leejh,yiyoon}@sm.ac.kr

Abstract. In recent, service providers would like to support actual feeling services for internet users to give a satisfaction. Since web environments are changed more newly, internet users want to satisfy their needs. For offering the satisfaction to users, we suggest a middleware to give an impressive media that is named *Harmonized Media Service Middleware* (HMSM). The HMSM can support the harmonized media by using some emotional knowledge for each user. The harmonized media is constructed with media contents, like video and emotional effects. The video content is made by individually users, so it has a just recorded data as a simple media. However, because the user wants a feeling of satisfaction, it is necessary to offer multiple media which include emotional effects for user's impression. In this paper, we suggest a way to offer a middleware for actual feeling multiple media, called the HMSM. The HMSM analyzes the input media and then extracts the effects which have compatibility with the input media from the emotional effect database. At the result, the HMSM will offer the actual feeling service to satisfy user's needs.

Keywords: harmony, emotional, media service, actual feeling, middleware.

1 Introduction

Recently, the concept of web2.0 that has ideal of participation, sharing and opening is revitalized on the web. Internet users are easily able to access the UGC (User Generated Contents) through the media sharing site like the Youtube.com [1]. Users are beginning to make contents rather than just consuming information that offered the web. In addition, users want to open their contents that were designed themselves. To reflect the flow of the user's preference, the media sharing sites are grown rapidly and UGCs are distributed on that site.

Despite of the growth of personal media contents industries, making contents by internet users has lots of lacks that an additional media to satisfy consumers hardly supply. If the making contents attach an additional media to supply a satisfaction of the consumers who want to fill their emotional, the using process that taken a media is harmonized with other media effects that can give consumers satisfaction in having the harmonized media.

In this paper, we suggest a new notion of the harmonized media service middleware which designed to give a satisfaction to consumers and to develop a simple

D. Ślęzak et al. (Eds.): GDC 2009, CCIS 63, pp. 176–183, 2009.

media that has only taken pictures into a multiple media that has the emotional effects.

Just using the Harmonized media service middleware is able to give consumers proper the harmonized media and can meet a consumer's satisfaction. The harmonized media service middleware analyzes an input media based on the ontology concept and then extracts some emotional media that would fulfill consumers through the analyzed knowledge [2]. Both the input media and the extracted emotional media are harmonized by the Harmonized media service middleware (HMSM) for offer consumer a satisfaction about a reproducing media.

2 Related Works

In order to use the video contents saving the departmentalized video contents based on the ontology and adding some proper effects to them, we can utilize the International Standard MPEG-7 that enables us to deal with multimedia contents effectively.

The semantic web technology realizes semantic interoperability based on the well defined meaning that a computer can recognize through widening the existing web and cooperative structure between computers and human being. The semantic web [3] technology is the next generation technology that not only expresses data for human being but also enables computers to understand, unify and recycle the data. The ontology offers the meaning of Domain languages as common typical naming structures. The ontology is a kind of knowledge expression. The computers only recognize and manage the Ontology data. The ontology axiom and rule are necessary to treat inference. The information related to the Ontology is useful because the theory is needed when we make contents based on the Ontology study and package them.

The MPEG-7 [11] is the international standard multimedia contents method that helps us to manage multimedia information effectively. It is the way to write multimedia contents, in other words, it is the standard for definition of the Metadata. The MPEG-7 provides the Visual description and the description of color, texture and texture. The Audio part of the MPEG-7 suggests a Fundamental of Audio description, information about Spoken Contents, and a Sound Classification Model. The MPEG-7 provides the Metadata about multimedia. However, the Metadata has only its own information, so it is impossible to provide actual feeling to the multimedia contents by using the MPEG-7. Thus, it is needed to add a model that makes the multimedia contents effective and rich to the MPEG-7 model.

3 Harmonized Media Service Middleware

Suggested the Harmonized media service middleware(HMSM) in this paper conducts to develop a simple media into a multiple media by fusing both an inputted media and an emotionally additional media. The type of additional media is varied. For example texts, sounds, images and music can be an additional media type. These events as the emotional effect based on ambience are extracted after grasp the relationship between an inputted media and effects.

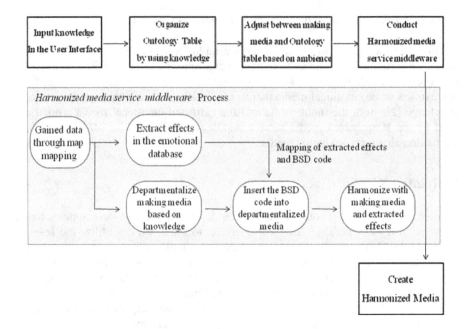

Fig. 1. Process of Harmonized media service middleware

The <Fig 1> shows process of the Harmonized media service middleware. As an advance step for giving emotional effects in substance, the obtained meta information by maker from a designed user interface. And then we consist of the ontology table based on the obtained information. It can conduct the mapping process between the ontology table and an inputted media by using the ambience data that one of the meta information. After former operation, the Harmonized media service middleware carry out departmentalize making media around the inputted knowledge. After that, it can obtain emotional effects from the emotional database through the map mapping step. For harmonizing between an inputted media and extracted effects, use the BSD (Bitstream Syntax Description) code of the MPEG-21 [12] specification. By inserting the BSD code into departmentalized an inputted media and extracted effects can be possible that to fuse an inputted media and extracts effect and to create a new media which has emotion.

3.1 Formation of *Harmonized Media Service Middleware*

For offering an emotional media, the Harmonized media service middleware consists of three parts as follows; the Analyzer, the Extractor and the Harmonizer. Through three steps, an emotional media can be serviced to customers. The <Fig 2> shows a formation of the Harmonized media service middleware.

The Harmonized media service middleware conducts these three steps to service an emotional media that has an actual feeling. First step, The Analyzer executes analysis

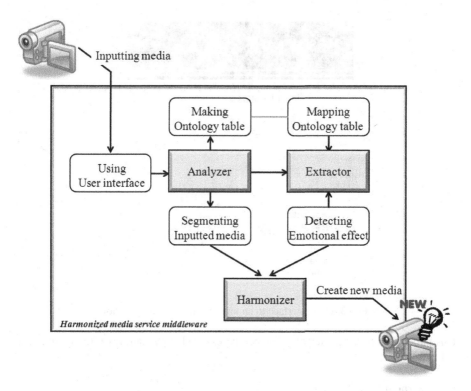

Fig. 2. Structure of the Harmonized media service middleware

about an inputted media contents by practicing techniques of the MPEG-7. The Analyzer should departmentalize an inputted media as a scene. It divides into the concept of the ontology and applies to a technique specification of the MPEG-7 based on the knowledge that obtained through the user interface. Second step, the Extractor executes process about effects. The Extractor should extract effects that have a relation to an inputted media from the emotional effect database. At last, the Harmonizer fuses a departmentalized media that gain by conducting the step one with emotional effects that gain by conducting the step two. The method of fusion uses the BSD code of the MPEG-21. Both departmentalized media and extracted effects have individual the BSD code that doesn't duplicate. Through the three steps, the inputted media can be developed a multiple media that includes the emotional context. As a result, the Harmonized media service middleware can create a new media.

4 Algorithm

4.1 Analyzer

The step of the Analyzer executes analysis of an inputted media that uploaded by maker as a internet user. The Analyzer step is able to take the user interface for obtain necessary knowledge about an inputted media. The <Fig 3> shows a user interface.

Fig. 3. User Interface to an input media meta information

This paper selects categories of ambience types like happy, sad, love, funny and cheer as key issue.

4.2 Extractor

The step of Extractor executes the Extraction of emotional effects from the emotional effect database. The Extractor should extract effects based on knowledge that is discovered through former the Analyzer step. Proper effects are selected by mapping between an ambience of information through the user interface and meta knowledge of stored effects into the emotional effects database. It can upgrade quality of the inputted media and increase satisfaction for customers. At first, an ambience of the inputted media and effects must correspond absolutely. Following, the selected type should correspond too. To select proper effects, this paper offers the ontology tables as shown in the <Fig 4>.

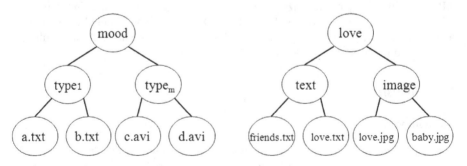

Fig. 4. Present as tree of the ontology mapping rule

Also, the ontology table can be accounted for a formula.

Following:

$M = \{happy \mid sad \mid love \mid \ldots \mid ambience_i\}$

$T = \{text \mid sound \mid music \mid image\}$

$MEDIA = \{ambience, type\}$

$ambience \in M, type \in T$

$S_m = ambience \cap type$

The Set M includes a variety of ambiences. The Set T includes a type of effects which will add media. The MEDIA consists of an ambience and a type which will be offered in substance. To detect proper effects, the S_m (serviced media) is designed to select with a satisfaction both elements.

4.3 Harmonizer

The step of Harmonizer executes a fusion of emotional effects and an inputted media. Through this step, the Harmonized media service middleware can create a new media that has an actual feeling. The inputted media divides into each scene and inserts extracted effects into a gap in the scenes. This process can present a formula.

Following:

$Scene = \{ S_1 + S_2 + S_3 + \ldots + S_{m-1} + S_m \}$

$Media = \{ E_1 + E_2 + E_3 + \ldots + E_{n-1} + E_n \}$

$HaM = \sum_{i=1,j=1}^{m,n} S_i + E_j$

The scene of the inputted media is divided from the Analyzer step and presents a set from 1 to m. The media of extracted the ontology mapping table is consisted of effects from 1 to n. The HaM means the Harmonized media which actualize fusion by adding scene and effects.

5 Realization of the HMSM

In this paper, originally a simple media can develop a multiple media by conducting the Harmonized media service middleware. To maintain compatibility between an inputted media and emotional effects, it adapts to the method that extract emotional effects by using ambience information and insert effects into a media. The media knowledge received through the user interface information match the effects.

Personally in the case of the content value of the grant can be realized. If you have a video content personality that recorded at a wedding, the media could have a lot of noise. In addition, it is difficult that give us a serious feeling rather than a recording media by experts. The Harmonized media service middleware is able to offer a new media that add emotional effects like sounds, images and texts etc. So consumers who offered a new media that has an actual feeling is serviced an opportunity that can feel an impressive media. The <Fig 5> shows a remake media. For remove noise inside media, proper music that selected the Extractor step add the original media. Of course, the music has compatibility with the original media.

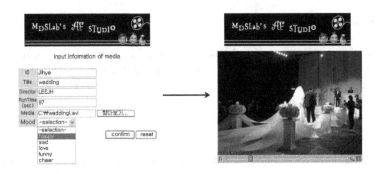

Fig. 5. Implement example through the HMSM

The way to add effects increase the quality of the media itself, and the satisfaction of both makers and consumers.

6   Conclusions

In this paper, we designed the Harmonized media service middleware which has a goal that offers consumers a new media. The new media service an actual feeling by using the emotional knowledge.

The Harmonized media service middleware processes three steps as follows; the Analyzer, the Extractor and the Harmonizer. Each step should execute its work itself. Content uploading by internet users just has simple information as the User Create Contents (UCC). However, by using the Harmonized media service middleware, the original inputted media can be changed an integrated feeling media as the User Generated Contents (UGC) that could present an actual feeling based on the emotional knowledge. As a result, we suggested the *Harmonized media service middleware* for grant harmonized media service.

Acknowledgments

This work was supported by the Korea Research Foundation (KRF) grant funded by the Korea government (MEST)(2009-0072275).

References

1. Yasnari, K.: WEB20. IINNOVATIION, wiznine (2006)
2. Welsh, T.: Ontologies and the Semantic Web. MIDDLEWARESPECTRA 21 (report 2), 2–9 (2007)
3. Berners-Lee, T., Hendler, J., Lassilia, O.: The Sementic Web. Scientific American (2001)
4. Gu, T., Pung, H.K., Zhang, D.: A service-oriented middleware for building context-aware services. Journal of Network and computer applications 28, 1–18 (2004)
5. Kim, S., Yoon, Y.: Video customization system using Mpeg standards. In: The 2nd International Conference on Multimedia and Ubiquitous Engineering, pp. 475–480 (2008)
6. Hossain, M.A., Atrey, P.K., El Saddik, A.: Gain-based Selection of Ambient Media Service in Pervasice Environments. Springer Science 13(6), 599–613 (2008)
7. International Organization for Standardization Organization International de Normalization ISO/IEC JTC1/SC29/WG11 Coding of Moving Pictures and Audio (October 2004)
8. Yoon, Y.-I., Kim, S., Lee, J.-W.: Universal video adaptation model for contents delivery in ubiquitous computing. In: Lee, S., Choo, H., Ha, S., Shin, I.C. (eds.) APCHI 2008. LNCS, vol. 5068, pp. 193–202. Springer, Heidelberg (2008)
9. Burrett, l.S., Pereira, F., Van de Walle, R., Koenen, R.: The MPEG-21 Book. Jone Wiley & Sons, Ltd., Chichester (2006)
10. Manjunath, B.S., Salembier, P., Sikora, T.: Introduction to MPEG-7 Multimedia Content Description Interface. Wiley, Chichester (2002)

A Trust Evaluation Model for Cloud Computing*

Hyukho Kim, Hana Lee, Woongsup Kim, and Yangwoo Kim[**]

Dept. of Information and Communication Engineering, Dongguk University,
Seoul, 100-715, South Korea
{hulegea,lhn1007,woongsup,ywkim}@dongguk.edu

Abstract. Cloud computing is a new paradigm in which dynamically scalable virtualized computing resources are provided as a service over the Internet. However, since resources are limited, it is very important that cloud providers efficiently provide their resources. This paper presents a trust model for efficient reconfiguration and allocation of computing resources satisfying various user requests. Our model collects and analyzes reliability based on historical information of servers in a Cloud data center. Then it prepares the best available resources for each service request in advance, providing the best resources to users. We also carried out experiments for reliability analysis with 4 data types, including an all data set, random data set, recent data set, and the data set within a standard deviation. As a result, using our trust model, cloud providers can utilize their resources efficiently and also provide highly trusted resources and services to many users.

Keywords: Cloud Computing, Virtualization, Trust Model, Grid Computing.

1 Introduction

Cloud computing [1], [2] is a new computing paradigm composed of Grid computing and Utility computing concepts together. It provides dynamically scalable virtualized computing resources as a service over the Internet and users pay for as many resources as they have used. The Cloud itself is a network of virtualized servers or virtual data centers that can deliver powerful applications, platforms, and infrastructures as services over the Internet. Actually Cloud computing already has been used for web mail, blog, web hard storage service and web hosting services. However, due to limitations in software technologies and network bandwidth in the past, Cloud computing could not guarantee service levels and scope that needed to be delivered over the Internet. Nowadays, Cloud computing can provide various levels of service and functions over the Internet, as software and network technologies develop [3].

Cloud computing has various advantages as follows: 1) Improved performance, virtualized servers in a Cloud computing system will boot up faster and run faster, because

---

[*] This work was supported by a Ministry of Education, Science and Technology (MEST) grant funded by the Korea government(S-2009-A0004-00006).
[**] Corresponding author.

D. Ślęzak et al. (Eds.): GDC 2009, CCIS 63, pp. 184–192, 2009.
© Springer-Verlag Berlin Heidelberg 2009

each virtualized server has fewer programs and processes loaded into memory; 2) Lower IT infrastructure costs, instead of investing in larger number of powerful servers, users can borrow and use the computing resources of the Cloud to supplement or replace internal computing resources. They need no longer have to purchase servers to handle peak usage levels; 3) Unlimited storage capacity, the Cloud offers virtually limitless storage capacity. Whatever user needs to store, the user can; 4) Less maintenance, Cloud computing can reduce both hardware and software maintenance including data center space and electricity; 5) Improved compatibility, universal access to documents, collaboration, dynamically shared computing power, etc. However, Cloud providers should efficiently provide their resources to users because resources in Clouds are limited [4]. Hence, we propose a trust model for efficient reconfiguration and allocation of resources according to the various user requests. The reliability of computing resource means availability of a computing resource considering its performance and status. In order to provide resources with high reliability, we need an accurate way of measuring and predicting usage patterns of computing resources whose patterns are changing dynamically over time. Our trust model aims to reconfigure servers dynamically and allocate high quality computing resources to users. The proposed trust model in this paper uses the history information of nodes in the Cloud environment. This information consists of each node's spec information, resources usage, and response time. Then the model analyzes this information and prepares suitable resources on each occasion, and then allocates them immediately when user requests. As a result, Cloud system can provide the best resources and high-level services based on the analyzed information and it is possible to utilize resources efficiently.

The rest of this paper is organized as follows. In Section2, we present the trust model's formation and implementation. In Section 3, we explain the experiments and analyze experimental results. And finally, we conclude in Section 4.

2   Trust Model Implementation

Our trust evaluation model aims to configure the complex set of services dynamically in a cloud environment, according to the predictive performance in terms of stability and availability of all resources that are to be provided as cloud services. Therefore, it is very important to build an adequate trust model for prediction of service's performance and stability.

Our trust evaluating model in the cloud environment is set as follows: $<S, T, R, C, D, U>$, where S is the service consumer (request), T is a set of time slot units where a day is divided by n, such as $T = \{T_1, T_2, ..., T_n\}$, R is {a set of resources} $\cup$ {a set of services}, $C: R \rightarrow V$ denotes the capacity of each resource/service and means that the capacity of each resource is represented as a vector of Integer V, $D: S \rightarrow V$ denotes the demand function of how much resource a service demands to complete the request and is represented as a vector of Integer V, and $U: R \times T \rightarrow [0,1]$, where U denotes the degree of resource availability at a particular time slot based on the requested service's demand capacity and is represented as a percentage. According to the above model, our trust model focuses on predicting the operational availability (noted as U in the above model) during particular periods. Based on this prediction, we could estimate the operating availability for each resource on demand during particular time slots. So a system could configure services dynamically and distribute tasks efficiently in such way that a system minimizes task failure and task migration rate. To this end, we utilize the statistical usage history for the pre-evaluation of each resource in order to make the correct prediction of service availability in the Cloud environment.

In our trust model, we employ Probabilistic Latent Semantic Analysis (pLSA) [5] methodology to estimate the availability of each service/resource provision from the history of statistical usage data. Using pLSA, we can estimate system availability during specific periods and hence we can allocate resources with a minimum failure rate and support a more reliable cloud computing environment. We formalize the pLSA based trust model (equation 1) as follows.

$$P\!\left(r_t > c_i \mid s_j, u_i\right) = \sum_{z \ni Z} P\!\left(r_t > c_i \mid z, s_j\right) P\!\left(z \mid u_i\right) \qquad (1)$$

where u_i is the service request, s_j is the resource ID, c_i is the minimum resource requirements for a service request u_i, r_t is the available capacity for the each time slice, and z is hidden space used for pLSA methodologies. If the expected satisfaction of users gets through this formula, the expected performance of the integrated services or functions can be anticipated, and the best services can be selected. For the purpose of performance prediction, various methods [6] are proposed and Petri Net [7], Process Algebra [8], And the Markov Chain [9] are the most common approach for performance prediction. However, these methodologies work under the assumption that the system clearly knows probabilities of the performance of service provision, which is almost impossible in a cloud environment. Therefore there are desperate needs for estimating resource based performance prediction methodologies specifically for a cloud environment. Therefore, in this paper, we only focus on the resources reliability analysis. In addition, even though pLSA methodology can provide accurate prediction operformance, pLSA intrinsically requires huge computation power. That could give us a large burden of system overhead. So we have to filter out unnecessary candidate resources to save pLSA's computational overhead. To this end, we must also develop a utility model and corresponding ranking algorithm to filter out unnecessary candidate service providers. Our approach helps to reduce overall computational overhead and enable fast analysis of node performance prediction, and hence provide trustworthy resource allocation and service provisioning in a better way.

3 Experiments

This section describes how to configure the Cloud system, and algorithms for performance evaluation, performance metrics used, as well as the experimental results.

3.1 System Configuration

As you can see in Figure 1, the proposed Cloud system environment in this paper consists of virtual machines, physical machines, and an SLA (Service Level Agreement)

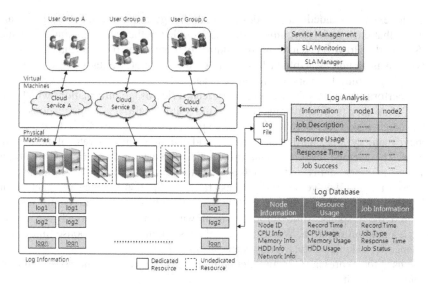

Fig. 1. Overall System Configuration

manager. Physical machines are the basic available resources and it is assumed that there are a limited number of physical machines. The physical machines provide a set of virtual machines which are configured dynamically according to user requests. When the limited physical machines are provided to users from a pool of resources, the provided resources have two types; one is the dedicated resources and the other is the undedicated resources to give some extra margin in case of sudden request rise as shown in the slash regions of Figure 1. In this Cloud system environment, if a new user requests resources when all of the resources are already assigned, then the undedicated resources allocated to others are provided to the new users via dynamic reconfiguration. At this time, providing the undedicated resources to new users shouldn't affect other dedicated resources' performance but it also should provide stable and high performance resources to new users. Therefore, in this paper we present mechanisms which sort high performance resources by analyzing the history information of the undedicated resources for providing highly trusted resources dynamically when the user requests arise.

3.2 Performance Metrics

We proposed mechanisms that sort high performance resources by analyzing the history information of the undedicated resources for providing highly trusted resources dynamically when the user requests arise. This is aimed to provide highly trusted resources to users based on the analysis of an idle server's history information together with the proposed algorithms. To maintain the current status of the system and provide the requested resources additionally, we analyze each node's log information at a regular interval so that we can sort and rank the resources and provide the best resources to a user as soon as possible. We designed and implemented the proposed algorithms with the Java programming language and for the experiments; we assumed that there exist 100 undedicated nodes in the slash regions shown in Figure 1. We also assumed that each node's log information is recorded at the same time interval which is 15 seconds. However, gathering real status log data from 100 real machines every 15 seconds is an unreasonable task so we randomly generated data for node specification (high, medium, low) and the resource usage, etc.

For performance analysis, we used resource/service usage information, which consists of node spec profile, average resource usage information, average response time, and average task success ratio. The node spec profile includes CPU type and frequency, memory size, hard disk capacity and the transmission rate of networking devices. The average resource usage information consists of the current CPU utilization rate, memory status and available hard disk capacity. To analyze the average response time and the average task success ratio, we applied our measurement to four task execution types - addition, subtraction, multiplication and division. We also measured the response time for calculation with eight ciphers which are created through a random function. We also regard the task failure if the response time is zero and hence we calculated the average success ratio of tasks.

We used the expression (2) for calculating the average resource utilization in terms of a node's capacity.

$$R_{i,t,usage} = \sum_{j \in activity(i)} \frac{R_{j,t}}{R_{i,t,capacity}} / K_{i,t} \qquad (2)$$

where i is node ID, j is a single usage activity in the system, t is a specific period of a day, $activity(i)$ is a set of all the resource usage activities at node i, K_i is the total number of resource usage activities at node i, R_j is the amount of resource usage from the activity j, and $R_{i,capacity}$ is the resource capacity of node i.

The best node is defined as a utility function utilizing four performance measures – node spec profile, average resource usage, average response time, and average task success rate – described above. We used the expression (3) to estimate the best node (Higher G_i from (3) implies better performance).

$$G_i = w_{Rc}Rc_i + w_{Ru}Ru_i + w_T T_i + w_S S_i \qquad (3)$$

where G_i is the utility of the node i, w_x is the weight for each term x (performance measure) of G_i, Rc_i is the resource spec profile of node i, Ru_i is the average resource usage of node i, T_i is the average response time of node i, and S_i is the average task success ratio. To calculate G_i, we extract all the available data from our system usage history and convert them to a normalized format with domain range [0, 1] such that each piece of resource information has effects on the utility G_i in fair way. In addition, we either assigned the same weight to each of four performance measures, or placed larger value to one of four weight coefficients while the three other three performance measures were assigned equal. G_i has the maximum value 1, and when we calculate with the same weight, w is 0.25. Otherwise, G_i is calculated using the weight 0.2 from the other 3 information types if one information type has the weight 0.4. After we obtain G_i, we then have node ranking information, and can select a few best nodes. Then we can obtain $R_{i,t,usage}$ (see equation (2)) for such nodes and convert it to r_i used in our pLSA based trust model (equation (1)) to predict the degree of service availability.

3.3 Experimental Results

We used 4 different types of data sets for a node's log analysis including an all data set, random data set, recent data set and the data set within a standard deviation. However, the node's spec information is fixed and doesn't change so it is not affected by the various data types used.

(Case 1) All data set
The first experiment is aimed at analyzing the average resource usage and the task processing capability without considering specific time slot. As shown in Figure 2 (a), this is the result of experiments with all data gathered for 7 days, showing the top 10 ranked nodes selected by the log analysis algorithm. Each bar in the graph shows the ranking for each node when we changed the weight from 0.25 to 0.4 for each affecting factor. As shown (a), node 84 ranked the highest among all the nodes when we

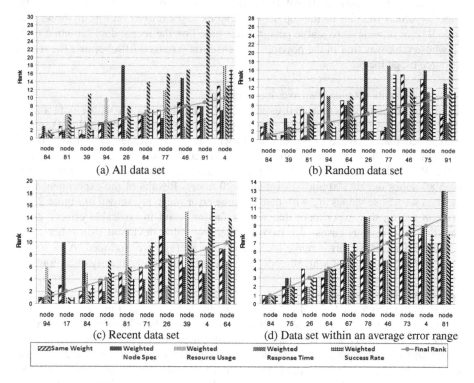

(a) All data set

(b) Random data set

(c) Recent data set

(d) Data set within an average error range

| ⬚Same Weight | ▓▓▓Weighted Node Spec | ▒▒▒Weighted Resource Usage | ░░░Weighted Response Time | ▦▦▦Weighted Success Rate | ━●━Final Rank |

Fig. 2. The Result of Experiments with the different data set

experimented with the all data set. Moreover, node 84 ranked high even when the weight of each factor was changed. On the other hand, node 91 ranked high overall even if it ranked low when the weight for response time was raised. This is because its basic spec is high and the current resources usage is low compared to the others.

(Case 2) Random data set
Figure 2 (b) shows the result of experiments with the random data set. A random data set consists of the specific amount of log data randomly extracted from the all data set. In this case we have similar result to case 1. This is because we selected data randomly from the all data set whose data is also randomly generated. Therefore, the random characteristic exists in both data sets. However, the result should be different if we conduct the experiment in a real computing environment in which real log data is collected.

(Case 3) Recent data set
Each node cannot maintain a consistent usage pattern over time. That is, the usage pattern changes over time, and the recent data set may reflect the future usage pattern better while reducing time spent on analysis. For this experiment, we only used data gathered for the last 24 hours. Figure 2 (c) shows the top 10 ranked nodes that resulted from the experiments with the recent data set. The experimental results with the recent data set are little different from the previous two cases. In this experiment, node 94 which was out of the top 10 in previous cases ranked on top. It shows that node 94 can provide most stable performance based on the recent data set while node 84 whose rank was first in the previous two cases only ranked fifth because the recent resource usage increased.

(Case 4) The data set within an average error range
In this experiment, we conducted experiments using the data set whose data values are within the average error range excluding nodes which are unstable (for example, unexpected load increase or system shutdown, etc). The average error range is the range in which the standard deviation value is added and subtracted from the average value. We excluded some nodes that have substantial margins of error. As a result, we used 80 nodes out of 100 nodes, excluding 20 nodes. Results of the experiment with the data set whose values are within an average error range are shown in Figure 2 (d). We can see on this experiment that weight factors result in ignorable effects, compared to the previous cases. We have smaller log value deviation than other cases because nodes whose error range are beyond the average are excluded. As a result, node 84 ranked the top among all nodes because it had the best capacity on average.

An Overall Ranking
Based on the above analysis of 4 data sets, we made the overall ranking as shown in Figure 3. The final top ranked node 84 has 4GHz CPU, 4.096GB of memory, 300GB of hard disk capacity and 100Mbps of Ethernet network capacity. The average resource usage is also quite stable around 20%, and the change in resource usage is also small, under the average standard deviation whose value is 20. Although node 84 ranked relatively low in the experiment with the recent data set, it achieved the top

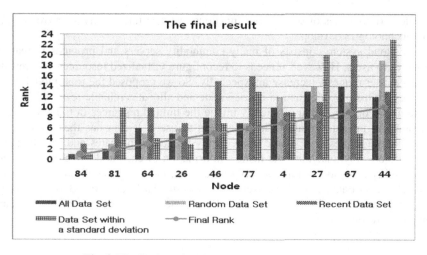

Fig. 3. The final results of experiment with all data sets

rank overall because the average resource usage is low on average and its deviation is also small. On the other hand, the ranking for node 67 is not so good in terms of the basic spec information and the average resource usage, but it was able to rank 9th because the change in resource usage is smaller than others, below the standard deviation. Similarly, node 44 maintained a better ranking when analyzed with the recent data set because its' recent memory utilization is 30% less than that with older data.

As a result, we found that all the nodes within the top 10 kept higher and better rankings than others no matter whatever data set is used. In our experiments we collected a diversity of information at regular intervals such as the node's basic spec, resources usage, response time, and average task success ratio. Those saved history information were then classified as the all data set, random data set, recent data set, and data set within the standard deviation. Since we evaluated and ranked the undedicated nodes with the various data sets, dynamic resource allocation considering recent resource status as well as resource availability is possible for highly trustable Cloud services.

4 Conclusions

Cloud computing is a new computing paradigm composed of Grid computing and Utility computing concepts together. It provides dynamically scalable virtualized resources as a service over Internet and user pay as much as they used. Cloud itself is a network of virtualized servers or virtual data centers that can deliver powerful applications, platforms, and infrastructures as services over the Internet. Actually Cloud computing already has been used for web mail, blog, web hard storage service and web hosting services. However, due to limitations in software technologies and network bandwidth in the past, Cloud computing could not guarantee service levels and scope that needed to be delivered over the Internet. Currently, however, Cloud computing can provide various levels of service and functions over the Internet, as software and network technologies develop.

The Cloud system consists of many commodity servers and provides virtualized resources to users. However, it needs to reconfigure virtualized resources dynamically when the user requests increase unexpectedly. So we proposed the trust model which analyzes the history information of each node and allocates reliable resources according to user requests. It can efficiently utilize the limited resources in the Cloud environment and provide reliable Cloud services to users. It also has the advantage of providing the requested resource immediately because it prepares and selects highly efficient nodes by analyzing the history information of each node. We experimented on reliability analysis with a diversity of data sets, including the all data set, random data set, recent data set, and data set within the standard deviation. By doing so, we can increase the reliability of overall Cloud system by providing highly trustable computing resources.

References

1. Buyya, R., Yeo, C.S., Venugopal, S.: Market-Oriented Cloud Computing: Vision, Hype, and Reality for Delivering IT Services as Computing Utilities. In: Proc. of the 10th IEEE International Conference on High Performance Computing and Communications (2008)
2. Vaquero, L.M., Rodero-Merino, L., Caceres, J., Lindner, M.: A Break in the Clouds: Towards a Cloud Definition. In: ACM SIGCOMM Computer Communication Review, vol. 39(1) (2009)
3. Li, H., Sedayao, J., Hahn-Steichen, J., Jimison, E., Spence, C., Chahal, S.: Developing an Enterprise Cloud Computing Strategy. Korea Information Processing Society Review (2009)
4. Vouk, M.A.: Cloud computing — Issues, research and implementations, Information Technology Interfaces. In: 30th International Conference (ITI 2008), pp. 31–40 (2008)
5. Hofmann, T.: Probabilistic Latent Semantic Indexing. In: Proceedings of the Twenty-Second Annual International SIGIR Conference on Research and Development in Information Retrieval, SIGIR 1999 (1999)
6. Kwiecień, A., Kwiatkowski, J., Pawlik, M., Konieczny, D.: Performance Prediction Methods. In: Proceedings of the International Multiconference on Computer Science and Information Technology, pp. 363–370 (2006)
7. Petri Nets World,
   http://www.informatik.uni-hamburg.de/TGI/PetriNets/
8. Baeten, J.C.M.: A brief history of process algebra. Theoretical Computer Science archive 335(2-3), 131–146 (2005)
9. Gokhale, S.S., Trivedi, K.S.: Analytical Models for Architecture-Based Software Reliability Prediction: A Unification Framework. IEEE Transactions 55(4), 578–590 (2006)

Multiple Reduced Hypercube $MRH(n)$: A New Interconnection Network Reducing Both Diameter and Edge of Hypercube

Hyun Sim[1,*], Jae-Chul Oh[1], and Hyeong-Ok Lee[2]

[1] Department of Computer Science, Sunchon National University, Sunchon, Chonnam, 540-742, Korea
{simhyun,ojc}@scnu.ac.kr
[2] Department of Computer Education, Sunchon National University, Sunchon, Chonnam, 540-742, Korea
oklee@scnu.ac.kr

Abstract. In this paper, Multiple Reduced Hypercube(MRH), which is a new interconnection network based on a hypercube interconnection network, is suggested. Also, this paper demonstrates that $MRH(n)$ proposed in this study is superior to the previously proposed hypercube interconnection networks and the hypercube transformation interconnection networks in terms of network cost(diameter × degree). In addition, several network properties(connectivity, routing algorithm, diameter, broadcasting) of $MRH(n)$ are analyzed.

Keywords: Interconnection network, routing algorithm, diameter.

1 Introduction

An interconnection network system to link multicomputer processors greatly influences performance and scalability of the whole system. Therefore studies on an interconnection network are a base for parallel processing computer development, and the need is continuously increasing. Interconnection networks that have been proposed to date are classified based on the number of nodes into meshes ($n \times k$), hypercube (2^n) and star ($n!$), and network scales to evaluate interconnection networks are degree, connectivity, scalability, diameter, network cost, etc [3,4,5,6,7,8,9]. In an interconnection network, degree related to hardware cost and diameter related to message passing time are correlated with each other.

In general, as degree of an interconnection network is increased, diameter is decreased, which can increase throughput in the interconnection network, however, it increases hardware cost with the increased number of pins of the processor when a parallel computer is designed. An interconnection network with less degree reduces hardware cost but increases message passing time, which adversely

---

* This work was supported in part by MKE & IITA (09-Infra, Industrial original technology development project).

D. Ślęzak et al. (Eds.): GDC 2009, CCIS 63, pp. 193–205, 2009.

affects latency or throughput of an interconnection network. Network scales being typically used for comparative evaluation of an interconnection network due to the said characteristic include network cost [3,4,5,6,7,8,9] defined as degree × diameter of an interconnection network.

A typical phase of an interconnection network is a hypercube interconnection network. A hypercube interconnection network is a representative interconnection network being broadly used in commercial systems in addition to existing studies by virtue of its merit of easily providing a communication network system required in applications of all kinds. Hypercube is node- and edge-symmetric, has a simple routing algorithm with maximal fault tolerance and a simple reflexive system, and also has a merit that it may be readily embedded with the proposed interconnection networks [10,11]. However, it involves weak points that network cost increases due to increase of degree with the increased number of nodes, and that a mean distance between diameter and node is not short as compared with degree.

To improve such weak points, Reduced Hypercube [12] that reduced the number of edges of a hypercube interconnection network, Gaussian Hypercube [13], and Exchanged Hypercube [14] have been suggested, and in addition, Crossed Cube [5] that improved diameter of a hypercube interconnection network, Folded Hypercube [9], HCN [6,11], HFN [3], etc. have been proposed. Many interconnection networks that have been proposed until now demonstrated that they have superior network cost to hypercube by reducing just one network scale of degree or diameter of hypercube.

In this paper, a Multi-Reduction Hypercube interconnection network $MRH(n)$ of a new interconnection network with superior network cost to hypercube-class interconnection networks is proposed while degree, diameter, and two network scales of hypercube are entirely reduced. And several properties of $MRH(n)$ - connectivity, routing algorithm, diameter, etc. - are analyzed. Also, this paper demonstrates that network cost of $MRH(n)$ is superior through comparative analysis of network cost between the proposed hypercube-class interconnection network and $MRH(n)$. This paper is composed as follows: Section 2 introduces $MRH(n)$, Section 3 analyzes the several properties of $MRH(n)$, Section 4 performs comparative analysis of network cost between a hypercube-class interconnection network and $MRH(n)$, and finally, conclusion is given.

2   Preliminaries

An interconnection network can be expressed as an undirected graph, which indicates each process in nodes and a communication channel among processors in edges. An interconnection network is expressed as an undirected graph $G = (V, E)$ as mentioned below. Here, $V(G)$ is a set of nodes that is, $V(G) = \{0, 1, 2, \ldots, N-1\}$, $E(G)$ is a set of edges, and a necessary and sufficient condition where an edge (v, w) is to be present as a pair (v, w) of two nodes v and w in $V(G)$ is that a communication channel exists between the node v and the node w. The network scales to evaluate an interconnection network include degree, diameter, symmetry, scalability, fault tolerance, broadcasting, and embedding [1,5].

Interconnection networks that have been proposed to date are classified based on the number of nodes into meshes having $n \times k$ nodes, hypercube having 2^n nodes, and a star graph having $n!$ nodes. Hypercube Q_n consists of 2^n nodes and $n2^{n-1}$ edges. The addresses of each node can be expressed in an n-bit binary number, and when the addresses of two nodes is exactly one bit different, an edge exists between them. The n-dimensional hypercube Q_n is a regular graph whose network cost is n^2 while degree and diameter are n, respectively. Hypercube has a strong point that it can easily provide a communication network system required in applications of all kinds since it is node- and edge-symmetrical and has a simple reflexive system, and is being used in Intel iPSC, nCUBE [12], Connection Machine CM-2 [13], SGI Origin 2000, etc [9]. In terms of embedding, it also has a strong point that other interconnection network systems can be efficiently embedded such as tree, pyramid, mesh, etc., however, it has a weak point that a mean distance between diameter and node is not short as compared to degree. This indicates that hypercube does not efficiently use edges. New interconnection networks that improved such weak point include Multiply-Twisted-Cube, Folded Hypercube [4], and Extended Hypercube.

Folded-Hypercube FQ_n is that one edge is added to nodes where addresses of each node are in complement relation in existing hypercube, and in this interconnection network, degree increases by 1 compared to hypercube but diameter of hypercube is improved by about a half.

3   Design of Multiple Reduced Hypercube ($MRH(n)$)

3.1   Definition of Multiple Reduced Hypercube

The nodes of a Multiple Reduced Hypercube $MRH(n)$ are expressed as n bit strings $s_n s_{n-1} \ldots s_i \ldots s_2 s_1$ consisting of binary numbers $\{0,1\}$ ($1 \leq i \leq n$). The edges of $MRH(n)$ are expressed in three forms according to connection method, they are called hypercube edge, exchange edge, and complement edge, respectively, and are indicated as h-edge, x-edge, and c-edge, respectively ($\lfloor \frac{n}{2} \rfloor + 1 \leq h \leq n$). Each edge is defined into when n is an even number and n is an odd number.

Case 1) When n is an even number: It is assumed that for edge definition, $s_n s_{n-1} \ldots s_{i+1}$ is α and a bit string $s_i \ldots s_2 s_1$ is β in the bit string of a node $U(= s_n s_{n-1} \ldots s_i \ldots s_2 s_1)$. Therefore the bit string of a node $U(= s_n s_{n-1} \ldots s_i \ldots s_2 s_1)$ can be simply expressed as $\alpha\beta$. Assuming that the nodes U and V are adjacent with each other, adjacent edges are as follows:

i) Hypercube edge : This edge indicates an edge linking two nodes $U(= s_n s_{n-1} \ldots s_j \ldots s_{i+1} s_i \ldots s_2 s_1)$ and $V(= s_n s_{n-1} \ldots \bar{s}_j \ldots s_{i+1} s_i \ldots s_2 s_1)$ of $MRH(n)$ ($\frac{n}{2} \leq j \leq n$).

ii) Exchange edge : This edge indicates an edge linking two nodes $U(= \alpha\beta)$ and $V(= \beta\alpha)$ of $MRH(n)$ if $\alpha \neq \beta$ in the bit string of the nodes.

iii) Complement edge : This edge indicates an edge linking two nodes $U(= \alpha\beta)$ and $V(= \overline{\alpha\beta})$ of $MRH(n)$ if $\alpha = \beta$ in the bit string of the nodes.

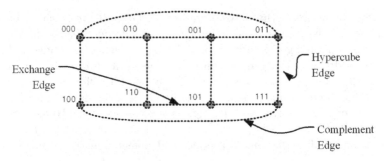

Fig. 1. $MRH(3)$

Case 2) When n is an odd number: It is assumed that for edge definition, $s_{n-1} \ldots s_{i+1}$ is α' and a bit string $s_i \ldots s_2 s_1$ is β' in the bit string of a node $U(= s_n s_{n-1} \ldots s_i \ldots s_2 s_1)$. Then the number of bit strings of α' and β' is each $\lfloor \frac{n}{2} \rfloor$. Therefore a node U can be indicated as $U(= s_n \alpha' \beta')$.

i) Hypercube edge : This edge indicates an edge linking two nodes $U(= s_n s_{n-1} \ldots s_j \ldots s_{i+1} s_i \ldots s_2 s_1)$ and $V(= s_n s_{n-1} \ldots \bar{s}_j \ldots s_{i+1} s_i \ldots s_2 s_1)$ of $MRH(n)$ ($\lfloor \frac{n}{2} \rfloor \leq j \leq n$).

ii) Exchange edge : This edge indicates an edge linking two nodes $U(= s_n \alpha' \beta')$ and $V(= s_n \beta' \alpha')$ of $MRH(n)$ in the bit string of a node.

iii) Complement edge : This edge indicates an edge linking two nodes $U(= s_n \alpha' \beta')$ and $V(= s_n \overline{\alpha' \beta'})$ of $MRH(n)$ if $\alpha' = \beta'$ in the bit string of a node.

By the above definition, it is found that the number of nodes is 2^n as the nodes of $MRH(n)$ are n bit strings $s_n s_{n-1} \ldots s_i \ldots s_2 s_1$ consisting of binary numbers $\{0,1\}$, and that $MRH(n)$ is a regular network whose degree is $\lceil \frac{n}{2} \rceil + 1$ since each node has $\lceil \frac{n}{2} \rceil$ hypercube edges and one exchange or complement edge.

Node(edge) connectivity is the least number of nodes(edges) that are required to be eliminated to divide an interconnection network into two or more parts without common nodes. Even if $k - 1$ or less nodes are eliminated from a given interconnection network, an interconnection network is linked, and once the interconnection network is separated when proper k nodes are eliminated, connectivity of the interconnection network is called k. An interconnection network having the same node connectivity and degree means that it has maximal fault tolerance [1]. It is known that node connectivity, edge connectivity, and degree of an interconnection network G are called $\kappa(G)$, $\lambda(G)$, and $\zeta(G)$, respectively, and $\kappa(G) \leq \lambda(G) \leq \zeta(G)$ [1]. This paper demonstrates that node connectivity and degree of $MRH(n)$ are same in order to prove that $MRH(n)$ has maximal fault tolerance, and based on the result, $MRH(n)$ has maximal fault tolerance.

Theorem 1. *The connectivity of $MRH(n)$ is $\kappa(MRH(n)) = \lceil \frac{n}{2} \rceil + 1$ ($n \geq 2$).*

Proof. Degree of each node composing $MRH(n)$ is $\lceil \frac{n}{2} \rceil + 1$. It is demonstrated that even if any $\lceil \frac{n}{2} \rceil$ nodes are eliminated from $MRH(n)$, $MRH(n)$ is not divided. It is assumed that in $MRH(n)$, X is a set of fault nodes, and the number of elements of the set X is $\lceil \frac{n}{2} \rceil$. Assuming that in $MRH(n)$, a network

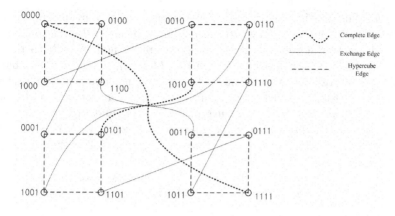

Fig. 2. $MRH(4)$

eliminating a fault node set X is a connected network, node connectivity of $MRH(n)$ is proven to be $\lceil\frac{n}{2}\rceil + 1$. Assuming that a node of $MRH(n)$ is S, an interconnection network eliminating a fault node set X from $MRH(n)$ is expressed as $MRH(n) - X$. It is assumed that $\lceil\frac{n}{2}\rceil$ nodes are included in X among nodes linked to a node S of $MRH(n)$. Degree of the node S is $\lceil\frac{n}{2}\rceil + 1$ therefore it can be found that S is linked to one node. It is assumed that $\lceil\frac{n}{2}\rceil$ or less nodes are included in X among nodes linked to the node S. Then it is found that S is linked to nodes of $\lceil\frac{n}{2}\rceil + 1 - \lceil\frac{n}{2}\rceil$ or less. Thus $\kappa(MRH(n)) \geq \lceil\frac{n}{2}\rceil$. In addition, $MRH(n)$ is a regular interconnection network whose degree is $\lceil\frac{n}{2}\rceil + 1$, therefore $\kappa(MRH(n)) \leq \lceil\frac{n}{2}\rceil + 1$. Accordingly, $\kappa(MRH(n)) = \lceil\frac{n}{2}\rceil + 1$. Similarly, $\lambda(MRH(n)) = \lceil\frac{n}{2}\rceil + 1$ can be demonstrated.

3.2   Routing Algorithm and Diameter

Assuming that in $MRH(n)$, an arbitrary node of the initial node $U(= u_n u_{n-1} \ldots u_j \ldots u_{i+1} u_i \ldots u_2 u_1)$ is $(\alpha\beta)$ $(\alpha = u_n u_{n-1} \ldots u_j, \beta = u_{i+1} u_i \ldots u_2 u_1)$ and an arbitrary node of the destination node $V(= v_n v_{n-1} \ldots v_j \ldots v_{i+1} v_i \ldots v_2 v_1)$ is $(\gamma\delta)$ $(\gamma = v_n v_{n-1} \ldots v_j, \delta = v_{i+1} v_i \ldots v_2 v_1)$, a routing algorithm is considered $(\lfloor\frac{n}{2}\rfloor \leq j \leq n)$. When two nodes are present in the same cluster, that is, the shortest routing when $\beta = \delta$ is determined by a hypercube algorithm because α and γ exist in the same internal module, node movement using a hypercube edge is indicated as $(\alpha\beta) \Rightarrow (\gamma\beta)$. In case of two nodes $(\alpha\beta)$ and $(\gamma\beta)$ $(\beta \neq \delta)$, the following three routing algorithms are proposed. Routing of the node $(\alpha\beta)$ in case of $(\alpha \neq \beta)$ is linked to the node $\beta\alpha$ by means of an exchange edge. If $\alpha = \beta$, the node $(\alpha\beta)$ is the node $\beta\alpha$ or the node $(\alpha\alpha)$, and then routing is linked to the node $(\beta\beta)$ or the node $(\alpha'\alpha')$. $\Rightarrow$ indicates an hypercube edge and $\rightarrow$ indicates routing between clusters as an exchange or complement edge.

Case 1) The routing algorithm A first moves α to β by means of a hypercube edge in order to move to clusters in which the destination node is included in setting a route to move from the initial node $U(\alpha\beta)$ to the destination node $(\gamma\delta)$, because in a graph of $MRH(n)$, a bit may be changed just at the α position. Movement $(\gamma\beta) \rightarrow (\beta\gamma)$ is done with an exchange edge to move from the current $(\gamma\beta)$ node to the cluster in which the destination node is located. Since the current nodes $(\beta\gamma)$ and $(\gamma\beta)$ are located in internal modules of the same cluster, movement $(\beta\gamma) \Rightarrow (\gamma\beta)$ is done with a hypercube edge to change β into γ. That is, a routing algorithm A to move from an initial node $U(= u_n u_{n-1} \ldots u_j \ldots u_{i+1} u_i \ldots u_2 u_1)$ to a destination node $V(= v_n v_{n-1} \ldots v_j \ldots v_{i+1} v_i \ldots v_2 v_1)$ is as follows: After movement from $(u_n u_{n-1} \ldots u_j \ldots u_{i+1} u_i \ldots u_2 u_1)$ to the node $(v_{i+1} v_i \ldots v_2 v_1 \ldots u_{i+1} u_i \ldots u_2 u_1)$ with a hypercube edge, the node $(v_{i+1} v_i \ldots v_2 v_1 \ldots u_{i+1} u_i \ldots u_2 u_1)$ is moved to the node $(u_{i+1} u_i \ldots u_2 u_1 \ldots v_{i+1} v_i \ldots v_2 v_1)$ with an exchange edge in order to move to clusters in which the V node is included. Since the current node $(u_{i+1} u_i \ldots u_2 u_1 \ldots v_{i+1} v_i \ldots v_2 v_1)$ is located in the same module as the V node, it is moved to $(v_n v_{n-1} \ldots v_j \ldots v_{i+1} v_i \ldots v_2 v_1)$ with a hypercube edge. Therefore it is found that the routing algorithm A is $(\alpha\beta) \Rightarrow (\gamma\beta) \rightarrow (\beta\gamma) \Rightarrow (\gamma\delta)$.

Case 2) The routing algorithm C is used when the number of different bits of γ and δ is least, meeting the conditions of $\beta \neq \gamma$ and $\gamma \neq \delta$. For algorithm method, an internal module of the destination node is preferentially matched in setting a route to move from the initial node $U(\alpha\beta)$ to the destination node $(\gamma\delta)$. To change α into γ with a hypercube edge, movement $(\alpha\beta) \Rightarrow (\gamma\beta)$ is done. Now, $(\gamma\beta)$ is moved to $(\beta\gamma)$ with an exchange edge to change β into the cluster in which the destination node is located. β is moved to γ with a hypercube edge that is, $(\gamma\beta) \Rightarrow (\delta\beta)$. To move to the cluster in which the destination node is located, movement $(\delta\gamma) \rightarrow (\gamma\delta)$ is done with an exchange edge, again. That is, the routing algorithm C moving from the initial node $U(= u_n u_{n-1} \ldots u_j \ldots u_{i+1} u_i \ldots u_2 u_1)$ to the destination node $V(= v_n v_{n-1} \ldots v_j \ldots v_{i+1} v_i \ldots v_2 v_1)$ is as follows: After movement from the initial node $(u_n u_{n-1} \ldots u_j \ldots u_{i+1} u_i \ldots u_2 u_1)$ to the node $(v_n v_{n-1} \ldots v_j \ldots u_{i+1} u_i \ldots u_2 u_1)$ with a hypercube edge, the node $(v_n v_{n-1} \ldots v_j \ldots u_{i+1} u_i \ldots u_2 u_1)$ is moved to the node $(u_{i+1} u_i \ldots u_2 u_1 \ldots v_n v_{n-1} \ldots v_j)$ with an exchange edge to move to the cluster in which the V node is included. The current node $(u_{i+1} u_i \ldots u_2 u_1 \ldots v_n v_{n-1} \ldots v_j)$ is moved to $(v_{i+1} v_i \ldots v_2 v_1 \ldots v_n v_{n-1} \ldots v_j)$ with a hypercube edge. To move to the destination node, the node $(v_{i+1} v_i \ldots v_2 v_1 \ldots v_n v_{n-1} \ldots v_j)$ is moved to the node $(v_n v_{n-1} \ldots v_j \ldots v_{i+1} v_i \ldots v_2 v_1)$ with an exchange edge. Thus it is found that the routing algorithm B is $(\alpha\beta) \Rightarrow (\gamma\beta) \rightarrow (\beta\gamma) \Rightarrow (\delta\gamma) \rightarrow (\gamma\delta)$.

Case 3) When $M = \beta$ in the route of the routing algorithm C, part 1 is the node $(\beta\beta)$, and when $M = \beta'$, part 2 is the node $(\delta\delta)$. The routing algorithm C has the shortest distance if the route of $(\alpha\beta)$ and $(\gamma\delta)$ uses a complement edge. For example, assuming that the initial node is 000000 and the departure node is 110111, if the routing algorithm A or the routing algorithm B is used, a routing distance n is 6. However, if a complement edge is used, 000000 $\rightarrow$ 111111 $\Rightarrow$

110111, therefore a routing distance $\frac{n}{2}$ is 3. Like this, the routing algorithm C is used if $(\alpha\beta)$ and $(\gamma\delta)$ use complement edges.

To find out the shortest route using a complement edge, a Hamming distance is used as mentioned below. $H(A, B)$ means the number of bits of different binary numbers for A and B, which is called a Hamming distance. It is also called $H(Q, P) = H(\overline{Q}, \overline{P})$ according to properties of a Hamming distance. Assuming that two n bit numbers are indicated as $A = A_n \ldots A_1$ and $B = B_n \ldots B_1$ as Hamming distance, the following equation is obtained:

$$H(A, B) = \sum_{i=1}^{n} A_i \oplus B_i$$

$\oplus$ indicates exclusive-or operator. The distances of R_A , R_B and R_C following the three routing algorithms below are as follows:

i) $R_A = H(\alpha\delta) + H(\beta\gamma) + 1$
ii $R_B = H(\alpha\gamma) + H(\beta\delta) + 2$
iii) $R_C = H(\alpha M) + H(\beta M) + H(\delta M') + H(\gamma M') + \theta$

If $M = \beta = \delta'$, $\theta = 1$, and if $M = \beta$ or $M = \delta'$ $(\beta\delta')$, $\theta = 2$. Otherwise, $\theta = 3$. M is a minimized cluster used to make a routing distance R_C to be the shortest distance, and M can be found as mentioned below. The cluster M, which makes a routing distance $Q = H(\alpha M) + H(\beta M) + H(\delta M') + H(\gamma M')$ to be the shortest distance, is called a Q-minimized cluster, and if the node P consisting of n bits exists, the bit of the order i of P is indicated as P_i. According to properties of a Hamming distance, $H(Q, P) = H(\overline{Q}, \overline{P})$, therefore $H(M'\gamma) = H(M\gamma')$ and $H(M'\delta) = H(M\delta')$, and based on this, the following equation can be obtained: $Q = H(\alpha M) + H(\beta M) + H(\delta'M) + H(\gamma'M) = \sum_{i=1}^{n}\{(M_i \oplus \alpha_i) + (M_i \oplus \beta_i) + (M_i \oplus \gamma_i) + (M_i \oplus \delta_i)\}$

A set of Q-minimized clusters satisfies the following conditions, and it can be obtained by searching for the bit string M_i to minimize the equation $(M_i \oplus \alpha_i) + (M_i \oplus \beta_i) + (M_i \oplus \gamma_i') + (M_i \oplus \delta_i')$:
If $\alpha_i\beta_i\gamma_i'\delta_i' \in \{0111, 1011, 1101, 1110, 1111\}$ then $M_i = 1$. If $\alpha_i\beta_i\gamma_i'\delta_i' \in \{0000, 0001, 0010, 0100, 1000\}$ then $M_i = 0$. If $\alpha_i\beta_i\gamma_i'\delta_i' \in \{0011, 0101, 0110, 1001, 1010, 1100\}$ then $M_i = X$. Here, X means that it can have any values of the 'Don't care' terms that is, (0 or 1). For example, two nodes are $(\alpha\beta) = (010001)$ and $(\gamma\delta) = (111101)$ in $MRH(3)$, and three 4-bit values $\alpha_i\beta_i\gamma_i'\delta_i'$ are 0000, 0110, and 1000. $M = 0X0$, and then X value may be 0 or 1, therefore Q-minimized clusters become 000, 010.

Lemma 1. *Assuming that two nodes of $MRH(n)$ are $(\alpha\beta)$ and $(\gamma\delta)$ (on condition of $\beta \neq \delta$) and that a route from the node $(\alpha\beta)$ to the node $(\gamma\delta)$ is P, if the route P includes 3 or more exchange edges, the route P is not the shortest distance.*

Proof. It is assumed that the departure node is $(\alpha\beta)$ and the destination node is $(\gamma\delta)$. If $\alpha = V_{-1}, \beta = V_0, \gamma = V_{x+1}$, and $\delta = V_x$, and the route P linking two nodes includes x exchange edges $(3 \leq x)$, the route P is composed as follows: $P = (V_{-1}V_0) \Rightarrow (V_1V_0) \rightarrow (V_0V_1) \Rightarrow (V_2V_1) \rightarrow (V_1V_2) \Rightarrow \ldots \rightarrow \ldots \Rightarrow (V_{x-1}V_x) \Rightarrow (V_{x+1}V_x)$.

A routing distance of the route P: $R_P = \sum_{i=1}^{x+1} H(V_i V_{i-2}) + x$.
It is divided into the following two cases according to x value.

Case 1) When x is an odd number : The route Q including one exchange edge is composed as follows:

$Q = (V_{-1}V_0) \Rightarrow (V_1V_0) \Rightarrow (V_3V_0) \Rightarrow \ldots \Rightarrow (V_xV_0) \rightarrow (V_0V_x) \Rightarrow (V_2V_x) \Rightarrow (V_4V_x) \Rightarrow \ldots \Rightarrow (V_{x+1}V_x)$.

A routing distance of the route Q: $R_Q = \sum_{i=1}^{x+1} H(V_i V_{i-2}) + 1$. $R_Q < R_P$, therefore it is found that length of the route Q is shorter than that of the route P.

Case 2) When x is an even number : The route Q including two exchange edges is composed as follows:

$Q = (V_{-1}V_0) \Rightarrow (V_1V_0) \Rightarrow (V_3V_0) \Rightarrow \ldots \Rightarrow (V_{x+1}V_0) \rightarrow (V_0V_{x+1}) \Rightarrow (V_2V_{x+1}) \Rightarrow (V_4V_{x+1}) \Rightarrow \ldots \Rightarrow (V_xV_{x+1}) \Rightarrow (V_{x+1}V_x)$.

A routing distance of the route Q: $R_Q = \sum_{i=1}^{x+1} H(V_i V_{i-2}) + 2$. $R_Q < R_P$, therefore it is found that length of the route Q is shorter than that of the route P. If the route P includes 3 or more exchange edges, the route P is found not to be the shortest distance.

Lemma 2. *If two nodes are present in the same cluster and the route P includes 2 or more complement edges, the route P is not the shortest distance.*

Proof. If two nodes are present in the same cluster and the route follows the routing algorithm A, it indicates routing in hypercube. If the route P linking two nodes includes x complement edges($x \leq 2$), the route P can be composed as follows:

$P = (\alpha\beta) \Rightarrow (V_1V_1) \rightarrow (V_1'V_1') \Rightarrow (V_2V_2) \rightarrow (V_2'V_2') \Rightarrow \ldots \rightarrow \ldots \Rightarrow (V_xV_x) \rightarrow (V_x'V_x') \Rightarrow (\gamma\delta)$.

A routing distance of the route P is as follows:

$R_P = H(\alpha V_1) + H(\beta V_1) + \sum_{i=1}^{x-1} 2H(V_{i+1}V_i) + H(\gamma V_x') + H(\delta V_x') + \theta$.
If $\theta \geq \delta$, at least, x complement edges are included. It is divided into the following two cases according to x value:

Case 1) When x is an odd number: The route Q including only one complement edge is composed as follows:

$Q = (\alpha\beta) \Rightarrow (V_1V_1) \rightarrow (V_1'V_1') \Rightarrow \ldots \Rightarrow (V_{2j}V'1) \Rightarrow (V_{2j+1}'V_1') \Rightarrow \ldots \Rightarrow (V_x'V_1') \Rightarrow (\delta V_1') \rightarrow (V_1'\delta) \Rightarrow (V_2\delta) \Rightarrow \ldots \Rightarrow (V_{2j}\delta) \Rightarrow (V_{2j+1}\delta) \Rightarrow \ldots \Rightarrow (V_x'\delta) \Rightarrow (\gamma\delta)$.

A routing distance of the route Q is as follows:

$R_Q = H(\alpha V_1) + H(\beta V_1) + \sum_{i=1}^{x-1} 2H(V_{i+1}V_i) + H(\gamma V_x') + H(\delta V_x') + \theta$,
If $V_1 = \beta$, θ is 1. Otherwise, it is 2. It is found that if $x \geq 3$, $R_Q \leq R_P$, therefore the route Q is shorter than the route P.

Case 2) When x is an even number : The route Q that does not include any complement edge is composed as follows:

$$Q = (\alpha\beta) \Rightarrow (V_1\beta) \Rightarrow \ldots \Rightarrow (V_{2j-1}\beta) \Rightarrow (V'_{2j}\beta) \Rightarrow \ldots \Rightarrow (V'_x\beta) \Rightarrow (\delta\beta) \rightarrow$$
$$(\beta\delta) \Rightarrow (V_1\delta) \Rightarrow \ldots \Rightarrow (V_{2j-1}\delta) \Rightarrow (V'_{2j}\delta) \Rightarrow \ldots \Rightarrow (V'_x\delta) \Rightarrow (\gamma\delta).$$

A routing distance of the route Q is as follows:

$$R_Q = H(V_1\alpha) + H(V_1\beta) + \sum_{i=1}^{x-1} 2H(V_{i+1}V_i) + H(\delta V'_x) + H(\gamma V'_x) + 1,$$

$R_Q < R_P$, therefore it is found that the route Q is shorter than the route P. Thus if the route P includes two or more complement edges, the route P is not the shortest distance.

Lemma 3. *In the routing algorithm A, the shortest route including one exchange edge exists.*

Proof. An exchange edge linking the two nodes $(\alpha\beta)$ and $(\gamma\delta)$ is a certain edge to link the clusters β and δ, therefore a route including one exchange edge must pass through an edge linking two nodes, certainly. A route following the routing algorithm A is a certain route including one exchange edge. Therefore the routing algorithm A is the shortest distance among routes including one exchange edge.

Lemma 4. *In the routing algorithm B, the shortest route including two exchange edges exists.*

Proof. The route P including two exchange edges is composed as follows:
$P = (\alpha\beta) \Rightarrow (V\beta) \rightarrow (\beta V) \Rightarrow (\delta V) \rightarrow (V\delta)(\gamma\delta)$, $(V \neq \beta$ and $V \neq I)$.
A routing distance of the route P is as follows:
$R_P = H(V\alpha) + H(\delta\beta) + H(\gamma V) + 2$
$R_B = H(\gamma\alpha) + H(\delta\alpha) + 2$ and $H(V\alpha) + H(\gamma) \geq H(\gamma\alpha)$, accordingly $R_P \geq R_B$. Therefore the routing algorithm B is the shortest distance among routes including two exchange edges. If $H(V\alpha) + H(\gamma V) = H(\gamma\alpha)$, the route P is same as the route length of the routing algorithm B, and also available as a substitute route of B.

Lemma 5. *In the routing algorithm C, the shortest route including one complement edge exists.*

Proof. Demonstration can be easily done based on definition of the routing algorithm C (case C) of the previous 4.

Based on the Lemmas 1-5, an optimal routing algorithm linking two nodes $(\alpha\beta)$ and $(\gamma\delta)$ on condition of $\beta \neq \delta$ in $MRH(n)$ could be found. The optimal routing algorithm is an algorithm having the shortest route among three routing algorithms A, B, and C. Distance d between two nodes $(\alpha\beta)$ and $(\gamma\delta)$ is the shortest distance among the three route lengths.
$d = min(R_A, R_B, R_C)$

Table 1. The values of R_{A_i}, R_{B_i}, R_{C_i}, and M_i

group	$\alpha_i\beta_i\gamma_i\delta_i$	R_{A_i}	R_{B_i}	R_{C_i}	M_i
1	0000, 1111	0	2	0	$M_i = X$
2	0110, 1001	0	2	2	$M_i = X$
3	0101, 1010	2	2	0	$M_i = X$
4	0011, 1100	2	0	2	$M_i = \beta_i = \delta_i'$
5	0010, 1101, 1000, 0111	1	1	1	$M_i = \beta_i = \delta_i'$
6	0001, 1110	1	1	1	$M_i = \beta_i \neq \delta_i'$
7	0100, 1011	1	1	1	$M_i = \delta_i \neq \beta_i$

For example, a distance d between two nodes $U=(000111101010)$ and $V=(011001101010)$ is obtained. The minimized cluster M between two nodes is 000111. The following three routing lengths are obtained.

$R_A = 3 + 3 + 1 = 7$.
$R_B = 4 + 0 + 2 = 6$.
$R_C = 3 + 1 + 2 + 2 = 8$.

R_B has the least value, therefore it is found that the routing algorithm B is a regular routing algorithm for two nodes (000111101010) and (011001101010). A distance between two nodes inside the interconnection network G indicates length of the shortest route between two nodes, and diameter of the interconnection network G means a maximal distance of the shortest route between two nodes.

Theorem 2. *Diameter of $MRH(n)$ is $\lceil\frac{n}{2}\rceil + \lfloor\frac{\lceil\frac{n}{2}\rceil+1}{3}\rfloor + 1$.*

Proof. It is assumed that the departure node is $(\alpha\beta)$ and the destination node is $(\gamma\delta)$. If $\beta = \gamma$, two nodes are present in one internal module, therefore a hypercube edge is used and maximal distance is $\frac{n}{2}$. If $\beta \neq \delta$, a distance between two nodes shall be the least value among three routing lengths R_A, R_B, and R_C. The three routing lengths can be expressed as follows:
M is a minimized cluster, and if $M = \beta = \delta'$, $\theta = 1$, and if $M = \beta$ or $M = \delta'$, $\theta \leq 2$. Otherwise, $\theta = 3$. R_{A_i}, R_{B_i}, and R_{C_i} are indicated as follows:

$R_{A_i} = (\alpha_i \oplus \delta_i) + (\beta_i \oplus \gamma_i)$
$R_{B_i} = (\alpha_i \oplus \gamma_i) + (\beta_i \oplus \delta_i)\delta$
$R_{C_i} = (M_i \oplus \alpha_i) + (M_i \oplus \beta_i) + (M_i \oplus \gamma_i') + (Mi \oplus \delta_i')$

Diameter D of $MRH(n)$ is as follows:

$D = max\{\alpha\beta, \gamma\delta\}\{d\} = max\{\alpha\beta, \gamma\delta\}\{min(R_A, R_B, R_C)\}$.
Since it is not easy to exactly express relation among R_A, R_B, and R_C expressed as exclusive-or operator ($\oplus$), relation among the three equations of R_A, R_B, and R_C is expressed with a plus (+) operator.

The values of R_{A_i}, R_{B_i}, R_{C_i}, and M_i based on the values of 4-bit $\alpha_i\beta_i\gamma_i\delta_i$ ($0 \le i \le n-1$) are indicated in Table 1. $\alpha_i\beta_i\gamma_i\delta_i$ of $\frac{n}{2}$ 4-bit values are divided into 7 groups by the values of R_{A_i}, R_{B_i}, R_{C_i}, and M_i. It is assumed that a_k is the number of 4-bit values obtained from $\alpha_i\beta_i\gamma_i\delta_i$ of the group k. For example, assuming that two nodes are $(\alpha\beta) = (0100110110)$ and $(\gamma\delta) = (1111000011)$, the five obtained 4-bit values are $0101, 1001, 0101, 0100$, and 1010, ($a_2 = 1, a_3 = 3, a_7 = 1$), and $a_k = 0$ for other k values. When all a_k values are not negative numbers, the sum of all ak values is $a_1 + a_2 + \ldots + a_7 = n$. If $a_6 = 0$, $M_i = \delta_i'$ or $M_i = X$ for i, therefore $M = \delta'$ and if $a_7 = 0$, $M_i = \beta_i$ or $M_i = X$ for i, therefore $M = \beta$. Thus, if $a_6 = 0$ or $a_7 = 0$, $\theta \le 2$.
The three distances can be expressed for a_k in the following equation:

If $A = a_5 + a_6 + a_7$, $a_6 = 0$, or $a_7 = 0$, $\theta \le 2$.
Otherwise, $\theta = 3$. The sum of all a_k is $\frac{n}{2}$, therefore $a_1 + a_2 + a_3 + a_4 + a_5 + A = \frac{n}{2}$. The upper limit of a distance is as considered below for four cases in order to find out diameter.
If $a_3 \ge a_2 + 1$ and $a_4 \le a_1 + a_3$, the routing algorithm B is an optimal algorithm, and an equation of a distance $min(R_A, R_B, R_C) = R_B = 2a_4 + 2a_2 + A + 2 \le 2a_1 + 4a_3 + A$ when $a_3 = a_2 + 1$ and $a_4 = a_1 + a_3$. Once the equation is concluded, $n = a_1 + a_2 + a_3 + a_4 + A = 2a_1 + 3a_3 + A - 1$ and $a_3 \le \lfloor \frac{n+1}{3} \rfloor + 1$.
Therefore $R_C \le 2a_1 + 4a_3 + A = \frac{n}{2} + a_3 + 1 \le \frac{n}{2} + \lfloor \frac{\lceil \frac{n}{2} \rceil + 1}{3} \rfloor + 1$.
The maximum value of the distance drawn from the result is $\frac{n}{2} + \lfloor \frac{\lceil \frac{n}{2} \rceil + 1}{3} \rfloor + 1$. Then diameter is pertinent to dimensions of an even number therefore diameter of a $MRH(n)$ graph including dimensions of an odd number is $\lceil \frac{n}{2} \rceil + \lfloor \frac{\lceil \frac{n}{2} \rceil + 1}{3} \rfloor + 1$. Thus $MRH(n)$ corresponds to about one third of existing n-dimensional hypercube diameter.

4   Comparative Analysis with Other Interconnection Networks

Network cost is indicated by a multiple of diameter and degree. Diameter indicates a maximum distance of the shortest route linking two nodes, which can be an effective reference to measure message passing as a lower limit of

Table 2. Hypercube variants vs Modified Hypercubes Interconnection Network Costs

	Nodes	Degree	Diameter	Network Cost
$H(n)$	2^n	n	n	n^2
$FH(n)$	2^n	$n+1$	$\lceil \frac{n}{2} \rceil$	$\approx \frac{n^2}{2}$
MTC	2^n	n	$\lceil \frac{n+1}{2} \rceil$	$\approx \frac{n^2}{2}$
$MRH(n)$	2^n	$\lceil \frac{n}{2} \rceil + 1$	$\lceil \frac{n}{2} \rceil + \lfloor \frac{\lceil \frac{n}{2} \rceil + 1}{3} \rfloor + 1$	$\approx \frac{n^2}{3}$
RC	2^n	n	$\lceil \frac{3n}{4} \rceil$	$\approx \frac{3n^2}{4}$

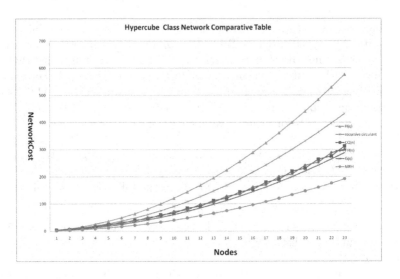

Fig. 3. Hypercube Class Network Comparative Table

latency required to disseminate information in the whole interconnection network, and degree is the number of pins composing the processor when a parallel computer is designed with a given interconnection network as a factor to determine the complexity of routing control logic, which is a reference to measure the cost of hardware used to implement an interconnection network. Therefore network cost is the most critical factor to measure an interconnection network. To demonstrate that $MRH(n)$ suggested in this paper based on the results of previous studies is suitable for implementation of a large-scale system for parallel processing, it is proven to be superior to the previously proposed hypercube classes of Hypercube $H(n)$, Folded Hypercube $FH(n)$, Multiply-twisted Cube MTC, and recursive circulant graph RC in terms of network cost as mentioned in Table 1. For analysis of network cost for an interconnection network, cases of the same number of nodes are compared in Table 2 and Figure 3.

5   Conclusion

In this paper, an interconnection network $MRH(n)$ with superior network cost while degree, diameter, and two network scales of hypercube are all reduced is suggested. Also, $MRH(n)$ connectivity is proven to be $\kappa(MRH(n)) = \lceil \frac{n}{2} \rceil + 1$, an optimal routing algorithm is suggested, and diameter is demonstrated to be $\lceil \frac{n}{2} \rceil + \lfloor \frac{\lceil \frac{n}{2} \rceil + 1}{3} \rfloor + 1$. In addition, it is demonstrated that $MRH(n)$ is a more superior interconnection network through comparative analysis of network cost if hypercube variants have the same number of nodes. This result proves that $MRH(n)$ is a very suitable interconnection network in implementing a large-scale system for parallel processing.

References

1. Akers, S.B., Krishnamurthy, B.: A Group-Theoretic Model for Symmertric Inter-connection Network. IEEE. Trans. Computers 38(4), 555–565 (1989)
2. Doty, K.W.: New Designs for Dense Processor Interconnection Networks. IEEE. Trans. Computers 33(5), 447–450 (1984)
3. Duh, D.R., Chen, G.H., Fang, J.F.: Algorithms and Properties of a New Two-Level Network with Folded Hypercubes as Basic Modules. IEEE. Trans. Parallel Distributed syst. 6(7), 714–723 (1995)
4. El-Amawy, A., Latifi, S.: Properties and Performance of Folded Hypercubes. IEEE. Trans. Parallel Distributed syst. 2(1), 31–42 (1991)
5. Feng, T.-Y.: A Survey of Interconnection Networks. IEEE. Trans. Computers 14(12), 12–27 (1981)
6. Ghose, K., Desai, K.R.: Hierarchical Cubic Networks. IEEE. Trans. Parallel Distributed syst. 6(4), 427–436 (1995)
7. Gupta, A.K., Hambrusch, S.E.: Multiple Network Embeddings into Hypercubes. J. Parallel and Distributed Computing 19, 73–82 (1993)
8. Harary, F., Hayes, J.P., Wu, H.-J.: A Survey of the Theory of Hypercube Graphs. Comput. Math. Appl. 15, 277–289 (1988)
9. Leighton, F.T.: Introduction to Parallel Algorithms and Architectures: Arrays, Trees, Hypercubes. Morgan Kaufmann, San Francisco (1992)
10. Mendia, V.E., Sarkar, D.: Optimal Broadcasting on the Star Graph. IEEE. Trans. Parallel Distributed syst. 3(4), 389–396 (1992)
11. Park, J.-H.: Circulant Graphs and Their Application to Communication Networks. Ph.D. Thesis, Dept. of Computer Science, KAIST, Taejon Korea (1992)
12. Reed, D.A., Fujimoth, R.M.: Multicomputer Networks: Message-Based Parallel Processing. MIT Press, Cambridge (1987)
13. Vaidya, A.S., Rao, P.S.N., Shankar, S.R.: A Class of Hypercube-like Networks. In: Proc. of the 5th IEEE Symposium on Parallel and Distributed Processing, pp. 800–803 (1993)
14. Wu, A.Y.: Embedding of Tree Networks into Hypercubes. J. Parallel and Distributed Computing 2, 238–249 (1985)
15. Yun, S.-K., Park, K.-H.: Comments on 'Hierarchical Cubic Networks. IEEE. Trans. Parallel Distributed syst. 9(4), 410–414 (1998)
16. Tucker, L.W., Robertson, G.G.: Architecture and Application of the Connection Machine. IEEE. Trans. Computers 21(8), 26–38 (1988)

Embedding Algorithm between $MRH(n)$ and Hypercube

Hyun Sim[1,*], Jae-Chul Oh[1], and Hyeong-Ok Lee[2]

[1] Department of Computer Science, Sunchon National University, Sunchon,
Chonnam, 540-742, Korea
{simhyun,ojc}@scnu.ac.kr
[2] Department of Computer Education, Sunchon National University, Sunchon,
Chonnam, 540-742, Korea
oklee@scnu.ac.kr

Abstract. In $MRH(n)$ interconnection network, which has been recently proposed as a new phase for parallel processing, network cost (degree $\times$ diameter) is improved by reducing diameter and edge at the same time, while existing hypercube transformation graphs reduce just one of diameter or edge. This paper suggests an embedding method between Hypercube Network Q_n and Multiple Reduced Hypercube Network $MRH(n)$. In addition, this paper demonstrates that Hypercube Q_n is embedded in $MRH(n)$ at dilation 3 and expansion 2, and that average dilation is 2 or less.

Keywords: Interconnection network, embedding, dilation, expansion.

1 Introduction

With development of computer technologies, the range of computer uses, which has been limited to scientific computing, is expanding into a direction of processing new forms of information such as letters, sound, image, etc. As problems in the fields of modern science and engineering with computers require performance of many calculations and at the same time obtainment of a solution in a short time, high performance computers having faster calculation abilities compared to existing computers are more increasingly required. As a method for performance improvement in the recent computer designs, parallel processing technologies are being broadly used. Parallel processing indicates that multiple processors share and simultaneously process the partitions of several programs or one program. A parallel processing computer is divided into a multiprocessor system having shared memory and a multicomputer system having distributed memory. Each processor of a multicomputer system has its own local memory device, processors are linked by a static interconnection network, communication among these

---

* This work is financially supported by the Ministry of Education, Science and Technology(MEST), the Ministry of Knowledge Economy(MKE) through the fostering project of the Industrial-Academic Cooperation Centered University.)

D. Ślęzak et al. (Eds.): GDC 2009, CCIS 63, pp. 206–214, 2009.

processors is done by message passing through an interconnection network, and calculation is done in a data-driven manner [6,15]. Interconnection networks are divided into a static interconnection network where linkage between nodes is fixed and a dynamic interconnection network where linkage between nodes moves according to conditions. The interconnection network suggested in this paper is for a static interconnection network. An interconnection network can be expressed as an undirected graph, which indicates each process in nodes and a communication channel among processors in edges. An interconnection network is expressed as an undirected graph $G = (V, E)$ as mentioned below [7]. Here, $V(G)$ is a set of nodes that is, $V(G) = \{0, 1, 2, \ldots, N-1\}$, $E(G)$ is a set of edges, and a necessary and sufficient condition where an edge (v, w) is to be present as a pair (v, w) of two nodes v and w in $V(G)$ is that a communication channel exists between the node v and the node w. An interconnection network system to link multicomputer processors greatly influence performance and scalability of the whole system. Therefore studies on an interconnection network are a base for parallel processing computer development, and the need is continuously increasing. Interconnection networks that have been proposed until now include mesh, hypercube [9,15,16], HCN [6,16], and a star graph [12], and network scales to evaluate interconnection networks are degree, diameter, symmetry, scalability, fault tolerance, broadcasting, embedding, etc [2,3,10,11,14]. Embedding is mapping of processors and communication links of an interconnection network G into those of another interconnection network H, which is one of fields to study whether or not an algorithm developed in an interconnection network G can be efficiently run in an interconnection network H. The scales for evaluating embedding cost include dilation, congestion, and expansion [1,7,14].

In this paper, we demonstrates that cost for embedding $MRH(n)$ in hypercube Q_n is $O(n)$. This paper is composed as follows:

Section 2 examines relevant studies on the interconnection network suggested in this paper, Section 3 analyzes embedding between Q_n and $MRH(n)$, and Section 4 gives a conclusion.

2   Preliminaries

An interconnection network can be expressed as an undirected graph, which indicates each process in nodes and a communication channel among processors in edges. An interconnection network is expressed as an undirected graph $G = (V, E)$ as mentioned below. Here, $V(G)$ is a set of nodes that is, $V(G) = \{0, 1, 2, \ldots, N - 1\}$, $E(G)$ is a set of edges, and a necessary and sufficient condition where an edge (v, w) is to be present as a pair (v, w) of two nodes v and w in $V(G)$ is that a communication channel exists between the node v and the node w. The network scales to evaluate an interconnection network include degree, diameter, symmetry, scalability, fault tolerance, broadcasting, and embedding [1,5]. Interconnection networks that have been proposed to date are classified based on the number of nodes into meshes having $n \times k$ nodes, hypercube having 2^n nodes, and a star graph having $n!$ nodes. Hypercube Q_n consists of 2^n nodes and n^{2n-1}

edges. The addresses of each node can be expressed in an n-bit binary number, and when the addresses of two nodes is exactly one bit different, an edge exists between them. The n-dimensional hypercube Q_n is a regular graph whose network cost is n^2 while degree and diameter are n, respectively. Hypercube has a strong point that it can easily provide a communication network system required in applications of all kinds since it is node- and edge-symmetrical and has a simple reflexive system, and is being used in Intel iPSC, nCUBE [12], Connection Machine CM-2 [13], SGI Origin 2000, etc [9]. In terms of embedding, it also has a strong point that other interconnection network systems can be efficiently embedded such as tree, pyramid, mesh, etc., however, it has a weak point that a mean distance between diameter and node is not short as compared to degree. This indicates that hypercube does not efficiently use edges. New interconnection networks that improved such weak point include Multiply-Twisted-Cube, Folded Hypercube [4], and Extended Hypercube.

The nodes of a Multiple Reduced Hypercube $MRH(n)$ are expressed as n bit strings $s_n s_{n-1} \ldots s_i \ldots s_2 s_1$ consisting of binary numbers $\{0,1\}$ ($1 \leq i \leq n$). The edges of $MRH(n)$ are expressed in three forms according to connection method, they are called hypercube edge, exchange edge, and complement edge, respectively, and are indicated as h-edge, x-edge, and c-edge, respectively ($\lfloor \frac{n}{2} \rfloor + 1 \leq h \leq n$). Each edge is defined into when n is an even number and n is an odd number.

Case 1) When n is an even number: It is assumed that for edge definition, $s_n s_{n-1} \ldots s_{i+1}$ is α and a bit string $s_i \ldots s_2 s_1$ is β in the bit string of a node $U(= s_n s_{n-1} \ldots s_i \ldots s_2 s_1)$. Therefore the bit string of a node $U(= s_n s_{n-1} \ldots s_i \ldots s_2 s_1)$ can be simply expressed as $\alpha\beta$. Assuming that the nodes U and V are adjacent with each other, adjacent edges are as follows:

i) Hypercube edge : This edge indicates an edge linking two nodes $U(= s_n s_{n-1} \ldots s_j \ldots s_{i+1} s_i \ldots s_2 s_1)$ and $V(= s_n s_{n-1} \ldots \bar{s}_j \ldots s_{i+1} s_i \ldots s_2 s_1)$ of $MRH(n)$ ($\frac{n}{2} \leq j \leq n$).

ii) Exchange edge : This edge indicates an edge linking two nodes $U(= \alpha\beta)$ and $V(= \beta\alpha)$ of $MRH(n)$ if $\alpha \neq \beta$ in the bit string of the nodes.

iii) Complement edge : This edge indicates an edge linking two nodes $U(= \alpha\beta)$ and $V(= \overline{\alpha\beta})$ of $MRH(n)$ if $\alpha = \beta$ in the bit string of the nodes.

Case 2) When n is an odd number: It is assumed that for edge definition, $s_{n-1} \ldots s_{i+1}$ is α' and a bit string $s_i \ldots s_2 s_1$ is β' in the bit string of a node $U(= s_n s_{n-1} \ldots s_i \ldots s_2 s_1)$. Then the number of bit strings of α' and β' is each $\lfloor \frac{n}{2} \rfloor$. Therefore a node U can be indicated as $U(= s_n \alpha' \beta')$.

i) Hypercube edge : This edge indicates an edge linking two nodes $U(= s_n s_{n-1} \ldots s_j \ldots s_{i+1} s_i \ldots s_2 s_1)$ and $V(= s_n s_{n-1} \ldots \bar{s}_j \ldots s_{i+1} s_i \ldots s_2 s_1)$ of $MRH(n)$ ($\lfloor \frac{n}{2} \rfloor \leq j \leq n$).

ii) Exchange edge : This edge indicates an edge linking two nodes $U(= s_n \alpha' \beta')$ and $V(= s_n \beta' \alpha')$ of $MRH(n)$ in the bit string of a node.

iii) Complement edge : This edge indicates an edge linking two nodes $U(= s_n \alpha' \beta')$ and $V(= s_n \overline{\alpha' \beta'})$ of $MRH(n)$ if $\alpha' = \beta'$ in the bit string of a node.

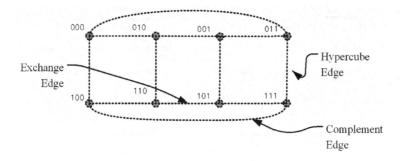

Fig. 1. $MRH(3)$

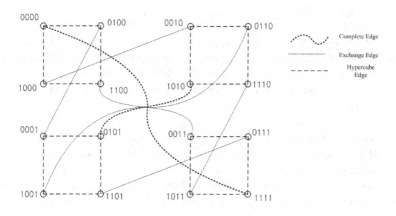

Fig. 2. $MRH(4)$

By the above definition, it is found that the number of nodes is 2^n as the nodes of $MRH(n)$ are n bit strings $s_n s_{n-1} \ldots s_i \ldots s_2 s_1$ consisting of binary numbers $\{0,1\}$, and that $MRH(n)$ is a regular network whose degree is $\lceil \frac{n}{2} \rceil + 1$ since each node has $\lceil \frac{n}{2} \rceil$ hypercube edges and one exchange or complement edge.

3   Embedding between Q_n and $MRH(n)$

An embedding algorithm between $MRH(n)$ whose network cost is improved compared to hypercube and n-dimensional hypercube Q_n is suggested and analyzed.

Theorem 1. *Embedding of n-dimensional hypercube Q_n in $MRH(n)$ at dilation 3 and expansion 1 is possible.*

Proof. It is assumed that the nodes $H = (h_n h_{n-1} \ldots h_j \ldots h_{i+1} h_i \ldots h_2 h_1)$ and $H' = (h'_n h'_{n-1} \ldots h'_j \ldots h'_{i+1} h'_i \ldots h'_2 h'_1)$ of n-dimensional hypercube Q_n are adjacent nodes by an i-dimensional edge $(1 \leq i \leq n)$, and the node $S = (s_n s_{n-1} \ldots s_j$

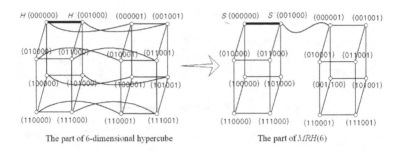

The part of 6-dimensional hypercube   The part of $MRH(6)$

Fig. 3. An example of Case 1

$\ldots s_{i+1}s_i \ldots s_2s_1)$ and the node $S' = (s'_n s'_{n-1} \ldots s'_j \ldots s'_{i+1}s'_i \ldots s'_2s'_1)$ of $MRH(n)$. Dilation is analyzed with the number of edges of $MRH(n)$ which is applied to connect the bit strings of S' in the bit strings of the node S of $MRH(n)$ when the node H of hypercube Q_n is mapped into the node S of $MRH(n)$ and the node H' of hypercube Q_n is mapped into the node S' of $MRH(n)$. Dilation is analyzed into the following two cases according to the bit strings of H' adjacent to the node H of hypercube Q_n.

Case 1) If $h_{i+1} \ldots h_2h_1 = h'_{i+1}h'_i \ldots h'_2h'_1$ and $h_nh_{n-1} \ldots h_j \neq h'_nh'_{n-1} \ldots h'_j$: The bit string of the node S of $MRH(n)$ where the node H of hypercube Q_n is mapped is $(s_ns_{n-1} \ldots s_j \ldots s_{i+1}s_i \ldots s_2s_1)$, and that of the node S' where the node H' is mapped is $(s'_ns'_{n-1} \ldots s'_j \ldots s'_{i+1}s'_i \ldots s'_2s'_1)$ $(n \geq j \geq \lfloor \frac{n}{2} \rfloor + 1)$. In the bit strings of the nodes S and S', only the bits of the order j are in complement relation with each other, therefore the nodes S and S' are nodes being in the same module of $MRH(n)$, and according to definition of $MRH(n)$, the nodes S and S' are adjacent nodes with each other. Consequently, the nodes S and S' are connected to one inner edge, and thus when the nodes H and H' of Q_n are mapped into the nodes S and S' of $MRH(n)$, they may be embedded at dilation 1.

Case 2) If $h_{i+1} \ldots h_2h_1 \neq h'_{i+1}h'_i \ldots h'_2h'_1$: The bit string of the node S of $MRH(n)$ where the node H of hypercube Q_n is mapped is $(s_ns_{n-1} \ldots s_j \ldots s_{i+1}s_i \ldots s_2s_1)$, and that of the node S' where the node H' is mapped is $(s'_ns'_{n-1} \ldots s'_j \ldots s'_{i+1}\bar{s}'_i \ldots s'_2s'_1)$ $(\lfloor \frac{n}{2} \rfloor \geq i \geq 1)$. In the bit strings of the nodes S and S', only the bits of the order i are in complement relation with each other, therefore the nodes S and S' are nodes being in different modules of $MRH(n)$. Dilation length from the node S to the node S' is analyzed through shortest routing from the node $S(= s_ns_{n-1} \ldots s_j \ldots s_{i+1}s_i \ldots s_2s_1)$ to the node $S'(= s'_ns'_{n-1} \ldots s'_j \ldots s'_{i+1}s'_i \ldots s'_2s'_1)$ of $MRH(n)$. The address of the adjacent node by an exchange edge at the node $S(= s_ns_{n-1} \ldots s_j \ldots s_{i+1}s_i \ldots s_2s_1)$ is $(s_{i+1}s_i \ldots s_2s_1s_ns_{n-1} \ldots s_j)$, and that of the node that took a 1 bit complement in $(s_{i+1}s_i \ldots s_2s_1s_ns_{n-1} \ldots s_j)$ is $(s_{i+1}\bar{s}_i \ldots s_2s_1s_ns_{n-1} \ldots s_j)$. In $(s_{i+1}\bar{s}_i \ldots s_2s_1s_ns_{n-1} \ldots s_j)$, the adjacent node to an exchange edge is $(s_ns_{n-1} \ldots s_j \ldots s_{i+1}\bar{s}_i \ldots s_2s_1)$, and the $(s_ns_{n-1} \ldots s_j \ldots s_{i+1}\bar{s}_i \ldots s_2s_1)$ node is same as the node $S'(= s'_ns'_{n-1} \ldots s'_j \ldots s'_{i+1}\bar{s}'_i \ldots s'_2s'_1)$. The mapped node $(s_ns_{n-1} \ldots s_j \ldots s_{i+1}s_i \ldots s_2s_1)$ of $MRH(n)$ is linked to $(s_{i+1}s_i \ldots s_2s_1s_ns_{n-1} \ldots s_j)$ by an exchange edge. The linked node $(s_{i+1}s_i \ldots s_2s_1s_ns_{n-1} \ldots s_j)$ is linked to the node $(s_{i+1}\bar{s}_i \ldots s_2s_1s_ns_{n-1} \ldots s_j)$ being in the module. The linked node $(s_{i+1}\bar{s}_i \ldots s_2s_1s_ns_{n-1} \ldots s_j)$ is linked to $(s_ns_{n-1} \ldots s_j \ldots s_{i+1}\bar{s}_i \ldots s_2s_1)$ by an exchange edge. Therefore it is found that embedding at dilation 3 is possible when the nodes H and H' of Q_n are mapped into the nodes S and S' of $MRH(n)$.

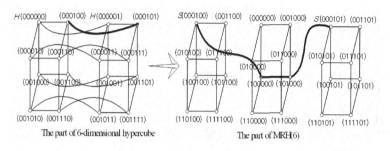

Fig. 4. An example of Case 2

Case 3) If $h_{i+1}h_i \ldots h_2h_1 \neq h'_{i+1}h'_i \ldots h'_2h'_1$ and $h_nh_{n-1} \ldots h_j = h_{i+1}h_i \ldots h_2h_1$: The bit string of the node S of $MRH(n)$ where the node H of hypercube Q_n is mapped is $(s_ns_{n-1} \ldots s_j \ldots s_{i+1}s_i \ldots s_2s_1)$, and that of the node S' where the node H' is mapped is $(s'_ns'_{n-1} \ldots s'_j \ldots s'_{i+1}\bar{s}'_i \ldots s'_2s'_1)$ $(n \geq j \geq \lfloor \frac{n}{2} \rfloor + 1,$ $\lfloor \frac{n}{2} \rfloor \geq i \geq)$, and $s_ns_{n-1} \ldots s_j = s_{i+1}s_i \ldots s_2s_1$ among the bit strings of the mapped node S, therefore it is unnecessary to use an exchange edge first linked in Case 2. Thus in this case, dilation is 2.

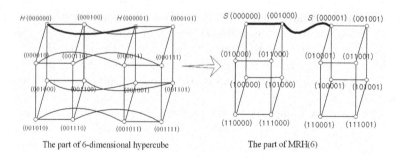

Fig. 5. An example of Case 3

As demonstrated in the above two cases, embedding of hypercube Qn in MRH(n) at dilation 3 is possible.

Corollary 1. *Average dilation of embedding of n-dimensional hypercube Q_n in $MRH(n)$ is 2 or less.*

Proof. When n-dimensional hypercube Q_n is embedded in $MRH(n)$, average dilation of embedding is obtained by dividing the sum of dilations of all edges of hypercube Q_n by the number of all edges. The nodes of hypercube Q_n are one-to-one mapped with those of $MRH(n)$, and the number of edges whose dilation is 1 among edges of hypercube Q_n is $n2^{2n-1}$, that of edges whose dilation is 2 is $n2^n$, and that of edges whose dilation is 3 is $2^n \times 2^{2n-1} - n \times 2^{2n-1} - n \times 2^n$, which can be found by Theorem 1. The number of all edges of Q_{2n} is $k = 2n \times 2^{2n-1}$. Therefore average dilation is $\frac{(n \times 2^{2n-1} + 2n \times 2^n + 3 \times (2^n \times 2^{2n-1} - n \times 2^{2n-1} - n \times 2^n))}{k}$ that is, $\frac{4 \times 2^{2n-1} - 2^n}{2 \times 2^{2n-1}} = 2 - \frac{1}{2^n}$, which indicates that mean dilation is less than 2.

Theorem 2. *Cost required for embedding $MRH(n)$ in n-dimensional hypercube Q_n is $O(n)$.*

Proof. It is assumed that the nodes $H = (h_n h_{n-1} \ldots h_j \ldots h_{i+1} h_i \ldots h_2 h_1)$ and $H' = (h'_n h'_{n-1} \ldots h'_j \ldots h'_{i+1} h'_i \ldots h'_2 h'_1)$ of n-dimensional hypercube Q_n are adjacent nodes by an i-dimensional edge $(1 \leq i \leq n)$, and the node $S = (s_n s_{n-1} \ldots s_j \ldots s_{i+1} s_i \ldots s_2 s_1)$ and the node $S' = (s'_n s'_{n-1} \ldots s'_j \ldots s'_{i+1} s'_i \ldots s'_2 s'_1)$ of $MRH(n)$. Dilation is analyzed with the number of edges of Q_n which is applied to connect the bit strings of H' in the bit strings of the node H of Q_n when the node S of hypercube $MRH(n)$ is mapped into the node H of Q_n and the node S' of hypercube $MRH(n)$ is mapped into the node H' of Q_n. Dilation is analyzed into the following two cases according to the bit strings of S' adjacent to the node S of $MRH(n)$.

Case 1) If $s_{i+1} \ldots s_2 s_1 = s'_{i+1} \ldots s'_2 s'_1$ and $s_n \ldots s_j \neq s'_n \ldots s'_j$: The bit string of the node H of Q_n where the node S of $MRH(n)$ is mapped is $(h_n h_{n-1} \ldots h_j \ldots h_{i+1} h_i \ldots h_2 h_1)$, and that of the node H' where the node S' is mapped is $(h'_n h'_{n-1} \ldots h'_{i+1} h'_i \ldots h'_2 h'_1)$ $(n \geq j \geq \lfloor \frac{n}{2} \rfloor + 1)$. In the bit strings of the nodes H and H', only the one bit of the order j are in complement relation with each other, therefore the nodes H and H' are nodes being in the same basic module of Q_n, and according to definition of Q_n, the nodes H and H' are adjacent nodes with each other. Thus when the nodes S and S' of $MRH(n)$ are mapped into the nodes H and H' of Q_n, they may be embedded at dilation 1.

Case 2) If $s_n s_{n-1} \ldots s_j = s_{i+1} s_i \ldots s_2 s_1$ and the nodes S and S' of $MRH(n)$ are in complement relation with each other: The bit string of the node H of Q_n where the node S of $MRH(n)$ is mapped is $(h_n h_{n-1} \ldots h_j \ldots h_{i+1} h_i \ldots h_2 h_1)$, and that of the node H' where the node S' is mapped is $(h'_n h'_{n-1} \ldots h'_j \ldots h'_{i+1} h'_i \ldots h'_2 h'_1)$ $(1 \leq i \leq n, n+1 \leq j \leq 2n)$. According to definition of Q_n, edges as many as the number of different bit strings are necessary to link the nodes H and H'. The number of bit strings for the nodes H and H' is n, therefore the number of edges required to link the two nodes is n when the nodes H and H' are in complement relation with each other. Thus it is found that embedding at dilation n is possible when the nodes S and S' of $MRH(n)$ are mapped into the nodes H and H' of Q_n. As demonstrated in the above two cases, dilation is $O(n)$ when $MRH(n)$ is embedded with Q_n.

4   Conclusion

Hypercube, which is well known as an interconnection network, has several strong points such as reflexive structure, node and edge symmetry, simple routing algorithm, embedding with other interconnection networks, etc., however, it has weak points including more network cost due to increased degree with the increased number of nodes and a relatively long distance between diameter and node as compared with degree. To improve such weak points, $MRH(n)$ have been suggested. In this paper, the broadcasting algorithm of $MRH(n)$ whose network cost was improved compared to hypercube was analyzed, how to embed between $MRH(n)$ and hypercube Q_{2n} was suggested, and based on the results, dilation was analyzed. As results of embedding, hypercube Q_{2n} could be embedded in $MRH(n)$ at dilation 3 and expansion 1, and mean dilation was 2 or less. Also, cost required for embedding $MRH(n)$ in hypercube Q_{2n} was found to be $O(n)$. These results imply that several algorithms, which have already been developed in hypercube, can be efficiently used in $MRH(n)$.

References

1. Akers, S.B., Krishnamurthy, B.: A Group-Theoretic Model for Symmertric Interconnection Network. IEEE Trans. Computers 38(4), 555–565 (1989)
2. Doty, K.W.: New Designs for Dense Processor Interconnection Networks. IEEE Trans. Computers 33(5), 447–450 (1984)
3. Duh, D.R., Chen, G.H., Fang, J.F.: Algorithms and Properties of a New Two-Level Network with Folded Hypercubes as Basic Modules. IEEE Trans. Parallel Distributed syst. 6(7), 714–723 (1995)
4. El-Amawy, A., Latifi, S.: Properties and Performance of Folded Hypercubes. IEEE Trans. Parallel Distributed syst. 2(1), 31–42 (1991)
5. Feng, T.-Y.: A Survey of Interconnection Networks. IEEE Trans. Computers 14(12), 12–27 (1981)
6. Ghose, K., Desai, K.R.: Hierarchical Cubic Networks. IEEE Trans. Parallel Distributed syst. 6(4), 427–436 (1995)
7. Gupta, A.K., Hambrusch, S.E.: Multiple Network Embeddings into Hypercubes. J. Parallel and Distributed Computing 19, 73–82 (1993)
8. Harary, F., Hayes, J.P., Wu, H.-J.: A Survey of the Theory of Hypercube Graphs. Comput. Math. Appl. 15, 277–289 (1988)
9. Leighton, F.T.: Introduction to Parallel Algorithms and Architectures: Arrays, Trees, Hypercubes. Morgan Kaufmann, San Francisco (1992)
10. Mendia, V.E., Sarkar, D.: Optimal Broadcasting on the Star Graph. IEEE Trans. Parallel Distributed syst. 3(4), 389–396 (1992)
11. Park, J.-H.: Circulant Graphs and Their Application to Communication Networks. Ph.D. Thesis, Dept. of Computer Science, KAIST, Taejon Korea (1992)
12. Reed, D.A., Fujimoth, R.M.: Multicomputer Networks: Message-Based Parallel Processing. MIT Press, Cambridge (1987)

13. Vaidya, A.S., Rao, P.S.N., Shankar, S.R.: A Class of Hypercube-like Networks. In: Proc. of the 5th IEEE Symposium on Parallel and Distributed Processing, pp. 800–803 (1993)
14. Wu, A.Y.: Embedding of Tree Networks into Hypercubes. J. Parallel and Distributed Computing 2, 238–249 (1985)
15. Yun, S.-K., Park, K.-H.: Comments on Hierarchical Cubic Networks. IEEE Trans. Parallel Distributed syst. 9(4), 410–414 (1998)
16. Tucker, L.W., Robertson, G.G.: Architecture and Application of the Connection Machine. IEEE Trans. Computers 21(8), 26–38 (1988)

Fuzzy Based Approach for Load Balanced Distributing Database on Sensor Network

Mohammad Zeynali and Mohammad Ali Jamali

Shabestar University, Tabriz, Iran
mo_zeynali@yahoo.com, Zadehhossein@yahoo.com

Abstract. A wireless sensor network consists of tiny sensing devices, with limited energy and processing ability. Some time we have to distribute a database on sensor network, because of limited energy in this sensor, load balanced distributing database can increase the lifetime of this networks. In this paper we propose Fuzzy based approach for Load balanced distributing database on sensor Network that prolonging the network lifetime. We use vertical partitioning algorithms for distributing database on sensors. First we clustering the network and then distribute partitions on clusters. A simulator was built and Results of various simulation runs are consistent with the hypothesis.

Keywords: sensor network, database, distributing, partition, load balanced, hit ratio.

1 Introduction

Wireless Sensor Network (WSN) comprises of micro sensor nodes with limited energy and processing ability. It is used in military as well as civil applications. Some time we have to distribute a database on sensor network, because of limited energy in this sensor, load balanced distributing database can increase network lifetime. In this paper we propose Fuzzy based approach for Load balanced distributing database on sensor Network that prolonging network lifetime. in proposed algorithm first we clustering the network and partitioning database then distribute partitions on clusters. The partitioning of a global schema into fragments can be performed in two different ways:

Vertical partitioning and horizontal partitioning [2]. This paper is concerned with vertical partitioning [1]. Partitioning based on attributes has been studied earlier in [4], [5], [6], [7]. Navathe et al used a two-step approach for vertical partitioning. In the first step, they used the given input parameters in the form of an Attribute Usage Matrix (AUM) to construct an Attribute Affinity Matrix (AAM) for clustering [9]. After clustering, an empirical objective function is used to perform binary partitioning iteratively. In the second step, estimated storage cost factors are considered for further refinement of the partitioning process.

Eltayeb Salih Abuelyaman [1] proposes a scheme for vertical partitioning of a database at the design cycle. The scheme determines the hit ratio of a partition. As long as it falls below a predetermined threshold, the partition is altered. Although no proof

D. Ślęzak et al. (Eds.): GDC 2009, CCIS 63, pp. 215–220, 2009.

is provided, experimental data showed that moving an attribute that is loosely coupled to a different Subset within a partition improves hit ratio. We use Eltayeb Salih Abuelyaman [1] algorithms for partitioning database. Only we change his mathematical formula to fuzzy sets as reduce The time of algorithm, also proposed algorithm can used in nondeterministic environment and on sensor networks. We know that skew distributing database on sensors cause inordinate use of some sensors, therefore reduced the life time of network, in this paper we effort to reduce the skew of distributing database partitioning as possible insofar. The rest of this paper is organized as follows: In the next section we will introduce the fuzzy sets. In section 3 we will discuss startphase. Simulation is given in Section 4. The conclusion is presented in sections 5.

2   Fuzzy Sets Overview

Fuzziness [8] is a way to represent uncertainty, possibility and approximation. Fuzzy sets are an extension of classical set theory and are used in fuzzy logic. In classical set theory the membership of elements in relation to a set is assessed in binary terms according to a crisp condition- an element either belongs to or does not belong to the set. By contrast, fuzzy set theory permits the gradual assessment of the membership of elements in relation to a set; this is described with the aid of a membership function:

$$\mu \rightarrow [0, 1]$$

The domain of the membership function, which is the domain of concern and from which elements of the set are drawn, is called the *'universe of discourse'*. For example, the Universe of discourse of the fuzzy set 'High Income' can be the positive real line $[0, \infty)$. The notion central to fuzzy systems is that truth values (in fuzzy logic) or membership values (in fuzzy sets) are indicated by a value on the range [0. 0, 1. 0], with 0. 0 representing absolute false and 1. 0 representing absolute truth. For example, let us take the statement: "Jane is old. " If Jane's age was 75, we might assign the statement the truth value of 0. 80. The statement could be translated into set terminology as "Jane is a member of the set of old people. " This statement would be rendered symbolically with fuzzy sets as :

$$\mu \, OLD \, (Jane) = 0. \, 80$$

Where μ is the membership function, operating in this case on the fuzzy set of old people, which returns a value between 0. 0 and 1. 0. The modifiers of fuzzy values are called Hedges. To transform the statement, "Jane is old" to "Jane is very old", the hedge "very" is usually defined as follows:

$$\mu \text{"very"} \, A(x) = \mu \, A(x) \, ^\wedge \, 2.$$

For example, If μ OLD (Jane) =0. 8 then μ VERYOLD (Jane) =0. 64. Every input value is associated with a linguistic variable. A linguistic variable represents a concept that is measurable in some way either objectively or subjectively, like temperature or age. Linguistic variables are characteristics of an object or situation. For each linguistic. Variable it should be assigned a set of linguistic terms (values) that subjectively describe the variable. Most of the times, linguistic terms are words that describe the magnitude of the linguistic variable, as "hot" and "large", or how far they are from a goal value as in "exact" or "far". Each linguistic term is fuzzy set and has its own membership function. It is expected that for a linguistic variable to be useful the union of the support of the linguistic terms cover its entire domain.

3 Startphase

The design of efficient database systems is not an exception because database partitioning is based on Frequencies of Queries (FOQ). In a distributed database, data must be collected from a large number of queries before partitioning. To avoid as a constraint, dependency on FOQ must be eliminated. One way to do so is to perform database partitioning at the design phase and immediately after completion of the schema. Comfortably, partitioning can be decided even before database tables are populated. For illustration of the proposed partitioning, the following definition will be necessary.

Description:

a) PNa : the total probability of attributes.
b) PNk : the probability of queries in the Set of Kickoff Queries SKQ[1].
c) PNf : the probability of queries in the Set of Future Queries SFQ[1].
d) SQ: the union of the set SKQ with SFQ.
e) SA = {A1, A2... ANa}: the overall set of attributes.
f) SQ = {Q1, Q2, ..., QNq} : the overall set of queries.

4 Simulation Phase

The simulator has the following two modules. Each of the modules is discussed separately.

a) fuzzy reflexivity
b) fuzzy symmetry

4.1 The Fuzzy Reflexivity Module

The module prompts a user to enter values for each of the first three parameters in above Description. The module then prompts the user to enter a percentage C that controls the number of attributes appearing in each query. If the designer enters the value 30 for example, then the module will generate a value of [0. 6, 1] with probability of 0. 3 and a value of [0, 0. 5] with probability of 0. 7 every one of entries in fuzzy RM matrix represent probability of existence one attribute in a query.

4.2 The Fuzzy Symmetry Module

The following equations were used to compute the fuzzy *Symmetry Matrix* (SM) on (see table. 2) which defines the desired relationships among attributes. There we change Eltayeb Salih Abuelyaman [1], mathematical formula to fuzzy formula that

Table 1. A randomly generated fuzzy Reflexivity Matrix

Attribute / Query	A	B	C	D	E	F	G	H
a	2 .0	8 .0	2 .0	2 .0	9 .0	1 .0	7 .0	6 .0
b	2 .0	1 .0	9 .0	7 .0	2 .0	9 .0	1 .0	4 .0
c	7 .0	1 .0	9 .0	7 .0	2 .0	1 .0	1 .0	4 .0
d	1 .0	1 .0	1 .0	7 .0	7 .0	9 .0	9 .0	7 .0
e	1 .0	9 .0	9 .0	3 .0	8 .0	9 .0	9 .0	4 .0
f	1 .0	1 .0	1 .0	3 .0	2 .0	2 .0	4 .0	3 .0
g	1 .0	9 .0	8 .0	3 .0	2 .0	8 .0	7 .0	6 .0
h	1 .0	2 .0	7 .0	9 .0	9 .0	8 .0	5 .0	4 .0

Table 2. Fuzzy Symmetry Matrix generated from the Reflexivity Matrix and equation 1

Attribute / Query	A	B	C	D	E	F	G	H
a	7 .0	2 .0	7 .0	7 .0	2 .0	2 .0	2 .0	4 .0
b	2 .0	9 .0	3 .0	3 .0	8 .0	9 .0	9 .0	6 .0
c	7 .0	9 .0	7 .0	7 .0	8 .0	9 .0	9 .0	6 .0
d	7 .0	3 .0	9 .0	9 .0	9 .0	8 .0	7 .0	7 .0
e	2 .0	8 .0	9 .0	9 .0	9 .0	8 .0	8 .0	7 .0
f	2 .0	9 .0	8 .0	8 .0	8 .0	9 .0	9 .0	7 .0
g	2 .0	9 .0	7 .0	7 .0	8 .0	9 .0	9 .0	7 .0
h	0. 4		6 .0	7 .0	7 .0	7 .0	7 .0	7 .0

firstly reduces the time of his algorithm and secondly we can use this formula in non-deterministic environment. Our proposed fuzzy based algorithm is:

The (see table. 1) provides the relationship between queries and attributes

Algorithm (1)

$$SM[i,j] = \overset{N}{\underset{K=1}{MAX}} (\ Min \ (RM[k,i], RM[k,j]) \ ) \qquad \text{for } j = 1 \text{ to } Na$$

for i =1 to Na (for j= 1 to Na) i ≠ j

for example, for computing SM[E,F] in (see table. 2), from (see table. 1), i=E, j=F and E=(0. 9,0. 2,0. 2,0. 7,0. 8,0. 2,0. 2,0. 9) و F=(0. 1,0. 9,0. 1,0. 9,0. 9,0. 2,0. 8,0. 8) from formula (1) we have : RM[E,F]=MAX(0. 1,0. 2,0. 1,0. 7,0. 8,0. 2,0. 2,0. 8)=0. 8 RM[E,F] represent the percent of query's that have attribute's e and f.

4.3 Partition Forming State

In general, the success of an algorithm depends on the strategy that sets criteria for choosing the best start point and the smartest move thereafter. we used the fuzzy SM on (see table. 2) to produce the partition P.

Initially As is equal to {(A, B, C, D, E, F, G, H)}.
from Eltayeb Salih Abuelyaman[1],partitioning Strategy and fuzzy SM matrix :

(a) S = {A} and As = {(B, C, D, E, F, G, H)}
(b) S = {(A,C)} and As = {(B, D, E, F, G, H)}
(c) S = {(A,C,F)} and As = {(B, D, E, G, H)}
(d) S = {(A,C,F,D)} and As = {(B, E, G, H)}
P = { (A, C, D, F) ; (B, E, G, H) }

In this state we compute the hit ratio using algorithm(1) if the value of hit ratio less than predetermined threshold (51%) then we move attribute's that closely coupled with partition to an other partition.

We use Eltayeb Salih Abuelyaman[1], algorithm to computeing hit ratio:Algorithm(1)

1. Compute the partition **hit ratio (PHR)**
2. If **PHR** is less than the predefined threshold
   then
   a) Find the attribute with the minimum **hit** to
      miss ratio and move it to a different subset
      using the attribute association table in the
      process
   b) Repeat from step (2)
3. End partitioning

Table 3. Attribute associate for P

	A	B	C	D	E	F	G	H
hit	6.1	2.3	2.3	2.2	2.3	1.9	2.4	2
miss	1	2.3	3.2	2.6	2.7	3.3	2.7	2.4

Hit ratio computing formula is: (hit/ (miss+hit))%100
result's equal (%45), less than preditermined thresold (%50) thus the partitioning will be changed (see table. 3). We know that skew distributing database on sensor cause inordinate use of some sensors as reduce the life time of network, therefore Now we move C attribute to an other partition and againe compute the new hit ratio.
P = {(A, C, D, F); (B, C, E, G, H)}

Table 4. Attribute associate for new P

	A	B	C	D	E	F	G	H
hit	0.9	4.1	3.2	1.5	1.3	1	3.3	2.6
miss	1.7	4.1	2.3	3.3	1.9	4.2	1.8	1.8

the new hit ratio is become (%52) that greater than preditermined threshold (%50).
Total partitioning is (see table. 4):

New P = {(A, D, F); (B, C, E, G, H)}
Now we distribute the (A, D, F) on one cluster and (B, C, E, G, H) on an other cluster.

5 Conclusion

In this paper we propose Fuzzy based approach for Load balanced distributing data-base on sensor Network. Same as we know that skew distributing database on sensor cause inordinate use of some sensors as reduce the life time of network in proposed algorithm, fragment's replaced in suitable cluster as reduce the energy consumptions of sensors and prolonging network lifetime. The result of our proposed algorithm evaluated in (see table. 3 and table. 4) that suitable for databases that attributes in query nondeterministic, for this reason we change the Eltayeb Salih Abuelyaman[1] algorithm's.

References

[1] Abuelyaman, E.S.: An Optimized Scheme for Vertical Partitioning of a DistributedData-base. IJCSNS International Journal of Computer Science and Network Security 8(1) (January 2008)

[2] Abbasi, A.A., Younis, M.: A Survey on Clustering Algorithms for Wireless Sensor net-works. Computer Communications 30, 2826–2841 (2007)

[3] Younis, O., Krunz, M., Ramasubramanian, S.: Node Clustering in Wireless Sensor net-works: Recent Developments and Deployments Challenges. IEEE Network (May/June 2006)

[4] Wei, D., Chan, H.A.: Clustering Ad Hoc Networks: Schemes and lassifications. IEEE, Los Alamitos (2006)

[5] Abdalla, H., AlFares, M.: Vertical Partitioning for Database Design: A Grouping Algorithm. In: SEDE (2007) (to appear)

[6] Özsu, M., Valduriez, P.: Principles of Distributed Database Systems, 2nd edn. (1st edn. 1991)

[7] Zadeh, L.A.: Fuzzy sets. Information and control 8, 338–353 (1965)

[8] Navathe, S., Ceri, S., Weiderhold, G., Dou, J.: Vertical Partitioning Algorithms for Database. Design ACM Transactions on Database Systems 9(4) (1984)

An Ontology-Based
Resource Selection Service on Science Cloud[*]

Hyunjeong Yoo, Cinyoung Hur, Seoyoung Kim, and Yoonhee Kim[**]

Dept. of Computer Science and Engineering
Sookmyung Women's Univ., Seoul Korea
{warmy79,hurcy,sssyyy77,yulan}@sookmyung.ac.kr
http://dslab.sookmyung.ac.kr/

Abstract. Cloud computing requires scalable and cooperative sharing the resources in various organizations by dynamic configuring a virtual organization according to user's requirements. Ontology-based representation of Cloud computing environment would be able to conceptualize common attributes among Cloud resources and to describe relations among them semantically. However, mutual compatibility among organizations is limited because a method applying ontology to Cloud is not established yet.

We propose to introduce a resource virtualization method using ontology. A new Virtual Ontology (VOn) is configured dynamically based on requirement of users, and the VOn is mapped to Cloud resources. Our service uses a Map/Reduce model for rapid and efficient merging a number of ontology. The execution environment is composed of selected resources on basis of a VOn, which is generated by Ontology Merge engine.

Keywords: Ontology, Resource Selection, Semantic, Science Cloud, Cloud computing.

1 Introduction

A virtual organization in Cloud computing provides a uniform views by virtualizing various resources [1, 2]. Cloud services are defined hierarchically by using Cloud computing ontology [6]. The layered approach represents inter-dependency and composability between the different layers in the Clouds. While this paper just defines concepts, a method of applying ontology to Cloud computing is not tangible. This paper, especially, does not refer to descriptions, specific policies, and management of resources.

However, it is difficult to provide perfect resources from various organizations because management policies and descriptions about various resources are different in each organization. These differences cause a problem about providing a uniformed view from various resources.

---

[*] This work was supported by Basic Science Research Program through the National Research Foundation of Korea(NRF) grant funded by the Korea government(MEST)(No.2009-0084669).

[**] Corresponding author.

D. Ślęzak et al. (Eds.): GDC 2009, CCIS 63, pp. 221–228, 2009.

Ontology-based resource description is proposed to solve these problems [3,4]. These researches are noticed as a novel method of a Grid resource description due to virtualizing common properties of resource based on ontology and representing relation among resources semantically. Moreover, there is research that produces a global ontology by merging each ontology existed in resource groups [5]. Currently, this research is at an early stage and is hard to provide interoperability among organizations because of merging resources from only static concepts in existed researches. In the paper [9], they propose a Semantically-Enhanced Resource Allocator (SERA) which is a scheduling system using customer requests and provides the ability of re-scheduling requests based on their priorities and considering advanced reservations. Nevertheless, the experiment is too limited to prove the proposed concept. The characteristics of target applications are not considered.

In this paper, we propose an Ontology-based Resource Selection Service (OReSS) which provides a method of resource virtualization using merged ontologies which is interoperable among virtual organizations and then selects resources based on the VOn. OReSS on Cloud computing, especially, selects ontology candidates by calculating a degree of similarity function based on user's requirements. Selected ontologies are merged and provided to a user as a new VOn.

The rest of the paper is organized as follows. Section 2 gives an overview of OReSS. In section 3, we describe an execution scenario of scientific applications in OReSS. Section 4 describes experiments and Section 5 discusses summary and future work.

2 Ontology-Based Resource Selection Service(OReSS)

We propose an ontology-based resource virtualization about various Cloud resources. This section describes the architecture of OReSS and each function in the OReSS.

2.1 Architecture of OreSS

The architecture of OReSS(Figure 1) consists of four layers: Physical Machines(PM) layer, Cloud Resource Virtualization(CRV) layer, OReSS layer, and End User(EU) layer. PM layer represents distributed and heterogeneous resource environments. CRV layer supports resources which adapted to Cloud by using virtualization and Ontology. OReSS layer generates VOn and selects proper resources among these VOns for satisfying the user's requirements. Finally, EU layer gets user's request about resources and supports an application execution service in the selected proper environment from OReSS layer. User's requests are information of resource components (CPUs, memory sizes, network bandwidth, or IP numbers) which they want to use and a degree of similarity for supporting resources which is closely related to resource component's spec.

OReSS layer can be categorized into: Virtual Ontology Manager, Ontology Repository which is a storage of resource ontologies, Job Monitoring Service, and Job Execution Environment. In detail, Virtual Ontology Manager consists of Ontology-Analysis engine for analyzing ontologies and Ontology Merge engine in order to create a VOn from a pool of selected ontologies. Job Execution Environment is made of Resource Selection engine and Job Submission.

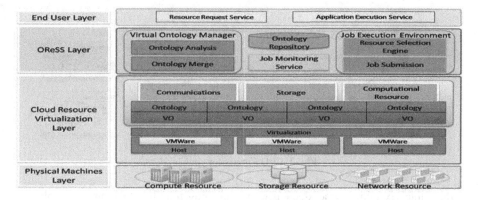

Fig. 1. Architecture of OreSS

2.2 Resource Selection Mechanism in OReSS

Ontology Analysis engine calculates similarity to user's requirement and makes a rank of ontologies, made from CRV layer, based on calculated similarity. In the analyzing ontology, Map/Reduce [8] computations is applied for rapid rank's calculation. We use a Similarity Computation Algorithm and a resource dictionary for finding ontology's concepts and synonyms of the reference [7].

After the rank of ontologies is calculated, Ontology Merge engine makes a new VOn by combining candidate ontologies which are over the degree of similarity. The degree of similarity is received from users and is used to merge associated ontologies which are resembled to required resource specification. For merging ontologies, we use a method of the reference [5].

When resources are scheduled for executing jobs, following three factors are considered: a VOn from Ontology Merge engine, status information of resources stored in a VOn's resource pool, and resource requirements from a user. Finally, jobs run on the selected resource.

3 Scientific Applications Execution Scenario on Science Cloud

Understanding properties of a scientific application is important. For example, a Computational Fluid Dynamics (CFD) application (Figure 2) has multiple experiments with various parameter sets. Each experiment needs highly efficient and enormous computational resources concurrrently because these experiments are computational intensive and can be executed independently. With these requirements, generating a VOn in advance helps reduce resource selection time for locating appropriate resources. In many times, total execution time of CFD applications depends on the number of assigned resources. To maximize performance of application execution, selecting appropriate resources for an application is important. When a user provides resource requirements for an application, many times we confront lack of resources which meet to the user's requirements. Small pool of resources causes longer job queuing time for an application to wait for its turn to use the resource. To

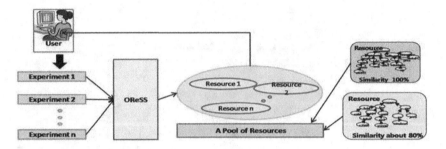

Fig. 2. CFD Simulation on Cloud

reduce total execution time, decreasing job queuing time by expanding a number of available resources based on user's requirements is more efficient than diminishing job execution time. For instance, when the degree of similarity sets above 80 percent, throughput increases because many computational jobs are executed concurrently on selected ontologies. However, providing resources with the degree of similarity, 100 percent, results in increase of total execution time due to large queuing time because of limited resources.

4   Experiments

A target application in our experiment is a batch application composed of lots of jobs requiring large scale computation with small size of input data. Typically, a scientific computational application requires high throughput computing and has no dependency among jobs. Therefore, this application depends more significantly on CPU performance, the number of resources, and memory size. However, network bandwidth or IO load to the application is not a major factor for performance. Therefore, in this experiment, CPU architecture, the number of CPU per a cluster, and MIPS based CPU performance are considered for computing similarity among clusters.

To show the proof concept, we experiment an ontology created by the several VOns in PRAGMA environment with information of resource's components and the specific degree of similarity, 90%. PRAGMA is Pacific Rim Application and Grid Middleware Assembly which has 35 institutions for establishing sustained collaborations and advancing the use of grid technologies. After calculating similarity with the specific information of resource's components and merging the VOns whose calculated similarity is above 90%, respectively the target pool for the application execution is shown Figure 3.

First, a user inputs requirements of resources' components, the requirements' priority information which is used in similarity computation phase, and the degree of similarity. In next similarity computation, Ontology Analysis engine calculates similarity among the requirements and resources based on the priority information. Then, resources are selected by the similarity, and these resources are merged by Ontology Merge engine for executing jobs. 100 percent is based on similarity computation, and clusters which are greater than user's requirements are re-calculated based on 100 percent because selecting and supporting similar clusters with user's requirements are economical to users in the cost sides.

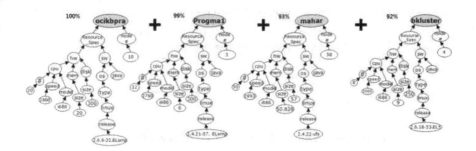

Fig. 3. The target pool for the application execution

We assume that the 100 percent matched cluster to user's requirement is ocikbpra and that the degree of similarity from a user is 90 percent. Moreover, the priority is set in order of CPU architecture, MIPS based CPU performance, and the number of CPU per a cluster. According to these conditions, selected resources are Pragma1 (99%), bkluster (93%), and mahar (94%). Figure 4 shows properties of these experiment clusters. When a job is assigned to these resources, Random scheduling is used. The number of assigned jobs in each experiment is 100.

Host Name	Node number	CPU number	Memory	Disk	CPU architecture	CPU clock	Similarity	Final Similarity
bkluster	4	8	9	250	i686	3000	107.14286	92.85714
mahar	50	50	50.828	57	i686	2993	106.89286	93.10714
Pragma1	3	12	6	472	i686	2790	99.642857	99.64286
ocikbpra	10	20	20	300	i686	2800	100	100

Fig. 4. Properties of selected clusters and a standard cluster

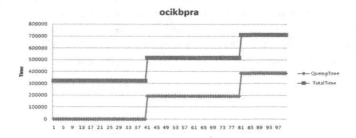

Fig. 5. Queuing time and total time in ocikbpra

We measure queuing time and total execution time in ocikbpra which is a 100 percent matched cluster to user requirements (Figure 5). In this result, there is no queuing time before 40th node, and, after 41th node, queuing time occurs about 200000. From 81th node, queuing time multiplies, and total time also increases.

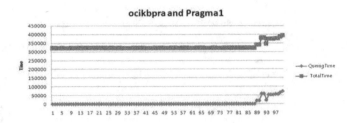

Fig. 6. Queuing time and total time in ocikbpra and Pragma1

In Figure 6, a merged cluster with ocikbpra and Pragma1, which is allowed to 99 percent similarity, shows better performance. There is no queuing time before 88th node. Compared with queuing time of Figure 5, queuing time after 89th node occurs, but is decreased because jobs are assigned to nodes of good performance in the expanded cluster. Moreover, average total execution time is decreased approximately by half compared with Figure 5 because the same reason.

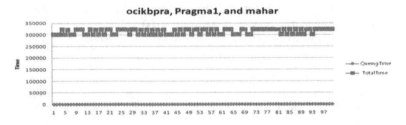

Fig. 7. Queuing time and total time in ocikbpra, Pragma1, and mahar

Figure 7 shows the result of job execution in unified environment which consists of ocikbpra, Pragma1, and mahar, which are included in above 94 percent similarity. There is no queuing time during job execution, and assigned jobs are totally completed between 300000 and 350000. The range of total execution time is made by difference between execution time according to CPU's performance.

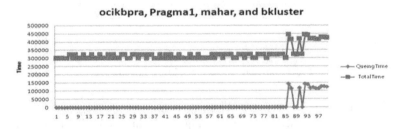

Fig. 8. Time and total time in ocikbpra, Pragma1, mahar, and bkluster

Figure 8 shows the result of job execution in totally merged environment which consists of ocikbpra, Pragma1, mahar, and bkluster, which are included in above 93 percent similarity. In this experiment, before 85th node, there is no queuing time, and total execution time is similar to formal experiments. However, after 86th node, maximum total execution time increases to 450000 when jobs are assigned to the last cluster, bkluster. The reason is that queuing time occurs in bkluster by the insufficient number of nodes for executing jobs.

Figure 9 shows the relation between size of clusters and the number of jobs having queuing time. The environment which is merged from three clusters, which are included in above 94 percent similarity, provides the best execution environment

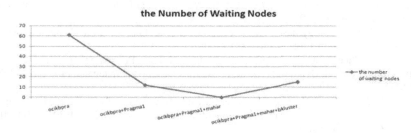

Fig. 9. Number of queuing nodes in four types of clusters

In conclusion, because of decrease of queuing time of job execution, adding resources according to calculated similarity value is more efficient than running jobs on the 100 percent matched cluster to user's requirement. Moreover, these results show that, when the degree of similarity is 94 percent, the best result is made, and queuing time increases in other cases.

Selecting the proper degree of similarity is important to make the best result during job execution through assigning proper resources and the number of jobs. Then, this similarity value is recorded in a job profile and is able to utilize similar job execution later.

5   Conclusion and Future Work

Resource management in Cloud computing is not easy. Managing distributed heterogeneous resources causes some problems: difficulty of resource information management, no standard definitions of resource requirements, and difficulty of guaranteeing compatibility of resource allocation. To solve these problems, we propose a resource virtualization method using ontologies in Cloud. A VOn is created by an ontology merge method based on the degree of similarity. From the experiment, expanding clusters with the proper degree of similarity shows guaranteeing the best execution time with minimize job queuing time. Merging cluster with the degree of similarity based on weighted factors according to application characteristics will be discussed near future.

References

[1] Nasser, B., Laborde, R., Benzekri, A., Barrère, F., Kamel, M.: Dynamic Creation of Inter-Organizational Grid Virtual Organizations. In: e-Science 2005, pp. 405–412 (2005)

[2] Cannon, S., Chan, S., Olson, D., Tull, C., Welch, V., Pearlman, L.: Using CAS to manage Role based VO sub-groups. In: CHEP 2003 (2003)

[3] Pernas, A.M., Dantas, M.A.R.: Using Ontology for Description of Grid Resources. In: 19th Int. Symposium on HPC Systems and Applications, Guelph, Canada, pp. 223–229 (2005)

[4] Xing, W., Dikaiakos, M.D., Sakellariou, R.: A core grid ontology for the semantic grid. In: CCGrid 2006, Singapore, May 2006, pp. 178–184 (2006)

[5] Lopes, J.G.R.C., Melo, A.C.M.A., Dantas, M.A.R., Ralha, C.G.: A proposal and evaluation of a mechanism for grid ontology merge. In: 20th HPCS (2006)

[6] Youseff, L., Butrico, M., Da Silva, D.: Toward a Unified Ontology of Cloud computing. IEEE, Los Alamitos (2008)

[7] Young, K.J.: Ontology-based Resource Selection Methods for Grid Computing, Master thesis, Sookmyung women's university (2008)

[8] Dean, J., Ghemawat, S.: MapReduce: Simplified Data Processing on Large Clusters. In: Proc. of the 6th Symp. on Operating Systems Design & Implementation, pp. 137–150 (2004)

[9] Ejarque, J., de Palol, M., Goiri, I., Julia, F., Guitart, J., Torres, J., Badia, R.M.: Using Semantics for Resource Allocation in Computing Service Providers. In: IEEE, 2008 MIPS based CPU performance (2008)

Author Index